THE CHRISTIAN EXPERIENCE
OF FORGIVENESS

Hugh Ross Mackintosh, born in 1870, was
in his day one of the best loved and
widely influential of Scottish theologians.
His distinguished university career in
Edinburgh was followed by specialised
studies in philosophy at Marburg. He had
great sympathy with movements in Ger-
man theology and made it one of his
chief objects to familiarise Britain with
them. His *Types of Modern Theology*,
published after his death, was an out-
standing achievement in this respect.

In 1904 he was appointed professor of
systematic theology at New College,
Edinburgh and was elected Moderator of
the General Assembly of the Church of
Scotland in 1932. In addition to the book
already mentioned he is well known for
The Doctrine of the Person of Christ and the
present volume.

Religious Books in the Fontana Series

Fontana Books make available, in attractive, readable yet inexpensive editions, the best books, both fiction and non-fiction, of famous contemporary authors. These include books up to 832 pages, complete and unabridged.

If you would like to be kept informed of new and forth-coming titles please apply to your local bookseller or write to:

WILLIAM COLLINS SONS & CO. LTD.
144 Cathedral Street, Glasgow, C.4

The Christian Experience of Forgiveness

H. R. MACKINTOSH

D.PHIL., D.D., D.TH.

COLLINS

fontana books

First Published by James Nisbet and Co. 1927
First Issued in Fontana Books 1961

Printed in Great Britain
Collins Clear-Type Press : London & Glasgow

TO

PROFESSOR H. A. A. KENNEDY
D.D., D.SC.

SCHOLAR ▪ COLLEAGUE ▪ FRIEND

CONTENTS

PREFACE

" The longer I live," said Rainy, " the more important and wonderful does the forgiveness of sins seem to me." In a series of works designed to present the great Christian doctrines afresh in their vital relations with experience, a treatment of Forgiveness may well find a place. It is a subject regarding which, except on the basis of experience, we should find it barely possible to say anything.

The experiential character of these pages may afford what justification is needed of the restricted space given to historical matter. I have made an effort to reduce narration of controversies, ancient and modern, to a minimum. But this element could not be wholly discarded. Modern problems in great part lose their meaning if we fail to set them against the background of the past. Also I have sought to develop the argument in its own light, without losing too much time on the refutation of other views. Nothing after all tells in discussion but the positive truth we elicit: the true idea, if we have it, pushed out the false one by its own momentum, and, without open hostilities, reigns in its stead.

The subject is one which admits of being handled in a large variety of ways, and for the order followed here I claim no more than a certain convenience. A start is made within individual Christian experience and the meaning of forgiveness there, as well as the need for it. Then the personality of Jesus is exhibited as the supreme guarantee of pardon for the sinful, and attention is called to the great convictions He inspired in believers like St. Paul and the Reformers. Forgiveness as a Divine act is then analysed for the conception of God it yields; the atonement is studied in its significance as the cost of forgiveness to God; a chapter is given to the psychological question how men take forgiveness; and finally something is said of the effects of felt pardon in individual and social life. At various points, it transpires that

9

so far from being easy to understand, as might be thought from the perfunctory treatment they occasionally receive, the problems of forgiveness gather up in themselves some of the gravest intellectual perplexities which Christian belief has to face.

To Principal Wheeler Robinson, D.D., one of the Editors of this series, who read the book in manuscript, and to my colleague, Professor W. Manson, D.D., who read it in proof, I owe a special debt of gratitude for their ready help and valuable criticisms. I desire also to thank the Editor of the *Expositor* for permission to use portions of the argument which, in an earlier form, had appeared in its pages.

H. R. MACKINTOSH

CHAPTER I

INTRODUCTORY

Unless we mean to drop confession out of Christian devotion —and in view of the Lord's Prayer, with its fifth petition, this is usually felt to be an extreme step—we are obliged to give the topic of Forgiveness a central place in the religious interest. Among the possible brief phrases in which the essence of Christianity might fairly be summed up, one certainly would be: I believe in God who forgives sins through Jesus Christ. Söderblom has well remarked that the idea of Love *may* be dragged down to the relatively unethical plane of natural religions: not so the idea of forgiveness. In this latter a spiritual salt is found which normally can be trusted to defy corruption. Forgiveness clearly is one of the *foci*—although not necessarily the only one— from which it is at once possible and natural to survey the whole circumference of Christian truth, and to determine the relationship which obtains between one conviction and another. It implies a distinctive view of God, of man, of sin, of the universe as supernaturally constituted, of Jesus. The believer, reflecting on other doctrines, finds that of them all none can keep the specifically Christian tone or quality if it has lost touch with the thought of pardon.

This doctrinal importance of the subject is of course owing to its importance for the practice of personal religion.[1] No man can properly rank as a Christian, in the sense of the New Testament, who has not received the forgiveness of sins, or who is not conscious that through its impartation something has happened of decisive moment for his relation

[1] Jeremiah's great anticipation of the Kingdom of God is only one of the prophetic utterances which give Divine pardon a central place: " I will make a new covenant with the house of Jacob and with the house of Israel. . . . I will be their God and they shall be my people. For I will forgive their iniquity and remember their sin no more " (Jer. 31.31-33).

to God. Missionaries, too, have often been apt to measure the depth and maturity of a convert's religious life by the sincerity of his interest in, and appreciation of, Divine pardon.

Above all, the forgiveness of sins has a fundamental significance in the teaching of Jesus Christ. History reveals no prophet or founder of religion who came forward, as He did, with the claim to have power under God to forgive sin. His contemporaries obviously were aware that in adopting this attitude His intention was not simply to proclaim the general truth or principle that forgiveness is a possible thing, but rather to offer Himself with pronounced emphasis as the guarantee and medium of its reality. In His person the Kingdom of God is here. This He said as a Jew to Jewish hearers. But by all the higher minds of Jewish religion forgiveness had invariably been regarded as foremost among the blessings which the advent of the Kingdom would secure.[2]

The place occupied by this topic in the history alike of Christian experience and of Christian theology is indicated by the close tie, if not the identity, which has long existed between the ideas of forgiveness and " justification." How these ideas, if rightly interpreted, really differ, is hard to see.[3] It may no doubt be held that forgiveness is only a negative thing, meaning no more than that past sin is blotted out and the slate as it were wiped clean, whereas justification as having positive implications lays down that God put the sinful right with Himself, not merely obliterating sin but receiving the penitent into fellowship as righteous in His sight. In this point of view it is easy to say that " justification is more and better than mere pardon." Every student of Protestant divinity knows that volumes used to circulate with authority in which this distinction, or something like it, was maintained. In theory the distinction may be possible; it has not the slenderest bearing on experience. We need

---

[2] We must not be pedantic, as though the meaning of forgiveness could not at least in part be represented by other terms. John 20.23 is the first passage in that Gospel where forgiveness is explicitly mentioned.

[3] St. Paul in Rom. 4.5-7 takes justification and forgiveness as equivalents.

not ask whether or not it might with consistency be urged at a moral and spiritual level beneath that of Christianity; what is certain is that the God and Father of Jesus Christ cannot be thought of as doing a barely negative thing, viz. cancel the sinner's guilt, except as in and by this act He takes him to His heart as a repentant child. To be justified, in the sense that counts for experience, is simply to be forgiven and accepted by God. Most of the famous debate about justification, therefore, and all of it that matters, has really been about forgiveness. Good reasons can unquestionably be pled for keeping the term "justification" in hand for purposes of precision here and there; thus it usefully suggests that pardoned men can make no claim, as of right, to God's acceptance. At the same time, "forgiveness" is evidently closer by far to human life; and to retain it as the normal word may help some people to believe, what seems too good to be true, that theology is simply a persistent and systematic effort to clarify the convictions by which Christians live.[4] We may not use the terminology of older thinkers, or practise their love of infinitesimal refinements of distinction, but at least they were toiling at a problem in regard to which every intelligent preacher of Christ has to make up his mind.

Is forgiveness the chief boon we owe to Christ? In the preface to the first edition of his great monograph Ritschl says it is; justification and reconciliation, he declares, is the central doctrine of Christianity, and to render it intelligible we need a virtually complete outline of theology. Others have held the chief gift to be sonship in Christ, or the sacraments, or moral inspiration; to Tennyson, one recalls, it was assurance of immortality. The frankest expression of the view that justification is not of the first importance is that of Paul de Lagarde, who had a trick of blurting out what many thought but scarcely cared to put in words. "The doctrine of justification," he wrote in 1890, "is not the Gospel, but a Pauline eccentricity. Even in Paul it is not the only or the most profound way of solving the problem of a man's rela-

---

[4] An excellent instance of how to make theology unintelligible is afforded by one writer who says: "The annulment of the old is called in the technical language of religion ' forgiveness.' " Technical language! Do we not forgive one another every day?

tion to his guilt. It was not the basal principle of the Reformation; and now, to crown all, in Protestant Churches it is dead. And rightly. The doctrines of justification and reconciliation are mythology which nobody believes save those who take ancient Trinitarianism seriously; and this to-day means nobody at all."[5]

But to ask what is best or second-best in the Gospel does not take us far. The Christian message is concerned not with a number of things but with the one comprehensive and infinitely precious gift of salvation, i.e. fellowship with God; and while this includes a variety of aspects, it is above all a spiritual unity. Unless we are to break every tie with New Testament religion, forgiveness comes into this, and comes in primarily, fundamentally, vitally. As Lincoln puts it, "no man can escape history." We are unable by this time to make Christianity over again; facts have settled its nature; in every age it has had this wonder of forgiveness at its heart. To quote the New Testament is needless; we should have to write out whole pages. But there is the Apostles' Creed, in which everything is supernatural, and which enumerates pardon among the other supernatural things: "I believe in the forgiveness of sins." There is the Epistle of Barnabas, at the close of the first century, assured in spite of its Alexandrian mysticism that "to this end the Lord endured to deliver His flesh unto corruption, that by the remission of sins we might be cleansed." There is St. Ambrose in the fourth century, with his ringing words: "I have nothing whereof I may glory in my works; I will therefore glory in Christ. I will not glory because I am righteous, but because I am redeemed; not because I am clear of sin, but because my sins are forgiven." In the Middle Ages there is St. Bernard, admonishing the hearer: "See that thou believe this also, that it is through Himself thy sins are pardoned: this is the witness of the Holy Spirit speaking in thy heart, Thy sins are forgiven thee." There is the great saying of Luther: "Where forgiveness of sins is, there is life and blessedness." The doctrine of justification by faith, not necessarily under that title, has a way of turning up with

[5] *Deutsche Schriften.*

new majesty and power in every period of revival; when religion sinks in apathy, its romance and glory dimmed, this is one of the first convictions to lose vigour and passion.[6]

St. Paul in the first instance, Luther as his disciple, have done more than any other follower of Christ to lead the Church to a full self-consciousness in this sphere. Each obtained clear insight respecting the terms on which sin is taken away as the outcome not of quiet or scholarly development, but of a desperate battle for his soul. Under new conditions, Luther was compelled to repeat St. Paul's conflict in order to regain St. Paul's truth. Water becomes steam only at a certain heat; and it looks as if there had to be an intense experience, a deep spiritual disturbance and fermentation, setting free great religious forces, before the unbought mercy of God to the sinful could be grasped anew and uttered with revolutionising power. Everything in Christianity is then apt to group itself round this truth. The certainty of forgiveness in Christ is, if not the sum, at least the secret of Christian religion.

But although forgiveness may be the keystone of the arch, it is none the less an idea which creates vast difficulties for the modern mind. Partly these are intellectual or what may be called æsthetic difficulties that confront the Christian view of things as a whole; partly they bear specially on the evangelical conception of Divine pardon.[7] In recent engagements with negative thought, the conception has had to bear the brunt of some of the hardest fighting. To the gravest of these objections let us now turn.

The problem of Divine forgiveness has occasionally been put aside as perfectly unreal, as indeed a moral puzzle of our

[6] Cf. Ihmel's article, "Rechtfertigung" in Hauck's *Real-Encyclopädie*. Forgiveness in some positive sense has always been central in each of the two great historical forms of Christianity; these have differed, rather, as to the conditions on which it is imparted and received.

[7] Essential mysticism has no message for the man who longs for Divine pardon. On the other hand, to take a great non-mystical thinker, Kant's moralistic view of good character as the *sine qua non* of forgiveness will be found in his *Religion within the Limits of Mere Reason* (Semple's translation), pp. 150-157, 176, 188-189, 261.

own making. To ask how forgiveness comes is to assume its necessity, but in fact it is not necessary at all. As Whitman says, the animals do not lie awake at night and weep for their sins; and neither need we. "Clear and sweet is my soul, and clear and sweet is all that is not my soul." It is of course evident that the notion of forgiveness is only relevant to the alarmed or burdened conscience; and in order that conscience should be alarmed, or at least that its alarm should be confessed, certain assumptions must in principle be in the mind. One of these assumptions is the reality of guilty sin, revealed by the consciousness of God, and of the obligation binding us to live according to His will of Holy Love. The alarm or sense of guilt, in other words, is no offspring of morbid complexes, nor is it evoked by a view of God that may be dismissed as legal and pre-Christian; it is a right kind of alarm, and is the response to a right vision of God. This assumption, however, without which the Christian doctrine of forgiveness becomes unintelligible, is far from being generally received. Apart from a universal distaste for sombre truths about ourselves, the materialistic or mechanistic monism which darkened the sky for a generation indisposes many of our contemporaries to take moral distinctions as in any real sense absolute, or as more than useful and provisional conventions of social life. Guilt has at best a psychological meaning for those who regard themselves as creatures, and even victims, of heredity, education and environment, no more accountable for character than barometer for storm. On such a view, our choices are made for us before we make them.

Whether this mood can be dispelled by reasoning is very doubtful. The man who urges the plea on his own behalf, protesting that in his case everything which religious people call sin may justly be put down to his parents' account, or his schoolmaster's, or his comrades', is commonly a humbug, and invariably is devoid of a sense of humour. Conceivably, however, the plea might be stated on behalf of others. "I am responsible, undoubtedly," it may be said; "but I know persons whose chance of goodness has been nil, and about whom you cannot use the word responsibility except in an erroneous or Pickwickian sense." This estimate of course is superficially kind but actually merciless, since it proposes to consider some men as on the moral level of animals, who are incorrigible because without responsibility; but in addition, it must be pointed out that the great literature of the world goes dead against it. Æschylus, Virgil, Dante, Shakespeare, Goethe—the atmosphere they breathe loses a vital ingredient if the fact of human responsibility be denied. If the evil things he has done, the evil person he has made himself, do not justly pierce and wound a man's conscience, the tragic dramatist cannot make a beginning. Besides, although the habit of penitence, or the capacity for it, might in one aspect be thought to have dropped out of the modern mind, in another it is keener and graver than before. More people now than at any time in history, it is probable, have a painful consciousness that socially they are involved in "man's inhumanity to man." This is the old sense of sin in a new garb. "Men," it has been pointed out, "are aghast at their own indifference to and acquiescence in the social wrongs by which they are surrounded. Men are appalled by their powerlessness to modify or remedy the iniquity and the suffering inherent in the modern industrial system. They are stung by a sense of guilt, they are overwhelmed by the feeling of impotence, they are distracted for a remedy. Social responsibility has become, like the law of old, a schoolmaster to bring them to Christ."

If we have come so far, the question whether our failure to treat each other as we ought requires to be forgiven, will depend for its answer solely on whether we believe in God. To hear a man who believed in the moral being of God say that he needed no forgiveness would affect us like the statement of a friend, in a picture-gallery, that for him the works of the great masters had no beauty. At once we should recognise that we cannot make him see. But, if we ventured on advice, it would be the suggestion that he should contemplate some great picture, should look and look again, at intervals, with the confidence that something would happen. New perceptions would emerge. The beauty spread before him would by degrees become visible. Similarly, let the insensitive man take pains to see Jesus, let him not withdraw his attention from that Figure, and inevitably he will learn the truth about himself. True, it is not through the realisation of Jesus only that God touches the spring of penitence in men; He may do it through many another deep experience; but the experience is always that of beholding a goodness that shames us.

A second objection to forgiveness is the fear, or even the conviction, that men cannot be forgiven because the thing is contrary to the nature of the world. Is not spiritual law if anything more rigid than physical, as being absolute for thought, not contingent; and what can this mean except that the consequences of sin cling to us for ever? We may reject the Oriental doctrine of Karma, binding this life to past lives by the chain of inflexible causation, but is not inflexible moral causation the very signature of the life in which we now are? Surely it is nature's last word that the effects of sin are irreversible, our future an inescapable conclusion foretold and fixed by the premises of the past. If, then, the universe reacts to sin with an inexorability of which the procession of the stars can be only a faint emblem, let us submit to fate. Let us consent to be what we have become. In resignation, without whining, let us live out our life at the level to which sin has brought it.

In this contention, clearly, there is an element of nobleness; if it errs, it does not err basely. It gives expression to the deep assurance that nothing in earth or heaven can tamper with the sanctions of moral law. Exemption from the effects of wrong cannot be had for nothing; we, or someone else, must pay. Being is so made that our sin will find us out. Nothing in talk about forgiveness can be so distressing or incredible as hints of a poor and cheap condonation. The man who has begun to face moral realities cannot be persuaded that the accounts of the past will not somehow be presented. If the teacher of religion does not keep him right on the point, the novelist and the dramatist will.

While, however, the contention is far from ignoble, it is none the less mistaken. To begin with, although plainly the past is unalterable in the sense that it has happened and to all eternity will have happened, yet its value, its ultimate significance for life, is still undetermined. That the future must decide. It is in the future that its significance will not merely appear but actually be made real. Later experience may impart a new and beneficent meaning to what formerly seemed unrelieved disaster, just as a musical chord frequently is qualified in tone and value by succeeding chords and phrases, or as a dreary stretch of country may from a more advanced point of view reveal itself as an exquisite factor in a fine landscape. Something like that can happen to our sins. Their final import, though not their occurrence, may change. As it has been put, " they may become occasions of some spiritual state of great value which could not have been reached without them. Till the power is known that can so transform them, they remain mere blots; and the man, in whose experience they are, feels the weight of an irremovable burden. But if there is known to him some transforming power his despair vanishes."[8] I am not at the moment arguing that evil is an element of good, or even that it is an indispensable means to good, both of which positions seem to me more than doubtful, since it is at least conceivable that *greater* good might have been realised through the refusal to sin; I am contending, rather, that in a spiritually constituted world we are not shut up to believe that sin must entail final or hopeless fatalities of evil consequence. And this for the good reason that life is perpetually betraying the presence within it of a power capable of so dealing with past events, which as events it cannot obliterate, as to transmute their value. Everything depends under God on how a man reacts to his own history, how he takes it, what he does with it. It depends, supremely, on whether his attitude to the past —its guilt, its soiling, its legacy of weakness—is simply moral, or also religious and believing. In the words of the old writer, " it is not sinning that ruins men, but sinning and not repenting."

In the second place, it is mistaken to hold that forgiveness is impossible, that a man must lie on the bed he has made, because there is a living God. In certain ways, when we are

[8] W. Temple, *Mens Creatrix*, pp. 173-174.

seeking to interpret life, it is simpler to leave God out. Even human personality is terribly trying to the system-maker, scientific or metaphysical. So wild an element in the universe puts out his logic, like a child asking odd questions in a drawing-room. But if man in this personal rôle confuses the theorist, still more does God. Fatalisms which might be plausible or even menacing if He were not there, become unimposing since He is there. It is because the Bible was written by men whose eye was on God from first to last, to whom indeed fellowship with God was the point of departure, that it has in it neither fatalism nor pessimism. Instead, it is full of an element which the mind both of fatalist and of pessimist has lost; it is full of wonder. How in Scripture we can often catch the marvelling spirit that lies behind the uttered voice, giving it triumph and exhilaration! And it is worth while to observe that what are perhaps the most remarkable instances of this exulting note have to do with the forgiveness of sins. First, to take one example, comes the great declaration: " I have blotted out, as a thick cloud, thy transgressions, and as a cloud thy sins: return unto Me, for I have redeemed thee." Something amazing and incalculable has occurred; something that can be known yet passes knowledge, and that can have no source but the creative love of God. And then in exultation the prophet calls Nature to his aid in celebrating the height and depth of mercy: " Sing, O ye heavens, for the Lord hath done it. Break forth into singing, ye mountains, O forest, and every tree therein."[9] This is a strain which Jesus prolongs and deepens. He more than any is sure there is such a thing as forgiveness, not because it is small, but because it is great and fatherlike. In the parable of the prodigal, He intended the hearers to perceive that the chief character in the story is not the younger son but the father. Had the father died, the wanderer would have returned to find the door shut and the possibility of reconciliation gone for ever. But the father lived and loved and waited. If then Christ is trustworthy, if there is a living God who loves and acts, the forgiveness of sins is the most stupendous, tragic and blessed possibility of life.

[9] Isa. 44.22-23.

Finally, it may be argued that forgiveness is essentially immoral, and that consequently by its insistence on Divine pardon the Christian religion betrays a serious ethical inferiority to other, more sombre, faiths. This, by the way, is an objection of unusual interest; for, although not sound, it does call attention to the fact that the doctrine of forgiveness, indicative as it is of our dependence rather than of our freedom, brings out clearly the difference of the religious from the purely moral standpoint. It is characteristic of religion to take a graver view of sin than that taken by morality, while at the same time asserting, as the other does not, the possibility of its being remitted. Accordingly, when it is urged that forgiveness is contrary to morality, this really is a dim and confused testimony to the truth that Divine pardon transcends ethics, because pardon is in kind peculiarly and distinctively religious. It is not immoral, but its origin lies beyond morality, just as poetry has a way of being above or beyond logic.[10]

When St. Paul was accused of encouraging laxity by his gospel of free gracious pardon, and had to meet the charge openly, he replied in effect that no one could imagine anything of the kind who knew what his gospel was or had observed its moral influence. He points out that faith, by which forgiveness is received, makes men one with Christ, i.e. attaches them by bonds of choice to One in whom God's holy love is personally present; and that while faith is not itself finished goodness of character, it is the condition out of which goodness naturally springs. In other words, he denied that God accepts us because we are good, but affirmed that the terms on which He accepts us ensure our becoming good. This is an argumentative consideration which, although very old, is not in the least obsolete. Forgiveness in point of fact does not do what, if it be immoral, it must do; it does not demoralise. Not that the gospel of forgiveness cannot be twisted into antinomianism; St. Paul admits this, and deals with it in its own place. But no instance can be found in which the man who is freely pardoned for Christ's

---

[10] What morality does is to send out an S.O.S.; it is the self-revealing God alone who can hear and answer.

sake and in virtue of his self-identification with the sinless
Son of God has thereby been infected with moral degener-
acy, enfeebled in character, or impoverished in ethical ideals.

What indeed is a demoralised mind? It is a mind which
increasingly is losing its horror of sin; which has come to
acquiesce in sin more leniently and to make terms with it as
an acknowledged part of life. Can it be seriously held that a
practised psychologist, invited to report on what took place
in the thought and feeling of the man who at the moment
was receiving Divine forgiveness, would conclude that the
total outcome and meaning of the experience was to induce
a laxer view of moral evil? The very question is its answer.
No true instance of pardoning and being pardoned, whether
between man and man or between God and man, could in
the nature of things be or be conceived which did not involve
in the pardoned self a quickened awareness of sin and an
intensified repudiation of it. Assume a mood of levity on
either side, and instantly the ethical conditions of the experience itself disappear. What remains may be defiance facing
weak conniving good-nature; it may be some other equally
melancholy distribution of parts; but forgiveness, in the
noble, subduing and cleansing import of the word, it cannot
be.

The same objection has been formulated, from the standpoint of ethical idealism, by spokesmen of moral education.[11]
To weaken moral impulse by insisting on the fact of pardon
is, it is held, a more than doubtful policy in pædagogics. You
cannot speak often and urgently of forgiveness without leading men to despair of success in the moral task, and thus
undermining their personal interest in obedience. The
proper end of all moral education is to induce men to develop
and exert their moral powers. It is to summon them to
" self-knowledge, self-reverence, self-control "; but to harp
upon the constant need of forgiveness interferes with the
hopeful discharge of this task and suggests that the moral
ideal is in fact unattainable. Not that the idea of forgiveness may not play a real if subordinate part. For the elas-
ticity of moral will it is of genuine importance that the

[11] On this point cf. Stange, *Die Vergebung der Sünden,* pp. 5-6.

memory of past transgression should not be permitted to destroy the confidence and gladness with which we face duty. At the same time, even Christianity has had to insist that the idea should be kept in its proper place. It has seen the dangers of making too much of it. Jesus Himself laid the chief stress on keeping the commandments. The Church has sought above all by its practice of discipline to engrave the claims of morality on the human conscience; we may virtually say that in proportion as the Church became conscious of its task as a contributor of immeasurably valuable elements to the civilisation of mankind, it has tended to relegate the thought of Divine forgiveness to the background. To assume that all men need daily to be forgiven is, at bottom, to assume that duty cannot be fulfilled, and that the effort to fulfil it, as being necessarily vain, is superfluous.

Probably the evangelical doctrine of pardon has to meet no more formidable argument than this, and much of what the following chapters contain will be offered as a reply to it, direct or indirect. But at the moment it may be pointed out that in effect it is the same objection as the Pharisees made to Jesus' receiving sinners. This is not to suggest that the Pharisees were superficial or merely deluded by habits of hypocrisy. They were mistaken, but they were not base. As it has been put, " it was ultimately an interest in the moral character of religion that prompted them. They could not understand how anyone could offer fellowship with God to people whose moral life revealed so glaring a deficit.[12] Culpable leniency of that sort was contrary to their view of God; a deep gulf separated Jesus' love for the sinful and the type of ethical idealism on which their religion rested. Few of us have the right to cast a stone at them; their attitude, when held to in defiance of higher suggestions, is simply that of the natural man from whose eyes the veil that Jesus removes has not yet been lifted.

Other difficulties about forgiveness may well be the unhappy legacy of old controversies. It has been maintained, for example, that a man can have fellowship with God only after a definite series of prescribed experiences—so much

[12] *Ibid.*, p. 7.

torturing contrition, so much exultant joy; and in some minds
this may have fostered the impression that the Christian
message of pardon calls on us to work up morbid and artificial emotions. Others are repelled and mystified by the
confession they suppose is looked for from the penitent to
the effect that he himself—his character, will, life—is worthless in the sight of God. But how can this be, if God is
Father; and how can we be expected to feel its truth? In
short, the precise meaning of the humility involved in seeking or taking pardon is deemed obscure. Or again, to others
it is incredible that God, the Infinite and Absolute, can enter
into such relations of intimacy with the individual as forgiveness denotes, or act towards him and upon him with
distinct, particularising love. With such difficulties it is not
hard to have sympathy; they are real, not fictitious or foolish;
and it is very doubtful whether the mind that cannot in some
degree enter into them and view them on the inner side has
itself appreciated the all but unbelievable wonder of Divine
pardon, or understood the cumulative effect which present-
day education, with its imposing conceptions of natural law
and inviolable causal sequence, is bound to exert on the
modern intelligence. After all, it is only in *faith* that we are
assured of pardon. It is so great a thing that no one rightly
believes in it except he who feels that in view of the dis-
closures made in Christ he has no choice but to cast himself
upon a love deeper than all his sin.

It is instructive at this point to refresh our minds by history.
What was it, in the end, which by its very meaning enabled
Christianity to triumph over and displace the rival religions
of the time? Holl has recently called attention to the true
explanation; viz. the fact that Jesus could be described, even
by enemies, as " the Friend of publicans and sinners." To us
this constitutes His greatness as Saviour; to His contemporaries it was disgraceful. Yet Jesus incurred the disgrace of
set purpose. He speaks with obvious irony of the " righteous,"
for whom His call is not meant, pictures the publican as
going down to his house justified, and announces salvation to
the penitent thief dying for his crimes. Such things count for

little if slurred over as more or less rhetorical, but taken seriously they mean a revolution in religion.

Certainly they were otherwise unknown in the world of that day. No other faith proclaimed a God who in love was ever seeking touch with the guilty and on whom even degraded men might have a special claim. This was the more disconcerting that Jesus' conception of the Father laid unequalled stress on His sublime holiness and impending judgment at the advent of the Kingdom. The holy and righteous Judge, He declares, yearns over His children and in His Son and Representatives has come to win them by kindness. In the light of common sense and of all the prevailing religious convictions, this message, the paradox of the Gospel, was an unheard-of and disastrous innovation.

It was new over against Judaism. True, the prophets had had wonderful things to say about Jehovah's compassion and mercy; it was mercy, however, to those who acknowledge themselves to be His people, and the transgression which He delighted to pardon was the transgression "of the remnant of His heritage." There is promise here for the sinful, but with reservations. Even so, the atmosphere has changed in post-exilic Judaism, in which Christ grew up. Now the commanding idea has become the holiness of God, a holiness so infinitely high and unapproachable that minute precautions are necessary for all who would come near Him. It was a period of ritual law designed to cleanse the defilement of sin. The priest atones and secures pardon; the means of atonement is the blood of sacrifice. But, most significant of all, not every sin admitted of expiation. Sins of error, of thoughtlessness, of human frailty—these were provided for. But for sins done presumptuously, "with a high hand," no sacrifice remained. The man had acted wilfully against better knowledge; he had left the shelter of the covenant, spurning its provisions, and was now beyond the pale. His sin was unforgivable in law. Doubtless as centuries passed the virtue of animal sacrifice lost hold on deeper minds; doubtless, too, the gleam of light cast by Is. 53 lit up the darkness with noble hopes; still, it remains true that for the religion of Jesus' day the righteous man, and he only, had access to

God. "Who shall ascend into the hill of the Lord? or who shall stand in His holy place? He that hath clean hands and a pure heart."[13] Yet it was not to the righteous but the sinful that Christ turned. This seemed to His contemporaries flat blasphemy, and they slew Him for it.

It was new also in comparison with the religion of Greeks and Romans. There all men regarded it as a commonplace that none but the pure could approach or have intercourse with Deity; and Celsus acutely fixed upon the kind of persons to whom Christianity opened its arms as proof positive that the new idea of God was immoral and despicable. Every other religion, he complains, invites only the blameless, the educated, the respectable; Christianity actually seems to put a premium on wrong-doing, so cordially does it welcome the evil and debased. Deity of the right kind can have no dealings with impure men. "It makes no difference to this," writes Holl, "that Greek religion too had the idea of atonement, that the Delphic God with its γνῶθι σαυτόν bade men search their own hearts, or that from Orphism onwards the notions of purification and asceticism had penetrated the Greek world, and the mysteries also had bound up with them purgation from defilement. At no stage of development did atonement mean that the God *forgave* guilt. No Greek would have felt anything of the sort to be intelligible. Guilt was a stain, an evil spell, in which man was entangled, and all the help a God could give was advice respecting the method of casting it off. Orphism went no further. True, it spoke of pre-temporal guilt, to be expiated in this life; but one could be rid of it by purifying oneself (i.e. the divine within) through leading an Orphic life; and anyhow the goal was not forgiveness but rather the proud consciousness of having become God oneself and now being a ruler like the Gods. Moreover, it was especially the mysteries that insisted with emphasis that none but the pure can share in the fellowship and blessing of Deity. The solemn formulæ which were spoken at the beginning of the action proclaim this: 'He that hath cleans hands,' 'He that is free from all crime,' 'He whose soul is unconscious of any evil,' 'He that has lived righte-

13 Ps. 24.3-4.

ously and well '—he, none but he, might draw near. Hence certain flagrant wrong-doers were excluded from the start, but even those admitted were subjected to a purification *before* they could see the Divine. The more the sense for the holy deepened on the moral side, the stricter became the conditions which must be fulfilled ere a man could have contact with Deity. Access to God vouchsafed to the impure and sinful could not but seem here too a perversion of all right notions of religion and morality, an attack on men's simplest feelings for the Divine in its dignity and elevation."[14]

To repeat it yet again: Christianity conquered through its message that in Jesus there is personally present a God Who receives sinners. It triumphed not because it was the religion most hospitable to fresh ideas, not merely because its moral and social doctrine was of higher character than its rivals, or because it was the faith best fitted to win educated minds. It is the new element in a faith that tells, and Christianity overcame by means of its message of forgiveness, in which it had no rival. It dared to proclaim that in the light of God's intense holiness no illumined conscience can ever insist on distinguishing men as "pure" and "impure," since before Him all are in the same condemnation, and all must cast themselves on His mercy.

> All the fitness He requireth
> Is to feel your need of Him.

The faith which ventures on a gospel so great has the future in its hand.

Not improbably to some whose sympathy with Christian religion is heartfelt and active, the importance which in the foregoing pages has been ascribed to the forgiveness of sins may seem so exaggerated as to be indefensible. Of this we need not complain. It is perhaps a hasty view that all beliefs are of equal value at all periods of life. True faith may coexist with temporary colour-blindness to this aspect or that

[14] K. Holl, *Urchristentum u. Religionsgeschichte,* pp. 20-21.

of the whole truth. Yet such blindness to the cardinal message of Christianity cannot last; some day the real meaning of the neglected thought peals through us for the first time, and everything has to recrystallise about it. In the Great War men not fundamentally irreligious woke up abruptly in many cases to the utter Sovereignty of God—the intense reality of an Unseen Power in Whose protection they could lose themselves, like eaglets nestling under the pinions of the mother bird. Till this discovery had been made, sanity itself was imperilled. Similarly, all religious men whose conscience is alive must awake at some time or other, slowly or in a flash, to the fact that unless they can reach pardoned fellowship with God, all is over with their inward life.[15] Till then they may have been half-fledged believers; but now into their unripe religion there breaks a new experience—some gross fall into sin, contact with a saint, a new awareness that Jesus Christ is present and is making them ashamed. Character at its best begins to look very drab and seedy in the light He casts; and they then know, once for all and without reasoning, that the one thing needful is to be forgiven; forgiven for what they have done but still more for what they are. When our eyes open to this, we are ready for the greatest of all gifts, and it becomes ours. *Habemus Deum, et Deus ipse noster est.*

[15] " Sincerely to give up one's conceit or hope of being good in one's own right is the only door to the universe's deeper reaches " (James, *A Pluralistic Universe*, p. 305).

CHAPTER II

WHAT FORGIVENESS IS

To be saved, for a Christian man, is to have trustful communion with God as His child and with men as a brother among brethren; and the position taken in these pages is that the fundamental and creative act whereby salvation in this sense is made and kept real, is the forgiveness of sins. Pardon is not the end of God's ways with men, but it is the blessing which leads in all others by the hand. It is a bestowal which, if in New Testament phrase they are to live " in the light," the sinful need not once merely, but from day to day. In what does forgiveness consist?

Notoriously it has too often been identified, or confused, with remission of penalty. To a certain extent we can understand this, and even sympathise with it; for, as is all but universally agreed, the gravest penalty attached to sin is forfeiture of fellowship with God, such an exclusion from that Divine intimacy as is morally unavoidable; and *this*, unquestionably, pardon does remit or remove. The forgiven man finds himself drawn close to the Father's heart. But most thinkers who fall into the confusion just referred to mean something quite different. What they have in mind is some definite penalty or penalties not apparently linked to sin by any spiritually necessary bond, like disease or the loss of reputation consequent on drunkenness, or financial ruin following upon neglect of worship; and they find themselves unable to conceive of Divine pardon except as consisting in, or at all events implying, the removal of such punishments. Despite the backing it often appears to have from common sense, this position may be shown to be untenable.

It is clear, to begin with, that in this external sense forgiveness and remission of penalty have no vital connexion with each other. Common usage brings out the fact that in a wide variety of circumstances they can exist quite separately.

It is within the competence of a judge, good cause being shown, to refrain from imposing the legal penalty of an offence and simply to call upon the culprit to give an undertaking for good behaviour in the future. Similarly, the Crown can remit punishment by way of clemency; a thief might be let off imprisonment who had gained military distinction for valour. But neither judge nor Crown as such can forgive wrong; only the injured person can do that. Again, willingness or unwillingness to forgive may be of crucial import in circumstances where there can be no question at all either of inflicting penalty or dispensing with it; for example, when children have been treated unkindly by parents, though not with physical violence. Or once more, we may forgive the dead, of whose wrong-doing we learned only after their death. Not only so, but where the injured party has forgiveness and punishment equally in his power, there need be no coincidence of pardon and remission. A father may resolve not to punish his child and yet remember his sin against him; on the other hand, he may forgive him wholeheartedly but also decide that penalty must be exacted, and in this view the child himself may concur.

When we take the problem up into the religious sphere, it is to find that so far from the forgiveness of God necessarily involving the abolition of all punishment, the truth rather is that over a certain area of experience pardon and retribution invariably go together, because the holy love that constitutes the Father's very being makes anything else impossible. In saying so, we must be on our guard against reviving the old misconception which divided the nature of God against itself, by deriving forgiveness from love and the punitive consequences of sin from righteousness. The point is that the Divine character is such that wherever it encounters moral evil, in saint or sinner, it cannot but react against it with repelling and retributive force. Love, that is worthy to be called love, confronts the evil thing with an inevitable and intrinsic purity. If God did not chastise sin in the very act of forgiveness, and in the persons of the forgiven as a sequel to forgiving them, He would not be more loving than He is; He would cease to be God.

At this point also it is important to distinguish things that differ. If alienation from the Father, accompanied by that painful sense of accountability and self-contempt which may broadly be designated "guilt," forms the primary consequence of transgression, then, as we have just seen, it is supremely and wonderfully true that this is swept away by the forgiving acceptance of God. Pardoned sin thereafter has no power to disturb or sadden our relation to God; or perhaps, since the self-torturing capabilities even of the Christian heart are incalculable, we may more wisely say that in God's loving intention no such saddening disturbance is contemplated. Forgiveness means, on His side, the untroubled communication of His love to unworthy men, whose unworthiness lasts on even after their forgiveness, and in spite of it. Our evil desires tear us from God, but the pure and deep kindness exhibited in Jesus reknits the bond as though its severance had never been, and there and then the misery and punishment of the estranged life is terminated. Whatever more of inward cure and rehabilitation may be still to come, it is the result of that creative act of love whereby the Father puts us right with Himself.

On the other hand, there are secondary consequences of sin which at least in many instances are not directly removed by pardon. Nor does the penitent invariably wish that they should be. The discipline of chastisement may indeed be welcomed; its solemn incidence has at times been confessed patiently and thankfully endured. But however few may reach this level of trustful insight, it is the fact that traces of the old sins persist in our lives, our memories, our imaginations, our opportunities, our health. Sin would not be sin if it did not steal something which cannot quite be recaptured. If in youth we waste our powers, if we yield habitually to deceit, if we soil the innocence of others or despise their affection, then, whatever God's later mercy may bestow, these things have left deep marks, not wholly to be obliterated, on thought and habit, on preferences and delights. There are *kinds* of service we might have rendered, which we now cannot render. There is an exemption from stained recollections we can never possess. Above all, if by our influence or example we have been the means of leading others into sin, we must feel with anguish the irretrievable loss we have inflicted on them. "Surely till memory sleeps, there must be something to trouble the bliss of forgiveness, to overshadow the joy even of souls redeemed from sin, in the thought that they have done irreparable wrong to the souls of others—a wrong for which there is no place for repentance, though we seek it carefully with tears."[1]

There are those no doubt who have argued that the conception of penalty has no rightful place in the Christian thought of God and His work, and who admit even the idea of fatherly chastisement only with a grudge. The notion of Divine punishment we shall examine later; it will suffice here to say that if only the element of passionate and irresponsible vengeance be eliminated from the conception of God, as Christ has taught it, no reason exists why we should not say that all punishment coming from Him is fatherly chastisement, and could be nothing else if in truth He is Father. The relevance of this to our present topic lies in the fact that those secondary punitive consequences of sin which, as we have seen, may persist even in the forgiven experience, possess so manifest an aspect of high and loving discipline that in their presence (at least in our best hours) we can give praise. What we then see and feel is no rigid impersonal law smiting us, no bare natural evolution of results which blindly and impassively administers pain. Far from being the dark blows of unconscious fate, these things are felt as elements in the very grace that forgives and cleanses. "When we are judged, we are chastened of the Lord, that we should not be condemned."[2]

It is true, no fixed limits can be assigned to the restorative efficacy of Divine love in bringing back even here what might seem to have been forfeited permanently. Who can say how far healing of soul may work healing of body, or in what measure the joy and serenity of fellowship with God and reconciliation with estranged friends may quicken anew the corporal powers that vice had wasted? In some measure, as life appears to teach, even the constitution undermined by

[1] J. Caird, *University Sermons*, p. 151.   [2] I Cor. 11.32.

evil ways may be built up again if the man be at peace with
the Life-giver; for soul and body are one indissoluble person.
Yet we speak here only in possibilities and peradventures. To
some terrible extent the price has to be paid, at times paid to
the uttermost farthing. It is so more often than not when we
sow to the flesh; but these may not be the worst sins of which
we accuse ourselves. We may have spread evil in other lives,
and retrospect may then yield the unavailing and all but
incurably sad conviction that most of its effects we cannot
trace, and those which are traceable we have no power to
counteract. Thus we cannot promise ourselves, with easy
optimism, that repentance of itself must bring the shadow
back upon the dial. There will always be substantial and awe-
inspiring reason to say that the God who forgives the sinful
is also a God who takes vengeance on their doings. The
degree in which Divine absolution carries with it deliverance
from evil fruits of past sin is not a subject for theological
reflection so much as an experimental problem which belongs
to the inner life of individuals, and to which at best deepening insight can supply only an approximate answer. To the
majority of Christian men this whole province will always
remain one of solemnising and humbling mystery.

As we encounter or practise it in human affairs, forgiveness
is an active process in the mind and temper of a wronged
person, by means of which he abolishes a moral hindrance to
fellowship with the wrong-doer, and re-establishes the freedom and happiness of friendship. Jesus once described
pardon, as it ought to be, as the forgiving of brethren " from
our hearts." What He has in view plainly consists not merely
in an alteration of behaviour to the trespasser, but of feeling
and inward attitude. The old tides of affection and confidence,
which had ebbed, must rise again to flow over the offence
and cover it out of sight. The fault is to be swept from our
thoughts; its influence on our emotions or actions must end;
pardon is illusory on any other terms. Those people who
say that they can forgive but not forget betray the fact,
unconsciously for the most part, that their " forgiveness " has
been accompanied by reservations and qualifications which,

morally, are fatal. It is of course true that the offending sin is remembered in the sense that we are still aware of it; when our mind recurs to the subject, we are conscious, and may always be conscious, that it once happened. But what has utterly changed for us is its value or personal significance. Before, it was a fact that provoked and maintained estrangement; now, if pardon is real, the injured man has wholly ceased to regard that past event as determinative of his personal relationships to the offender. Self and neighbour are now at peace. In this sense all true forgiveness forgets the guilt which it pardons.

Thus it hardly needs saying that forgiveness differs by a whole moral universe from the mere abandonment of revenge. It demands more by far than self-mastery enough to veto retaliation. Yet in practical life, where we ignore conscience or bribe it not to speak, the two are frequently confused. In our resentment at injury we will not strike back; we dislike the customs of the secular, whose frankly avowed maxim is to give as good as they get, and in addition the command of Jesus keeps down our hands; but in the private world of feeling we are our own masters and may please ourselves. We have a long memory, and, once wronged, we intend to show the spared offender very plainly that he can never again be the same to us. Grievance, too, has a taste of luxury which lies as a sweet morsel under the tongue. Hence if accident or a good man's guile should bring us into the offender's company, there is that in our demeanour if not our language which openly proclaims that positive reconciliation is not to be thought of. To call this forgiveness would be absurd. It is a temper largely composed of scorn, and scorn is one of the emotions on which, firmly and inexorably, Christ set His ban.

Similarly, forgiveness is emphatically more than the ignoring of a trespass. For in this latter case no element of passion is involved. No suffering has been endured as the medium of reconciliation; nothing is present in the mind of either party which might not be the outcome simply of prudential and calculating policy. Faults may come to be overlooked provisionally or tentatively, with a moderation to be changed again later, if the cautious plan should fail.[3] Such a relationship between persons could obviously be no more than external or tolerantly civil; it would imply no communion of spirit, no pity, no love, no mutual interchange of inner feeling or sharing in moral experiences and aims.

All this goes to adumbrate our conception of what the forgiveness of God, if real, cannot but be; at least it must prove as full, as unqualified and overpowering in generosity, as the forgiveness of good men.[4] The Christian religion has suffered gravely in the past because on too many occasions it has been supposed to stand for a conception of Divine pardon less noble than that which the best moral opinion would look to see exemplified in the life of any ethical pioneer. And an instinct which cannot err has raised the protest that man cannot be better than God. Theology will do well to accept such admonitions. While its first impulse may be to retain old views of God which in their time moved the world, second thoughts must suggest that the Gospel itself has forged the weapons, and handed them to men, by which in every successive age imperfect expositions of its meaning and scope are successively destroyed. To say that God's pardon must not be less great and deep than man's at his best is, after all, a platitude; though the platitude may be one which ought to be cried aloud. The real truth is that man's forgiveness, at its noblest, is no more than a faint echo or imitation of that eternal and transcendent Divine pardon made ours in Jesus, with which everything began. The mercy of God is from everlasting, and one of the later fruits which its revelation in time has ripened is man's dawning thought of what mercy, as he is called to practise it, may indeed be.

The New Testament comes forward with a presentation of the forgiving love of God which, in quality and range, has neither rival nor predecessor. It exhibits God as forgiving

[3] Cf. the story of the man who, fearing that he was on his death-bed, sent for an acquaintance with whom he had fallen out years before, and made overtures of peace. They shook hands in amity. But as the other left the room, the sick man roused himself to say, " Remember, if I get over this, the old quarrel stands."

[4] See note on Herrmann's theology at the close of this chapter.

with a sublimity and a universality of intention which display all the characteristics of human pardon at its highest pitch; but in addition it adds certain elements of Divine infinitude and wonder that open vistas into a new realm. The forgiveness is such as, apart from its manifestation in Jesus, we could neither ask nor think. This immeasurable aspect of pardon, as the Father imparts it, is worth study.

God is here represented as desirous, whatever it may cost, of living with Human children in the supreme and final relationship—the moral communion of persons. One bar to this exists: that spirit in them of distrust and selfishness which we call sin. The will of God is bent first and last on the realisation of a universal community all of whose members, as the Father's sons and daughters, love and trust each other; sin thwarts this will and, as thwarting it, is the object of His displeasure. He moves against it with all the intensity of His being. In speaking of the Divine "wrath," religious men have been throwing out their minds at a huge, dark and commanding fact, not to be affected or removed by any complacency of ours. Now the forgiveness of God peals out always in one unified chord along with this solemnising undertone, and would lose more than half its meaning if detached from it. It signifies that despite this sin against which His indignation flames, as it must if the world's pillars are not to be based on rottenness, the Father takes the amazing step of receiving sinful men into His life of friendship, that within that life there may be actualised in them His purpose of a loving brotherhood. To the man who asks: "Can I be cleansed? Must I for ever bear this load? Can there be no piercing of this alienating barrier between God and me?" an answer comes and makes itself credible: "I am thy salvation; only believe." He who grasps and holds this fast is a pardoned man. He is justified; he is righteous, in the sense that he is right with God and in inmost spirit is as God would have him be. He has peace with the Father and can know it, and the Father is at peace with him. The New Testament has no meaning if it does not mean this, and mean it as the staple of its message.

But this is a very wonderful conception, which mere

logical reasoning has always found it virtually impossible to
interpret in the transparent terms that reasoning must employ.
Many phrases of the Bible urge its astonishing character;
they ask "Who is a God like unto Thee, that pardoneth
iniquity?" Since God is holy, with a towering purity that
condemns our lusts without appeal, forgiveness sounds too
good to be true. At first sight Jesus makes it not more
credible but less. We must not, as Otto reminds us, turn the
Gospel of Jesus into an idyll. His message of the Kingdom
had aspects of awe-compelling and overwhelming greatness;
even in His presence men trembled at the word of God. Yet
it is pre-eminently in Jesus that forgiveness appears and
approaches. As it has been put: "How could Christ have
had need of teaching what was simply the primary, self-
evident fact to every Jew, and especially to every believer in
'the Kingdom,' namely that God was 'the Holy One in
Israel'? He had rather to teach and to proclaim what was
not self-evident to the Jews, but His own original discovery
and revelation that this very 'Holy One' is a 'heavenly
Father.'"[5] The wonder of Christianity lies in this, that the
Holy God receives sinners. To say so uncompromisingly is in
line with the language of the Bible, which customarily fixes
on the astounding fact without attempting to explain it otherwise than by referring it, adoringly, to the grace of God—
which is of course only to "explain" a marvel by a marvel.
It speaks of God's "removing" transgression, of His "blotting it out," of His "covering" sins or "casting them into
the sea," of His not mentioning a man's sins to him, of His
remembering sins and iniquities no more. So, in the final
instance, what Jesus gives to the men who hung upon His
words or touched His garment, what Luther in his agony
heard and rejoiced in as he laid his ear to the New Testament, is assurance that to long for peace with the Father is to
have it. It is all but unbelievable that the Righteous One
should forgive unrighteousness, yet the Church knows it to be
the commonest thing in all the world. The reality of pardon,
imparted by such a God, can never be demonstrated to one
who has not known it from within, nor can it be shown to

[5] R. Otto, *The Idea of the Holy* (E. T.), p. 86.

follow necessarily, as Y follows X, from any rational notion of God that might figure in a metaphysical argumentation. But though not to be explained, it can none the less be experienced as something irresistibly borne in upon the mind that submits itself, with candour, to the impression of Jesus Christ. The point, however, is that it *is* experienced as that which passes all understanding. It is the breaking of eternity into time, the intervention of a love beyond all measures, a supernatural event not deducible by any human calculus from the nature of the universe but rather the spontaneous and unanalysable deed of God. We do not reach it by hard thinking, we are confronted by it. It emerges from pure love as an inexplicable gift to the unworthy which conveys the solution of our sorest problems, in the sense that we can now endure their weight unmurmuringly and perhaps even with joy, since God has forgiven us and is our Friend. He has done all; the love and the glory are His alone.

What chiefly comes home to us, in such moments, is that the initiative is altogether with God. He is the Living One. He has acted, has interposed to open His heart to us, and has thereby made all things new. Of His own movement He has altered our relation to Himself. *We* could not have altered it, any more than by sheer intensity of wish the sinking castaway can draw himself up beyond the devouring surf. God must put forth His arm and work mightily. And this He does in fact; He, the Judge of men, brings the guilty sinner, as he is, into the enjoyment of His love, provided only that he chooses to be brought in and responds to the love willingly. Henceforth it is for us to live in the attitude and mind of a child whose fault has been forgiven. Gratitude, gladness, exhilaration is the only fit temper for all who have been thus blessed. And with the gratitude will go, naturally, the quiet and unselfish confidence that the Father who pardons will never abandon His work of love and pity. We are still sinful, it is true; but God " has for ever."

For sound and wholesome Christianity it is, I think, impossible to emphasise too much the fact that in this whole field of experience the first step is, and remains, with God. It is to Him, manifestly, that we owe the existence of the

Gospel; whatever obscurity may surround the place and contribution of the human will in the experience of being saved
and however natural the protest against an all-absorbing
fatalism of grace, it remains true that the reality of Jesus
owes nothing to us but is a simple gift of the Father. When
our eyes open spiritually, the first object on which they
light—an object they do not make but *find*—is a gracious
God, who is calling sinners to Himself. In responding by
faith to His call we act indeed, but it is the activity of
taking. It is not otherwise in later Christian life. There we
are still receivers, and He the Doer of all. A communion
has arisen between God and sinful hearts whose permanent
quality is identical with that of its inception; to the end it is a
communion resting not on any self-produced activities of
pardoned men but perpetually and exclusively on their response to the movement of God's creative love. At each point
the one right thing for the sinful to do is to cast themselves
on that reconciling mercy of God which from the first has
made them debtors. Thought, feeling and endeavour are to
find basis and inspiration in the constant mercy of the
Father.

Thus the wonder of forgiveness does not cease but rather
grows and gathers intensity once the first glow of realisation
has passed.[6] To the saint it is a daily discovery that God
does not cast him out. Christian as he is, he remains a
sinner; saved, doubtless, in respect that he is now in filial
communion with the Father, yet not translated magically into
a sphere where temptation is unknown, but set to develop
moral freedom through struggle and discipline, under the
leadership of God and in His enjoyed love. Recurring faults
are met by a mercy which he would not dare to claim in
right and which excludes the notion that " salvation," given

[6] Even so rewarding a writer on the psychology of religion as
Professor Pratt can rest satisfied with the conclusion, in his *Religious
Consciousness* (1921), that the " sense of sin " has been given too
prominent a place in normal schemes of conversion. Here he is quite
possibly right, but he hardly inquires whether it is not in the course
of the Christian life, perhaps years after conversion has taken place,
that conviction of sin may become most acute, and the need for
forgiveness, accordingly, most intensely felt.

freely at the start, could be sustained in being by meritorious performance. In the family of God all are in this sense "unprofitable servants" to the end, costing more than the worth of any service.

We reach the conclusion, accordingly, that the ground and spring of forgiveness is in God, not in man. The source and presupposition of its occurrence lies in His being what He is—faithfully and unchangeably the Lover of men. But this implies that the sweep of His mercy must not be narrowed at any stage. When Jesus spoke of the goodness of the Father who sends rain on the just and the unjust, and is kind to the unthankful, He uttered a trust which evangelicalism has been tempted to ignore, or defend in tones of apology. It is not only the good, thank God, who live as His beneficiaries. Mercy is His being, and streams forth to all in uninterrupted kindness. To all, however evil, He continues the gifts and possibilities of life, with a throng of varied powers and impulses suited to the development of personality in the kingdom of free and loving spirits; this also is grace to sinners, given not reluctantly but willingly; in a sense it is forgiveness, manifesting His untiring will to save. How men often reflect on this in a marvelling temper when they have found God in Christ, and look back across years of dull insensibility! How many things in that old life become expressive, witnessing to the ceaseless patience that had pursued us! Even then we were not forsaken by the Father. He surrounded us with persons, influences, appeals which are a proof, in retrospect, that He had never turned from us. That is a fact revealed to us through personal and individual experience, but it must hold good for the whole world. He who was merciful to our folly is merciful to all.

However this may be, it does not entitle us to ignore a plain and momentous distinction. Things reveal their nature by what they do, and what forgiveness in the specifically Christian sense does is to establish communion between God and forgiven men. In fact, however, this does not at all necessarily follow from the merciful and universal Divine forbearance that broods over all men everywhere. Long-suffering is shown to the impenitent, that they may come to a better mind, but the capacity of sin to hinder communion with God is not thereby removed; they do not enter, *eo ipso,* into the friendship of a Father with forgiven sons. Hence if we speak here of " pardon," we do it in a sense so excessively wide as to be misleading. It is less pardon than the permanent possibility of pardon as bestowed in Jesus. In contrast to the forgiveness set forth in the Gospel, it is inchoate and rudimentary.

The significance of modern psychology for our problem, especially in its practical issues, may justly rank as one of the most actual of our preliminary questions. What is the bearing on our subject of the most recent study of mind? Can psychology tell us what forgiveness is?

Here more than one reply seems to be possible. To begin with, psychology may elect to leave forgiveness alone, as falling outside its province. Psychologists as such, it may be held, have no means of deciding whether there is or is not a forgiving God, whether the belief on the sinful man's part that he has been forgiven is or is not an objectively true belief. They can do no more than describe the mental processes or machinery by means of which the consciousness of forgiveness comes to be uppermost in the inner life, together with the conditions psychical, environmental, and even physiological which precede (some would say, produce) this result —e.g. the instincts striving towards satisfaction, fulfilment and completeness which thereby are assuaged. It will appear, I think, that this at least points in the right direction.

Or again, it may be argued that psychology is only concerned with what happens in the mind of one who believes himself to be a subject of Divine forgiveness, but that this includes the important consequences for mental pacification and rejuvenescence which flow from the inrush of the new certainty. Attention is drawn to the obstacles to power and freedom found in the universal human experience of guilt, to the paralysing effect of remorse upon our moral energies, and the vast psychological importance of having repressed moral secrets brought up into the open, in order to relieve the patient of some hidden complex by which he has been haunted. Such a view does not rest content with processes but in addition tries to decipher their meaning. This meaning, however, is construed as a purely immanent one. It consists in the value realised by the new readjustment of the self to its own desires, memories, perturbations and divisions, as well as to its social surroundings, whether these other be people or institutions. To a large extent this seems a sound and defensible position. It is only when forgiveness is taken as having no transcendent significance—as a question of mental hygiene but not of objective Divine relationships—that difficulties arise.

Once more, it has been contended that, by exhibiting the origin of belief in sin and guilt, the moral law, and God, as well as their gradually acquired social predominance in history, psychology can let us see their merely subjective import. They remain, perhaps, but they remain as detected illusions, of which psychological treatment can relieve us, and which at a high level of reflection it is our duty to discard. This, stated briefly but not unfairly, is the general hypothesis now being set forth by a good many representatives of what is called the "New Psychology," though not by all. If the hypothesis be sound, clearly the belief that one can be forgiven and know it is no better than a hallucination. But obviously the hypothesis in itself is not psychology at all; it is a dogma of naturalistic metaphysic, illegitimately tacked on to a study of mental life which (rightly for its own purpose) had ignored everything in mind but necessitated processes. In this point of view, the newer psychology is just the latest edition of a very familiar theory—psychological determinism.

Not that the inquirers of this new school have not thrown new light upon sin. They have placed valuable emphasis on the emotional aspects of sin, reminding us that feeling enters into it as well as volition; they have shown us, at all events with a new vividness, how the raw material of sin is latent in that deranged balance of instincts with which all start in life, and how actual sin consists in their misdirection; they have underscored the fact that the moral organism, like the physical, may be thrown out of gear in a manner for which we are not responsible in the usual sense of that word. Such insight may not be as new and original as we are frequently invited to suppose, but it is worth having. What Freud and his disciples tell us concerning dreams and moral perversities does, after all due allowance, deepen our sense of what is meant by " the corruption of man's heart." We realise afresh some of the actual elements in our psychical make-up at which the theologians of an older day were pointing when they insisted on " total depravity," even though they turned a blind eye to the fact that, in agreement with St. Augustine as with Goethe, we are justified in predicating congenital good of man no less than congenital evil. Also the new psychologists have drawn needed attention to the distinction between sin and moral disease. It is well to be reminded that things like kleptomania, sexual obsessions, morbid fears, and genuinely ungovernable tempers are, like functional nerve disorders, due to unconscious repressed complexes; they are disorders of conduct, to be dealt with by the mental physician.

Even so, however, representatives of the newer psychology at its best will have it that moral disease is one thing, and sin another. For Dr. J. A. Hadfield,[7] to take one example, moral diseases are due to causes over which we have little or no control, while sins " result from a deliberate and conscious choice of the self, and depend upon the acceptance of a low ideal." Or, as he puts it elsewhere, the essential psychological distinction between the two is this, that " sin is due to *wrong sentiments,* moral disease is due to *morbid complexes* giving rise to uncontrollable impulses." Waiving the not unimportant question whether the best Christian opinion would endorse the view that sin is always voluntary, and may not at times consist of unwilled outbursts of feeling, like jealousy or hate, and this occasionally at least where there cannot reasonably be any talk of a complex, we note the fact that on such terms room is definitely made for sins which can only be " cured " in so far as they first are pardoned.

This, however, is not the aspect or form of the New

[7] *Psychology and Morals,* chap. vi.

Psychology which for the moment has succeeded in imposing itself upon the public mind. Freud, Jung and possibly (in a more popular vein) Tansley are the best-known names, and it is undeniable that some of their theories concerning the origins and intrinsic nature of religion, make the consideration of Divine forgiveness wholly superfluous. In regard to these theories in general it has been said with point that in reality " they represent the suppressed complexes of certain psychological writers and obtain credence only through the belief that they rest on scientific inquiry." We may reasonably beg leave to put aside as unimportant the arguments on religion of a writer who can actually make it a strong point against faith that no one has ever seen a God![8] Clearly if the power of rational choice be denied, whether in the name of instinct or the unconscious, sin as understood by Christianity is a chimera. Or if the moral law be denuded of all objective validity and reduced merely to the level of social utilities, if conscience be no more than an emotional response to circumstances prompted by herd-instinct, so that the sense of obligation loses its sublime absoluteness of imperative, again sin is a delusion. And, finally, if God be *only*[9] a projection of the human mind, and the affirmation of His reality a mere device by which the human self endeavours, more or less successfully, to escape from the discomforting realisation of its own weakness and from the conflicts engendered by opposed instincts; if, as Tansley graphically puts it, " the mind, like the Indian juggler, can climb up a rope the end of which it has thrown into the heavens "—then once more it is vain to speak of sin or pardon. Sin has now become no more than mental uneasiness, and religious people may quite justly be described as abnormal neuropaths who persist in an infantile attitude to life and to themselves. But it must have

[8] See Jung, *The Psychology of the Unconscious*, p. 30 (quoted by Balmforth, *Is Christian Experience an Illusion?*, p. 88).

[9] Two remarks may be made: (1) Of course, like every objectively true idea, the idea of God *is* a projection, in the sense that the ideal content is in the judgment referred to reality, (2) in certain instances, no doubt, " God " is for a child nothing (or little) more than a " projection " of his father. But this *is* childish, and can quite well be transcended.

occurred to readers of these crude and at times unintelligent hypotheses that the recipe of auto-suggestion, thus peddled about like quack medicine, is applied in a strangely fortuitous manner. It is natural to ask: is religion peculiar in owing its existence to auto-suggestion? May the same be said of morality, of the belief in an external world, possibly even of science? Is it quite inconceivable that the theory of auto-suggestion as explanatory of religious faith may itself be the offspring of auto-suggestion? For my part, I cannot see why the fool who said in his heart, " There is no God," should not have been afflicted by auto-suggestion at least as much as He who said: " I am not alone, for the Father is with Me." Perhaps, after all, what we have before us is little more or better than an example of the incurable tendency of men to suppose they have solved a problem when they have but indicated the difficulty by a new big word. Certainly it is hard to understand how herd-suggestion or infantile fantasy could produce anything so bitterly mortifying to human pride as the Christian sense of sin and unworthiness. Is it not more credible that this painful consciousness of ill-desert re-emerges unfailingly, throughout the generations, because in every age men have found themselves confronted by the Holy One, who shows them what in fact they are?

Speaking broadly, then, we may conclude that large and fruitful as the most modern psychological discussions in this field have often been, they have not invariably been accompanied by the perception that on certain ultimate issues, concerned with our attitude to those fundamental personal relationships which are the core of reality, psychology can have nothing to say. It is as much the fact now as ever before that religious truth, if it be truth, can as little as truth of a moral or scientific nature be undermined by psychological analysis, however searching. Of course, if people insist on defining man as *essentially* a gregarious animal, inspired by a herd-made morality, and ignore the really interesting fact that moral pioneers have been those who revolted against the tyranny of the " herd," it is not surprising that they should reach hardly any positive results in Social Psychology, except those which are plainly false or inadequate. As a whole the verdict of Dr. E. J. Bicknell is sound: "Psychology can teach us nothing about the essential nature of sin or original sin. It has thrown much light on the psychical machinery of sin. . . . But from the standpoint of pure theology the idea of sin still remains unaffected. Our acceptance or rejection of the Christian view of sin must be determined on other grounds than those of psychology."[10] The chief problems, in short, remain exactly what they were. In that case it is manifest that no considerations based upon the alleged findings of psychology can at all lessen the urgency of the problem of forgiveness.

Note

THE THEOLOGY OF HERRMANN

No modern thinker has made a more profound study of forgiveness, human and Divine, than Herrmann of Marburg; and it may be convenient that we should bring together some of his leading thoughts.[11] He is chiefly interested in the pardon accorded to man by man in so far as it casts light on the crucial experience of the sinner entering into communion with God. The one has a real analogy to the other; it is indeed its herald and preparation.

He points out that in human intercourse itself there is a mutually exclusive relationship between holiness and kindness, righteousness and love, when these qualities are interpreted strictly. They cannot be reconciled with each other by pure thought. It is only in some concrete instance that we discover how righteousness and love *can* unite in a real fact which is at once incomprehensible and undeniable, a fact which wins from us an equally mysterious and inevitable self-surrender. The act of human kindness in which we are

[10] *The Christian Idea of Sin and Original Sin,* p. 78. The whole of Section IV there should be read.

[11] Cf. some paragraphs in de Boor's excellent article in the *Zeitschrift für Theologie und Kirche* (1926), pp. 41-45.

pardoned is an act both of exclusion and inclusion, of rejection and acceptance, paradoxically yet most definitely combined. " The moment," he writes, " in which these two experiences, of the power of goodness as it judges us and of love as it seeks us, meet as the effects within us of one and the same personal will, is the experience of forgiveness. Only so do we receive the forgiveness of a person. What is essential is that we should perceive that owing to our guilt and the other's moral goodness, fellowship between us is excluded, while yet we experience the contrary fact that the other is not merely inflicting punishment on us but seeking us for ourselves."[12] "Everyone knows the experience of this power as it works upon him. It is the most effectual thing in education; apart from it we should not become men at all. We are not really educated save as we make the discovery that others, whom we regard as better than ourselves, are sparing no effort to aid us. In presence of such self-sacrificing goodness, our eyes open to the one and only thing to which we can make unreserved submission. It is then we perceive a reality which is no longer alien to our deepest life, and to which our nature opens. In freely surrendering to it we realise our utter dependence on it, while at the same time we are lifted into a triumphant freedom of life such as we find nowhere else."[13]

Now, just because this human experience of being pardoned is so strange and inexplicable, we can learn what it means only by coming up against it in fact. The vital thing is the concrete event, and its place cannot be taken by any generalisations about human love or about man's plain duty to forgive his neighbour. The reality of our guilt makes all such theorisings or sententious hopes seem mere culpable levity. The man who takes his friend's pardon for granted, as a thing of course, is morally bankrupt. But what we cannot arrive at by hard thinking is brought home to us as an amazing reality by the event. Forgiveness in idea is unconvincing; forgiveness as happening to us in real life changes everything and is its own evidence. In human intercourse, therefore, forgiveness and kindness to be real must be his-

[12] *Ethik*, p. 130.   [13] *Gesammelte Aufsätze*, p. 347 f.

torical; that is to say, except as they *happen* concretely between persons, they are nothing. Their validity is not that of general principles but of actual occurrence. No universal proof of them could be given, nor can they be made the objects of a necessitating demand. In short, there is something religious about them. In themselves they contain the two essential marks of that which alone can satisfy the religious mind: they contain holiness and love as a single unity. "Both, we experience in our contact with persons who enrich us by their kindness yet humble us by the depth of their sacrificial fellowship of spirit."[14] "The man who had never known anything of a love that gave itself for him, would be incapable of believing in God."[15]

And yet this experience, as between man and man, is not in itself a revelation or discovery of God. It does not take us all the way. For one thing, man's pardon of man is sharply limited to the circumstances of a particular offence; it does not and cannot cover the man's whole life. No one can forgive his neighbour's sin. What appears to me in others as pure goodness does make clearer to me the fact that goodness alone can help me; yet it is just this goodness that erects a barrier between me and these my benefactors, and renders them incapable of meeting my sorest need. Our sin, indeed, may come to blind us utterly to the human goodness we once perceived, and quench in us the trust and reverence it had evoked. For another thing, man's power to forgive man is undermined by his own sinfulness, which leaves him with nothing more than ability to condone this or that particular fault or shortcoming. The goodness we are conscious of in others is invariably submerged again in our awareness of their sin, and we are left in doubt whether what we have before us is moral personality in the strict sense or only a certain blossoming of natural good temper. "Those Christians whose moral bearing and faith have stimulated our own faith into activity, may break our faith again by weakness of character. Thus our trust in the forgiving power of goodness may be quickened and killed by our intercourse with the same human persons. Hence the religious experience in

14 *Gesammelte Aufsätze*, p. 209.   15 *Ibid.*, p. 423.

which we apprehend the pardoning love of God can only arise through contact with One who evokes an utter reverence unclouded by any doubts, who shames us by holiness yet lifts us up by love, who forgives in sheer purity with a pardon that covers, not this or that fault merely, but our personality as a sinful whole."

Such reverence, it is clear, must owe its rise in the soul to an encounter, definite and historical, with a concrete fact capable of evoking and sustaining it. Such forgiveness is only credible when we actually have it imparted to us. The guilt of which we are conscious even as against a fellow-man will not yield to mere ratiocination; it is removed (though at best in a relative degree) only when he takes the initiative and seeks us out for friendly reconcilement. *A fortiori* the forgiveness that is to cover our whole life must impinge upon us through a concrete reality, present in the time-series of events, which we find it impossible to negate or evade. At what point in our existence do we meet with a reality answering to this description? Where in all being is the fact that overpowers us as an irresistible proof of the power and grace of God, and so wins us for the Father? It is the Person of Jesus, set forth in the New Testament. "Forgiveness only becomes ours when we actually behold God Himself in the Christ who is for us an indubitable fact. The only way we can receive the forgiveness of God is this, that He makes us feel the penalty of our sin, and yet at the same time brings home to us the incomprehensible fact that He is seeking us and not giving us up. . . . The forgiveness of God is not a demonstrable doctrine, still less a notion that can be appropriated by an act of will. It is a religious experience. It must stand before us as an incomprehensible reality that the same fact that increased our grief for our unfaithfulness and weakness of will nevertheless is also perceptible to us as a word of God convincing us that He has stooped down to us. The appearance of Jesus can become for us this expression of God's forgiveness as soon as we perceive in Him, as nowhere else, the nearness of God. It is not through long-winded dogmatic reflections that we reach the sense that we receive the forgiveness of God through Jesus; that comes into our consciousness as soon as we understand religiously, or lay hold of as a work of God upon us, the fact that the Being of this Man is part of our sphere of existence. For then His death, as He bore it and as He expounded it in words at the Last Supper, becomes to us the Word of God that overcomes our feeling of guilt. The God who comes near us in Christ reconciles us with Himself by that death."[16]

No one at all closely acquainted with Herrmann's theology can feel any doubt that such typical passages as these contain the secret and power of his thought. In a sense he was a "one-idea'd" man; he was determined to know nothing, as a pathway to God, but the Person of Jesus. On this he dwelt with prophetic insistency; and whatever be the defects of his argument, from the standpoint of a fully systematic thinker, it was this which stamped his message as—in a rare degree and in the great sense—evangelical.

[16] *Communion with God* (Eng. trans., slightly altered), pp. 140-142.

CHAPTER III

SIN AND GUILT

We are unlikely, it will be granted, to reach valid or impressive conclusions about forgiveness till we have first gained a clear insight that there exists something real and grave to be forgiven—something in which personally we are implicated—and also have in essence ascertained what this something is. Now to that in man which must be put away by remission, if fellowship with God is to be real, the Christian mind gives the name " sin " or " sins." Those who deny the need for forgiveness obviously do so because they deny the reality of sin, and this again they do because they doubt or deny the being of God as Holy Love. These three terms, " God," " sin," " forgiveness," interpreted in a Christian sense, are in meaning such that they indissociably involve each other, and the negation of any one of them logically carries with it the negation of all.

There are, however, several questions relating to sin which it is superfluous for us to treat of here. We are only concerned to understand sin as it forms the object of Divine pardon. What is meant by the sin or sins which, as Christian experience proves, cry out for absolution? Or rather, as " sin " after all is an abstraction, and the only reality in the case is this person or that in personal relationships with God, what is meant by describing men as " sinful "? Why does their sinfulness constitute a need for being forgiven? But this question, if answerable at all, can be answered apart from any effort to solve various other problems which inevitably arise out of reflection upon sin, and which have filled a large place in the literature of the subject. The reality and character of the Fall, the nature of original sin, the genesis of sin—these are aspects of the larger topic which may be put aside as on the whole irrelevant to our purpose. The characteristics of sin which make pardon a necessity can in a real degree be understood irrespectively of the opinions we may form on those more outlying and perhaps insoluble matters. Here, accordingly, we shall leave them untouched.

The chief end of man, in the Christian view, is to turn into conscious and willed obedience, throughout all the powers of his being, that absolute dependence upon God by which he lives. He is man at all in virtue of that principle of reason and self-determination which links him to the Supreme Reason of the world, which moves within him as an infinite and mysterious element that sets him apart from the animal creation and gives him a place in nature all his own. Thus viewed, man has at once affinity to God and value for God— an affinity that forms the basis and possibility of fellowship, a value incommensurable with that of all created "things." The worst and weakest men are conscious, however dimly, of being subject not merely to natural but to ethical and Divine law. And the best within us is explicable, not by reference to the system of immanent causality within which the laws of energy hold good, but by the immediate and constitutive relation in which the human spirit is set to the transcendent life of God. Try to explain ourselves as we may, there is a vast residue that finite causes will not account for. It is to these potentially infinite factors that Scripture points in the great words: "God created man in His own image." And what the man thus fashioned is called upon to achieve is the autonomous development of his whole being under the control of that creative and holy Will. Our happiness lies in obedience.

When, however, we survey the world of humanity, when we look into our own breast, what is it that we find? Anything else than such a normal and continuous development of life, unfolding to the fulness of perfected powers. We find, instead, the universal phenomenon of man's nature divided against itself, at variance with neighbour and with God. If our true destiny is to obey, it is a destiny we are obviously unable to accomplish. It is not simply that we freely reject the Higher Will; we discover that to accept it gladly is beyond us. All who reach moral personality learn, on the faintest self-scrutiny, that their moral being is somehow wrong and crooked; that alongside of the commanding sense of obligation there are fermenting within them a set of half-blind and half-perverted instincts, evil tendencies which solicit their choice, lead their will astray, and often master it shamefully. In short, we cannot begin the life of moral struggle and consent to face ourselves without feeling within us the dreary pain of *the bad conscience*—without becoming aware, that is, that our will is evil. It is not wholly evil, as we shall see, but evil taints it in every element. Thus the fatal distinction between what we are and what we ought to be comes home to us. We are forced to look with open eyes on the one hand at our moral obligations, on the other at our moral incapacity. Both experiences are our own—the sense of what we should be, imposed on us by God, and the sense of what we are, thrust on us by a corrupt nature. It is an internal schism, a rupture in the unity of the self; and in consequence the self becomes so far a scene of anarchy and impotence. And in the last resort we are divided in ourselves because we are sundered from Him in whose will is our peace. To be alienated from God, for whose service and obedience we were made, is the invariable antecedent of alienation from self and neighbour; and the breaking of that unseen tie, if unrepaired by forgiveness, will bring every candid man to the avowal that he is dragging with him through life a weight of unmanageable and perverse evil, which in some sense he must own as his and cannot disown.

This wrong state or attitude of the will is called " sin " by all who acknowledge its reality, and what is distinctive of the Christian religion in this area is not so much its recognition of sin as the new estimate placed upon it. Recognition there has always been. It has not usually been denied that men do steal, or lie, or hate, or indeed that in the main human history has been a record of tragic failure. St. Augustine and Huxley, leagues apart as they may be, are in agreement here. But the religion of the Bible is original and final in its contention that the distinctive quality in sin lies not chiefly in its antagonism to our higher life, or to the welfare of society, but in its antagonism to the will of the living God. That will was fully disclosed through the compassionate love of Jesus. Accordingly, we now detect and measure sin by its unlikeness to the spirit of Jesus; we know sin when we see it by its difference from Him. Men had other serviceable criteria of sin before His day, but these are antiquated now. It is in the light of Christ that we see sin clearly and can in some real degree understand how it looks to God, whose estimate of it we are bound to share so far as we discover it. In proportion as a man grows familiar with the fact of Christ and lets the illumination of that pure spirit fall on his own soiled nature, he will become more sensitive to the horror of sin; also with growing insight he will discriminate more surely what is sin from what is not.

Historically, we can scarcely overrate the importance of this fact, that every closer approach to true knowledge of God has been accompanied by deeper insight into sin, though not by any means, as some thinkers have supposed, by an increase in the attention given to sin. We are wise if we " shut our eyes from looking upon evil," and decide that it is unprofitable to meditate on our own wrong-doing. But apart from this practical maxim, it remains emphatically true that every growing apprehension of God's reality and its meaning for our lives brings us to a profounder realisation of the sheer evilness of all that exiles us from Him and from blessedness. And here the limiting case, to repeat it once more, is the effect upon us of Jesus, who shows us God and therefore *ipso facto* shows us ourselves. In His light, we begin to understand what sin is and also why it is sin. Moral evil instantly ceases to be something arbitrary and incomprehensible, as it is in many religions and even at times in the Old Testament, where the worshipper cannot tell why certain things are wrong and need pardon in the sight of God, because the commandments he is bidden to keep have no intrinsic or self-evidencing rightness. All such arbitrariness is at an end for the man who has met with Jesus Christ. If, as He has taught us, to be one with God means confiding in the Heavenly Father with unqualified trust and in the service of His other children, it follows that sin means every disposition and action which lack faith and love. Sin, essentially, is selfish failure to trust and obey God.

In technical language, the predication of sin is a judgment not merely of existence but of value. It asserts both a fact and its character. What conscience is expressing in such a judgment is condemnation of an attitude or act as exhibiting a certain kind of will or person. The condemnation may start from the outward action, but it does not stop there; it includes the agent and his motives, for the act *has* a character and is what it is only as it phenomenalises a personal will or choice. Though colloquially we use it more broadly, sin strictly is a religious term, as is indicated by the fact that when condemning anything in ourselves or others as sin we assume without reasoning that we are dealing with it as it is "in God's sight." It has been done against Him; He sees it in its real colours; our judgment, if sound, is an echo of His. We may pass relatively valid judgments upon ourselves and our neighbours; in comparison with our neighbours we may even feel justified in assigning to ourselves or to them certain comparative degrees of goodness; but the absolute truth concerning our lives or theirs can only be pronounced by God. We are sinners in His eyes, though before men we might be without reproach, and even our own heart may not condemn us.

The nature of sin becomes perhaps more clear if we contrast it, in the first place, with misfortune. Between the two there are resemblances but also cardinal dissimilarities. Misfortune we deplore, at times bitterly, and its onset we normally do our best to resist or avert. But we do not consider it to arise, like sin, from within our very self, nor does the most crushing visitation of calamity necessarily rob us of self-respect. We feel that it is possible for men to rise in triumph over suffering; nay, that they may do so in the very article of pain; and the consciousness may justly be uppermost that by enduring disaster worthily it may be given them to realise nobler moral values and fulfil higher ends than would otherwise have been attained—ends and values that in themselves may conceivably be of infinite importance. But when we charge ourselves with sin, we are covered by our own judgment with reproach and censure, which we are compelled to believe is a reaffirmation of the censure of God.

In the second place, sin is to be carefully distinguished from error or ignorance. We have often to reprimand ourselves for blundering thought or action, and the annoyance or grief caused by these mistakes may have all degrees of intensity and duration. But error in and by itself is not sin; after erring, we blame our ideas but not our will, our insight but not the ruling energies of our being. What was wrong was our conception of the facts rather than the motives or principles by which in action we were guided. We distinguish between our self and the ideas that filled consciousness and were erroneously identified with realities; the second we chide morally, but not the first.

Among the positions familiarly associated with the name of Ritschl is the contention that sin essentially is ignorance, and that on any other terms God's forgiveness of it would be unintelligible. The only form of sin not to be described as ignorance is the act or attitude of those who resolutely and definitely reject Christ. Now it cannot be denied that ignorance or error is present in all sin. As it has been put: " No man if he fully understood himself, if he took everything into account, if he looked at God and at his own nature—what he was made for—and at the final issues, could sin." In choosing evil, we are imperfectly aware of all that our choice entails. " Father, forgive them," Jesus said, " for they know not what they do." This saying amply proves that ignorance enters, as a palliating factor, into many sins, perhaps into all; but we must not give it a range of meaning far beyond the speaker's intention. It cannot mean that those who killed our Lord were totally unconscious of wrong-doing, for the experience of Judas is evidence of the contrary. Not only so; we must ask whether it was mere short-sighted prejudice that blinded these men to Jesus' greatness. The Gospels plainly show that scribes and Pharisees had in some degree felt the wonderful power of Jesus' words, so that their rejection of Him in the end could not be wholly due to misunderstanding. He had not spoken of His mission obscurely or hidden from them His works of compassionate mercy. The truth is that like ourselves they were able to shut their eyes to the holy love that stood before them; the call to penitence and submission had wounded pride too sorely, and vengeance claimed its prey. Let him who has never rejected or betrayed the Saviour first cast a stone at them.

But apart from this historical example, two considerations insist on being allowed for. First, in the hour of penitence we find it impossible to urge that our sin has been no more than error. To describe it so is a reading of facts which even in the case of our neighbour is unconvincing and in our own is self-evidently false. At times, perhaps not very infrequently, we wilfully disobey God with open eyes; we see His will with perfect clearness, yet are aware of selfish or perverse impulses which drive us to oppose it advisedly and directly, and to these we yield. Malice, self-indulgence, unbelief—we sin in all these ways, knowing for certain that we are doing wrong. Doubtless in choosing the evil we do not resolve to be done with God for ever; we cheat ourselves, or bribe conscience to be silent, by protesting that this sin is an exception to the rule, which we intend shall not affect our permanent relationship to God; yet thus voluntarily to ignore the meaning of our sin is itself an act implying both knowledge and will. Had sin been mere ignorance, enlightenment would have sufficed; yet it is simple psychological fact that the clearest knowledge is often unable to break the fetters of evil habit. We must therefore reject a view which is really only explicable in a Christian teacher by the lingering influence of Greek thought—which in general Ritschl so much deprecated—in this case the idea that virtue is knowledge. The penitent as he pours out his confession is aware that to exculpate himself by pleading ignorance would be to aggravate the wrong, not lessen it. And a theory which breaks down just at the moment when we get our clearest look at sin can scarcely approve itself to a calm judgment.

But again, the motive underlying Ritschl's view is equally unsound. He is obviously of the opinion that the grace of God as Forgiver resides in this, that He regards our sin as ignorance and therefore pardonable. Sin done intentionally and with premeditation, it is suggested, would be unpardonable, as in Hebrew religion were "sins done with a high hand"; it reaches a pitch of enormity to which Divine mercy does not and cannot extend. The assumption is that if we could but share God's view of sin we should realise it to be less grave than we had supposed, because more excusable. And this is contrary to Christian experience; the movement of thought in the mind of a true penitent is exactly the reverse. So far from learning to regard sin as less serious because now justly interpreted as the product of misconception, he perceives with an ever deepening insight that sin is definitely rebellious, even though the rebellion may be for a time beneath consciousness. We have sinned because we meant to sin. When two people quarrel, we do not describe the facts accurately by saying that they differed in opinion, one of the opinions being erroneous; we recognise that what has broken up their friendship is a collision of wills, and that reconciliation, instead of being facilitated by the benevolent pretence that "it was all a mistake," can only be brought about by action which presupposes the existence of a real hostility. In like manner, open acknowledgment of the willed character of sin, of that element of deliberateness in it by which our personal relationship to God was broken, is a psychological prerequisite of truthful desire for pardon and of its glad reception.

Further, the view to which Ritschl leans can hardly fail to obscure the wonder of forgiveness, as transcending all we could ask or think. By characterising pardonable sin as ignorance, he more than half implies that the Divine mercy, while equal to the remission of smaller sins, will not rise to the height of forgiving the greater. This is not the teaching of the New Testament. The God who has sought and found men in Christ is a God who forgives to the uttermost, with a mercy that will bear any strain. He pardons, for Christ's sake, not merely those who have sinned inadvertently, but those who know they have sinned with all their might, exerting their whole force and thrusting the will of God aside. No sin to Him is unpardonable but that of refusing to ask pardon.

But if sin is neither misfortune nor error, although it contains elements of each, how shall we fix its meaning exactly? There is much to be said for the position that sin, as a simple datum of experience, is indefinable, in the sense that we cannot express its significance by any terms in which that significance is not already implied. But at least we may describe it as indifference or opposition to the will of God, that will being identified with the morally highest that we know. Sin is the lack or refusal of faith and love. The gravity of sin, so conceived, is manifestly relative to the character of God before whom and against whom the sin is knowingly committed; and, as we have already seen, this means that since Jesus Christ has been here, the hues of sin have grown darker. Outside Christendom sin may be folly, or ugliness, or disease; but these ideas cannot be taken as exhaustive or even as usefully descriptive now that sinners have faced the height and depth of love unveiled by the cross of Jesus. The difference is not superficial but radical, for it is occasioned by a new thought of God. Sin then is the claim, explicit or implicit, to live independently of God and to put something, whether self or world, in His place. It is in fact *godlessness,* the will that for us there should be no God at all; and while the chief moral forms in which this spiritual attitude finds expression are selfishness and sensuality, yet these terms do not bring out the fact, as a working conception should, that sin is what it is in virtue of its bearing on God and His will for men. It is a crucial point that sin has vitiated our personal relationships with Him, because all such relationships take their meaning and colour from the inward disposition, and it is in the disposition that sin resides. Thereby we have got wrong with the Father, and the supreme question in religion is how we may get right. If rectification is possible, do we take the initiative, or must the first active steps be taken by God Himself? This in brief is the problem for which the Christian message of forgiveness proposes a solution. It declares that the Father puts us right with Himself in pure grace, at an inward cost of which Calvary is the measure.

To the student of forgiveness and its problems, the one hopeful answer to the question: Where does my sin come from? is, curiously enough, From myself. Unless its source lies there, to speak of its being pardoned is meaningless and irrelevant. We might as well talk of logical error being cured by drugs. If sin does not arrive through me, if its traces cannot be followed up till they lose themselves in my act and nature, it does not require to be forgiven nor could forgiveness by any conceivable method be brought to bear. But let us not fail to register the fact that by tracking sin to the secret places of the human spirit we are not in reality *explaining* sin; we are not looking through a microscope, as it were, and watching the spectacle of the non-moral being transformed into the immoral. The problem *why* we sin, *why* we misuse our moral freedom, still confronts us as implacably as ever. Sin in the last resort is radically unintelligible; it is incapable of being interpreted in terms of rational purpose; it is irreducible to factors which in a moral sense can be made transparent and self-accrediting. As we contemplate the sin we have done, it confronts us as a thoroughly irrational entity, impervious to light—inexplicable to the mind, and to the conscience inexcusable. We can find no real place for it in the theoretical or the practical world. All the possible aids to reflection do not enable us to make sin satisfying either to reason or to love, but we stand with bowed head in presence of the accusing fact: "The good that I would I do not, but the evil that I would not, that I do."[1] We have no option but to conclude that that abandonment of God in which, by its nature, sin consists is the mysterious outcome alike of necessity and of freedom. It springs from natural tendencies which, so far as can be seen, are unavoidable, but none the less it is a thing of personal choice, for which we reproach ourselves. To put sin down to the account of external influences is not to lessen but to increase our sin by covering it with false excuses and poisoning the springs of truth within. On this subject Jesus has said the last word: "There is nothing from without a man, that entering into him can defile him."[2]

Forgiveness in the Christian sense is relative not merely to "sin" but also to the idea of "guilt"; yet before passing to a brief study of this second idea we ought to glance at one long-discussed problem which in this context has an importance of its own. The psychological fact that in repenting the best

[1] Rom. 7.19.   [2] Mark 7.15.

Christians ask pardon not only for what they have done, but even more for what they are, signalises the truth that " sin " is predictable, strictly and in the ultimate sense, of the *self* rather than of isolated acts. *We* are sinful. Does this mean that we are purely and exclusively sinful, untouched by good? Probably some candid minds have revolted against the thought of forgiveness on the ground that to ask for it is implicitly to confess that we are wholly and unrelievedly bad. This unmitigated badness in God's sight they deny, and we must inquire how far their denial is justified.

The position thus rejected, which is often supposed to be Scriptural, undoubtedly appears to introduce a fatal duplicity in the utterances of conscience; for it will not be questioned that conscience does pronounce some of our actions right and others wrong. But if right, they must be right in God's judgment and not merely in our own. The distinction of right and wrong is not a figment of human thought; it is valid for the Divine mind. If I have behaved justly to a neighbour, it was an act willed by God, and as done it receives His approval. Not that the manner of its doing may not be faulty, but the core of justice in it, which entitles it to bear the epithet " just," is what He commands. On the other hand, what awakens His displeasure cannot be right from the human standpoint. Further, we may reasonably ask whether the position now in view really is Scriptural. I cannot suppose that the unbiassed reader of the Gospels will conclude that in Jesus' sight men were *wholly* evil, even if destitute of the faith that gave entrance to the Kingdom. To the rich young ruler, for example, He would not have said, " One thing thou lackest," had He regarded him as totally depraved. St. Paul, too, in Romans definitely speaks of Gentiles whose conduct, at any rate in some cases, proved that they possessed a Divine law written on the heart. The Bible is always perfectly frank, much franker than theology has often been; and when it distinguishes good and evil in human practice, recognising the one no less than the other, it does so not from a weakened feeling for sin but because of its insight into facts. Writers of Scripture had so unflinching a view of sin that they could afford to acknowledge openly what in human life was praiseworthy; but more, and perhaps more important, their sense of the living God kept them perpetually aware that no man is ever absolutely without the knowledge of God's will or utterly deprived of His enabling impulse to goodness. If there is good, as there is, in lives not blessed by faith, this is not owing to self-made human virtue, but to the inescapable love and presence of the Father.[3]

There is however another side to the question, and one very relevant to forgiveness. In man as such there is something else than sin; but it is no less true that good, even when present, does not excuse the evil also present; the sinner is not justified for his evil because he has done good as well. If it be true that the power of our evil will does not extend so far as wholly to abolish our relationship to God or utterly destroy His activity within us, this may demand our gratitude, but it will not entitle us to self-righteousness. If we are so made and come in such a history that, by God's mercy, impulses to good are constantly reaching us, which in some measure can be accepted, all the more damning is the indictment which declares truly that we have all, without exception, been guilty of wilful and repeated sin. The good has been acknowledged; let the evil be acknowledged equally, and the need for pardon is evident.

When Kant replied to the facile optimism of eighteenth-century philosophers and essayists by rightly asserting the presence of radical evil in human nature, what he thus affirmed was not total depravity, but for practical purposes it was no less grave. Total depravity, as commonly understood, means that we are sinful and nothing else—"utterly indisposed, disabled, and made opposite to all good, and wholly inclined to all evil."[4] The incredible picture is drawn in pure black. Radical evil means that there is nothing purely good in man, nothing clean or untainted, but evil is unfailingly mixed with good. This surely is a perfectly accurate

---

[3] Cf. Augustine, Enchiridion XII: quamdiu itaque natura corrumpitur inest ei bonum quo privetur . . . quocirca bonum consumere corruptio non potest nisi consumendo naturam.

[4] *Westminster Confession*, chap. vi.

statement of the case. Can we point to any thought or feeling that is wholly undefiled? Which of us knows by inward experience what is meant by purely disinterested love, of God or man? We need not tell disparaging lies about ourselves to the effect that we are nothing but sin. This honest men will deny, but the truth they may be brought to own is sufficiently dark.

Theology has always been haunted by the fear that the frank admission of partial good in man will nourish pride and make humility and faith impossible. But it can never be harmful to follow Christ in recognising facts. To tell men they are evil only may actually hide from them how evil they are. To deny degrees of sinfulness may blind men to the one truth here that matters, viz. that *every* sin is blameworthy and forfeits communion with God. Each sin, major or minor, is mortal sin in this sense, that the possibility of its remission comes not from its smallness but from the mercy of the Father.

Thus far we have chiefly spoken of our relationship, in sinning, to God Himself; for this is the constitutive element in sin, on which all else must depend. But in addition to repelling God by sin, we antagonise others and we destroy ourselves. In all these respects we come as sinful persons to occupy a permanent and habitual state or condition; the life we live is one of alienation from the Father, of dispeace with men, or an inability we cannot cure to restrain in ourselves "the lusts of the flesh." These aspects of personal experience are indissociably bound up together in the life of sin; in the life that has received forgiveness they are no less inseparable. When in pardon we have become one with God, it transpires that to be on terms with Him of forgiven sonship has made all things new. Our relationships with others and with our own nature have now been reconstituted; having peace with God, we can in ever-increasing measure build up a life of self-control as well as of authentic fellowship with those whose existence we share.

When a Christian man seeks to give himself an account of his experience in being pardoned, he is compelled to fix on the idea of his *guilt*. Thus it has often been pointed out that forgiveness bears directly on the guilt of sin, indirectly on its power. The aspect or quality in sin which we designate guilt is its power to force us to condemn ourselves, with the accompanying consciousness that God is condemning us. To look at the Holy One with realising mind is to become aware that there is in us an impurity and impotence for which we are answerable. The paradox confronts us: because we are answerable, there can be for us no excuse, yet because we *are* answerable, and sin has not merely happened to us as an infection might, it is possible for us to be forgiven. Only guilty sin can be pardoned; there has taken place a disturbance of our personal relationship to God, and this He can rectify. Indeed, the sense of guilt is of itself a token of hope; it proves we are not hopelessly lost to goodness, because our eyes are not fast closed to the reality of God. Willingness to accuse ourselves is evidence that He has not wholly forsaken us.

The man to whom the holiness of God has become known cannot but be aware of his guilty sinfulness, yet he will not affirm its inherent necessity. Here we must start from the voluntary character of sins that come home to us most poignantly; underlying them all is a certain attitude of our will towards the will of God, an attitude which we find it impossible to explain by the influence of fate. This state of affairs is in no way modified by the circumstance that notoriously we cannot, by any effort of volition, however strong or lasting, produce any fundamental alteration in the sinful bent of our will; thus we cannot simply by trying hard come to love ourselves less and God supremely. Or to put it otherwise, we dare not make the reality of guilt conditional on some imaginable but problematic solution of the question of free will; indeed, we may at this point feel ourselves shut up to an antinomy, which from our present standpoint we are unable to resolve. We are born self-centred and egoistic, yet when we express our egoism in act or feeling we feel ashamed before God. In the hour of repentance we envisage our will as blameworthy; and this with an intuition which is not provisional but absolute in its perceptions, an intuition which can in no sense be conditioned by any further light we might conceivably obtain on a supposed neutral state of our will antecedently to the sinful act, but fixes the character of our will as it *is*. Things are what they are, be their antecedents what they may, and to be conscious of God in Christ is to pronounce an irrevocable verdict of " guilty" upon ourselves. If we have a will at all, it is guilty, free or not; and it is guilty just as being a will, i.e. something original which is no product of exterior constraint, but veritably our own. We are chargeable with sin—behind this fact we cannot go. No ulterior explanations can affect it. When we refuse to sophisticate ourselves, we derive our own sin from willed decision against God, in whom the moral law is alive. This conviction that we are in a state of sin for which we are liable, this direct imputation to ourselves of our sinful being and doing, is the sense of guilt. No burden can equal it: *der Übel grösstes ist die Schuld.*

Guilt has two aspects: it bears on ourselves and also on our relationship to God. It signifies, first, that the doer of the wrong is permanently owner of the deed; the fact that he once did it is a standing attribute of his character. In other words, it is persons, not acts, of which in strictness guilt can be predicated. And this for more reasons than one. To begin with, no act can be conceived which simply as an occurrence in space and time is, in itself, reprehensible. Killing may be no murder. The guilt which in familiar speech we attach to this or that action goes back in reality to the person who committed it. Furthermore, persons not acts are the true subjects of guilt because acts pass, but persons persist, continuously responsible for their doings. As it has been put: " Because it is part of the character of the very self, and the self remains, therefore the past sin remains, for me and in me, still. The guilt of that which has been guiltily done seems to be abidingly contained in the fact of my self-identity with the past. It is part of that continuity which personality means."[5] That the doer may forget the deed leaves its condemning quality unaffected, for under stress he may recall it again; and while there is forgiveness there is no

[5] Moberley, *Atonement and Personality,* p. 34.

forgetfulness with God. How great the doer's guilt may be depends on variable circumstances, and supremely on the extent to which he put himself into the deed. "This act is sinful" is a judgment on the content of the volition we are characterising; "this act is guilty" is a judgment on the conditions in which the volition occurred. And the degree of guilt must be determined by the share, the personal and inalienable share, which we took in what was done. Obviously out of a situation of this kind problems may spring which we cannot solve. None of us can measure his brother's guilt; it is indeed precisely true to say that he cannot measure his own, for he is incapable of discriminating the thoughts and intents of his heart with that just accuracy which would admit of his attaching the right co-efficient of guilt to each individual action. But in a study of forgiveness such refinements of calculation possess little or no importance. All guilt is destructive of that fellowship with the Father which pardon alone can recreate.

This, in fact, is our second point: that guilt does indicate the actual relationship between the sinful and Him whose will they have violated. True, there is a moral consciousness of guilt which forces us to condemn ourselves for wrong, irrespectively of any sense of the condemnation of God. When however the tokens of God's presence, and of His personal concern with our lives, wakens us up to the fact that in sinning we have thrust *Him* aside, the moral consciousness of guilt takes on a new and keener poignancy. The feeling that we are in self-chosen antagonism to the Person with whom we have to do gives a fresh edge and weight to compunction, intensifying our distress over moral failure. Not only so: it appears to be psychologically true to say that the bad conscience inevitably produces what we can only describe as resentment or enmity against God. He now assumes such an aspect in our thought that we can feel towards Him neither confidence nor gratitude. Trust Him we cannot, for now He is too far off to be confided in; we have banished ourselves from His company and therefore find it impossible to conceive of Him as other than menacing and hostile. Nor can we cherish gratitude to One whose holiness we dislike to recall, since it shames our defilement; we have nothing to thank Him for, for now He is our enemy, and the antagonism of direction necessarily obtaining between His good will and ours changes before our blinded eyes into personal ill-will on His part against us. He bars our path; He opposes our madness; He thwarts our desire: it is impossible but that in this mood we should reckon Him a dark and threatening adversary.

In these circumstances, there are natural objections to the reality or seriousness of guilt at which we grasp readily, cheating ourselves out of this feared and hated responsibility. We are tempted, for instance, by the plea that to impute guilt is to exhibit a deficient understanding of facts, and that in the familiar words "to know all is to pardon all." In proportion as we see into the play of causal factors out of which the evil deed grew, we can perceive more and more clearly (the argument runs) that the deed was unavoidable, that incredible as it may sound nothing was possible except the actual; so that "guilt," for the enlightened mind, is a pointless and obsolete term. So-called sin, the undesirableness of which need not be denied, is in reality only moral disease. As disease, it may be hereditary, the real source of what we are and do lying not in our character, even as determined by contemporary environments, but actually outside the frontiers of our own life, in the calamities or mistakes of bygone generations. Our function, then, is not to blame ourselves but to accept ourselves. Not the imputed act is reprehensible in the last resort, but rather our feeling of guilt about the act. The "sin" is normal; the compunction is eccentric. For anyone who persuades himself that the moral consciousness is not to be believed, this is an alluring hypothesis; and who can say how wistfully we may not all of us have glanced at it, as we searched for excuses and refused to make confession?

The modern way of rightly bringing action into a vital relation with character may at times appear to lend confirmation to this general view. If my action, it is urged, is in sober truth the outcome and offspring of my character, and thus expressive of what I am, must it not be a necessary action, such that the person I am could do nothing else? It acts itself, we may say; my choices are made for me by my nature before I myself (in appearance) make them. Yet on the whole this does not seem to harmonise with the utterances of conscience. So far as can be ascertained, conscience does not declare to the sinner, after his sin: You are bad, for you could only act in this way and could not act otherwise and as you ought. Its pronouncement rather is: You are bad, and your badness has come to the surface in the fact that you could do, and did, what you have actually done. Your act reveals the sinful disposition which is yours. It is not an unavoidable expression of your character, but it is a real expression of elements that go to make it what it is.

But however this may be, no coercive argument can be framed whereby the man who categorically denies his own guilt shall be proved in error, by a proof valid for all normal minds. The question is to be decided under the converging lights of moral and religious experience; in asserting our own guilt, or that of another, we are performing an act of faith in which we *vote* for that theory or interpretation which preserves the facts of the moral consciousness in their full meaning and reality. It is certain, in any case, that one to whom God has become known experimentally as holy will refuse to treat the bad conscience as illusory; to him it will be evident that by negating his responsibility to God and before his own mind he becomes not less guilty but more. Let the doubter but reflect upon his own explosive and unquestioning reaction against a deliberate wrong done to one he loves, the indignant rising of his moral being to condemn the outrage, his worthy impulse to confront the wrong-doer with his act and bring him to account, and he will find it intelligible enough that, notwithstanding the most modern theories of morality, men still use the word "guilt" with intense and serious meaning. To renounce it is to surrender all belief in the real character of the human will, as well as in the possibility of fellowship between moral persons. On those who hold, then, that the consciousness of guilt is illusory, falls the onus of proof. Their proof must fail, for, as

Bergson puts it, "all they can do is to extend arbitrarily to voluntary actions a law verified in cases in which the will does not intervene."

The significance of the feeling of guilt for the individual's moral and spiritual life it is impossible to exaggerate. Once it has struggled into wakefulness, its atmosphere spreads everywhere, and a deep shadow of felt inability dogs our thoughts of good. If we are guilty, what avails it to dream of happy moral triumph? Doubtless the ideal still remains to beckon us, to exact on occasion a burst of moral heroism or animate slow and persevering obedience; but the question cannot long be shirked whether in fact we are able to cope with the bad conscience so long as we remain within the boundaries of ethics. Can even the loftiness of the ideal be expressed in moral terms; can moral thought do justice to the depth of our distress over failure to attain it? Must not "the good" in what seems its impersonal cold and high distance become "God" if our conviction that the Universe is now unfriendly is to be accounted for, and if there is to be substantial hope for our escape and victory? In itself "the good" is simply hostile to the bad; it does not raise up the fallen or impart the promise of new strength. It is as men have beheld God in Jesus' love for sinners—without the fear of inexactitude we may say *only* so—that they have had courage to believe that "the good" is in reality but a less full and less glorious name for a gracious Father who has taken active steps to visit our need and open for us a door of hope. In His presence the bestowal of forgiveness has once for all made goodness "an assured career." Nor is this the whole. On the human spirit have always lain the two great burdens of guilt and fate; the weight of our own evil past, the weight of this unintelligible world. And to have the first removed is to be freed, *eo ipso,* from the second. When in His pardon God takes us for His own, doing at His own cost everything for our ransom, we thereby know Him, we possess Him by faith, as the Father who will give us all we need. This argument lies implicitly behind the great words, which link redemption to providence: "If God be for us, who can be against us?"[6] In forgiveness, definitively, we have been persuaded that God is "for us"; therefore the fateful terror of the world is gone. All things work together for good to those whom His exceeding mercy has brought to love God.

If we scrutinise the mind of one who in the Pauline sense has been "justified," who, that is, has received an initial assurance of God's love which goes deeper than all his sin, what thoughts regarding his guilt, and the changing sense of it in experience, are we likely to come upon? Probably there will be different stages to recall. One of the earliest, it may well be, is the dull, heavy, virtually irresistible and automatically registered consciousness that we are answerable for all we have done and have become; and this may be accompanied by a sombre gloom. On this, in many cases by occasion of some distinct and startling act of sin, there often supervenes an acute feeling of compunction, of the past as that which we can no longer bear and which must be got rid of; and here the words rise unbidden to the lips : " O wretched man that I am."[7] If thereafter we are confronted with Jesus Christ, if in Him we discover how awful goodness is and how great is the love we have violated, two kinds of change occur in the consciousness of guilt we are considering: first, its gravity is painfully increased by the new perception of our sin as antagonism to utter goodness, but along with this comes a joyful and wondering knowledge that none the less His great love is receiving us, and that the estranging power of guilt has been abolished. Only, be it noted, between these two last points, the intensification and the relief, there is no logical road. No kind of analysis theoretically dissecting the first will produce the second, any more than the lover's anxious wish for love yields of itself the assurance that he *is* loved. It is revelation alone that can bridge the distance, or change guilt deeply felt into guilt none the less removed; in response to the impression of God which Jesus makes there is a leap of the soul to the triumphant certainty that sin has no longer power to separate us from the Father. Guilt will never

6 Rom. 8.31.   7 Rom. 7.24.

yield to abstract ideas; it gives way only to self-evidencing fact, the fact of Christ.

Not even here does the story end. In one who knows God as faithfully and unchangeably Redeemer, there is an *abiding* sense of guilt. Forgiveness does not destroy the knowledge that we are, and have done, evil. Hence the statement that pardon abolishes guilt is not false, but it is an abbreviated, and as such an intelligible, expression of the truth that the power of our former guilty sin to banish us from communion with the Father has been taken away. He remembers our sin no more for ever, yet we remember it against ourselves; and indeed it is more than doubtful whether in any real sense a Christian can ever "forgive himself" for wrongdoing. This settled sense of unworthiness is commonly more profound, though less emotionally piercing, in the old than the young. But whereas before reconciliation with God the feeling of guilt is purely disabling and suffuses the moral life with the consciousness of radical failure, later, as an undertone of felt unworthiness, it aids in fostering that humility and receptiveness apart from which the life of God cannot be ours.

CHAPTER IV

FORGIVENESS PRESENT IN JESUS

The preceding chapters have been concerned first with the place of forgiveness in the Christian message as a whole, then with the general meaning of forgiveness in experience, and the need for its bestowal. It was necessary, without unduly anticipating the course of argument, to clarify our ideas regarding the importance and scope of the problem we are discussing. Now we come to a point which, if taken seriously, must be decisive for our outlook over the whole field. It is this, that forgiveness of the kind received and enjoyed within the Christian fellowship is possible and credible only in view of Jesus. It is only as we envisage Him that we can positively believe it to be true that " there is joy in heaven over one sinner that repenteth." There could be no more urgent or momentous subject. No problem is more crucial than to determine how, as men live in the modern world, " sinful, and sad because sinful, and sorrowful in sinning," they can be sure that God pardons freely, accepting them at once and before they become any better as His reconciled children; and this in such a manner that they can face life with serenity, and can offer to all who have been defeated in the moral struggle the same distinct personal assurance of the Father's forgiving love.

The brief answer to this question is that we acquire this certainty of fatherly pardon, and in the full sense acquire it only, in the presence of Jesus Christ. The Old Testament sense of forgiveness was indubitably real and profound, yet even it may be called precarious in this respect that it was liable to be undermined or wholly destroyed by the onset of personal calamity. Even the devout believer was apt to interpret sickness or the loss of goods as proof that God was no longer at peace with him. Adversity all but unavoidably took on the aspect of judgment. And in addition, there were

72

nationalistic demarcations which sharply divided those to whom from His very nature God would be gracious from those to whom, again from His very nature, He would not. The Greek or Persian could not count on His mercy.[1] But, apart from this, it is the religious man to-day we have in mind, and in his search for assurance of pardon he is unlikely to rest satisfied with what even the best Hebrew faith can offer. It is to Christ alone that he can be pointed with confidence.

It is not denied, of course, that elsewhere men may attain to unconfirmed gleams of hope, varied degrees of probability, daring conjectures. But these can hardly bear up against the worst occasions of doubt—the mood of sick remorse which follows upon intentional sin, or the sense of hopeless insignificance so often produced by unmerited misfortune. When no creative source of trust stands out before our vision, external to ourselves and reinforcing our powers of faith triumphantly by its very meaning, it is hard for the guilty or troubled soul to cling to the conviction that God is merciful. He may strain after the conviction, but the effort soon is vain; so far from his faith carrying him, he carries it as he might a heavy weight.

Moreover, as soon as we leave academic abstractions and come to reality, we discover that there are certain human situations which our thought of Divine forgiveness must take account of, if it is to stand the acid test of life. We may think, for example, of a chaplain in the Great War standing beside a dying man whose one concern is to know whether God receives the sinful or casts them out. It is true that death-bed religion is a poor substitute for Christian living; it is also true that in such an hour unworthy spiritual fears may assail the bravest men. Yet we are ignoring facts if we cannot recognise that this particular situation is as real as any other in human life, and has as insistent a claim to be considered and provided for. What shall we say to such a man? How shall we answer his question: Can I be forgiven?

[1] This is not to deny the dawning of a larger catholicity in the Old Testament, based on humanity. Cf. the Book of Jonah, Is. 19.24-25, 25.7, Mal. 1.11.

There need be no hesitation in declaring that any religious message which is radically inapplicable to his case is unfit to survive in a world like this.

But it would be affectation to pretend that the question at issue has a bearing only upon other people. If our cogitations busy themselves only with the pardon so terribly needed by someone else, they will be empty and foolish. The only thing that is profitable is for each man to consider the relation of God's mercy to himself. "I need to be forgiven. Can the thing be done, and how, and on what grounds do I know it?" We are none of us worthy to stand before God.

> O! how shall I, whose native sphere
>   Is dark, whose mind is dim,
> Before the Ineffable appear,
> And on my naked spirit bear
>   The uncreated Beam?

This cry is written out of our own heart. We require to know, each of us, what is the mind of God towards the unworthy. And it is solely in the person of Jesus that clear light is found.

Other sources of assurance have been proposed. It has been suggested that an adequate impression of Divine mercy to the sinful may be derived from Nature, from an inductive reading of history, or from the efforts of speculative argumentation or the logical analysis of ideas. But no great hardihood is needed to affirm that people who wished to know whether their sins could be pardoned, and who later reached a clear certainty on that subject and gained the power to live in communion with the Father, have never turned hopefully in any of these directions or at all events have never found their hopes come true. The simple fact is that no one sufficiently in earnest to raise the question of forgiveness at all would to-day dream of looking for a satisfying reply to his eager longing in Nature, or in general history, or in metaphysical speculation.

Not that Nature does not seem to speak, often, of a higher benignity; not that for many of us it may not be true that in hours of vision we discover behind and within the greatness and glory of the material universe a diviner greatness and a diviner glory. But we cannot forget that Nature, as it confronts the sinner, is either silent or equivocal; if there are phenomena that may reasonably be viewed as indicative of mercy, there are also those which suggest indifference or even cruelty. The appeal of Nature, moreover, is limited in range; it does not touch or move all sorts of mind; and if those on whom we press it choose to call it an illusion, we should find it hard to make adequate reply. But in addition—and for us at the moment this is fairly decisive—the impression of the presence and power of the Eternal that comes home to men through the beauty of the world, while in itself subduing and profound, is not in the majority of cases such as to assuage the sense of guilt, relieve conscience, or communicate the inspiriting assurance that they are now in the relationship to God of dear children to a Father. What the experience of discerning God in Nature can do for a man is either to enrich a consciousness of pardon already present, or to make him long more deeply for a pardon he has not yet obtained. But of itself it cannot mediate forgiveness.

Nor does history give us what we need. It is more than difficult, it is in fact impossible, for one who surveys the multifarious and interwoven events of the past, the varied fortunes of mankind, or even the plain tokens in history that righteousness exalts men and nations while vice and crime exact inevitable penalties, to gain through this survey an assured knowledge that the Power supreme over the changes of human life is prepared to forgive *his* sin. It is true that the operation of a higher Sovereignty and Wisdom may be divined in the process of the generations. But no such intuition makes anything certain to a sinful man concerning himself, or concerning the possibility of his being drawn into fellowship with God. Past events may be enough to show that God is, and that history does not lack His surveillance and control. Yet for the penitent this is not enough; it does not convince him of God's love to him individually. This failure of history in general to furnish an adequate medium of evangelisation rests on the fact that no response on our part to its implied teachings can bring us into a fully personal relationship with God. We are still left in the region of probabilities. If there are historical events which may plausibly be held to demonstrate the Divine pity (and to faith do demonstrate this), there are events also which might not unreasonably be taken as proving that His attitude to those who openly violate His will is that of crushing and awful judgment, in which He not only avenges wrong with unflinching austerity but may even visit the transgressions of the fathers upon the children. In short, if we had to discover God's character from the course of historical development, taken as a whole and unillumined by faith, we should not know what to think. He might be merciful, but also He might not. And who can tell, a repentant man might ask, which side of His incomprehensible nature may be turned towards me and my sins?

Once more, no one who takes our problem seriously will adopt the advice of those who bid him *postulate* the Divine forgiveness. For it is a point of vital importance that *ex hypothesi* the man we are thinking of has felt what may become the agony of the guilty mind, of that inward uncleanness which he knows must place a barrier between him and the Holy One. And that can never be overcome by the mere appeal to first principles, however sound. The religious man feels it as a mockery that in his deep concern he should be invited to take pardon for granted; this is by implication to tell him that were he only to place himself at the synoptic view-point of philosophy, he would see that union with God is timelessly and eternally real, and that to be assured of this he has only to open his eyes. But you cannot thus talk a man out of his shame. That is not to be dispelled by general considerations, of which in any case it cannot be known whether they apply to him. Nor will you persuade him that if only he will pull himself together and make a great effort, the burden now depressing him can be " thrown off " and left behind. No one ever knew what " guilt " means to a sensitive conscience who did not feel that another hand than ours must lift away the heavy mass that bears us down. If we are to believe ourselves free, another voice must speak, and speak in such a way that we know it to be the voice of God.

It is simple psychological fact, I am persuaded, that the only people in the world to-day who live in the glad consciousness that their sins have been forgiven are those who have encountered Jesus. They have met Him in the lives of the good; above all, they have stood face to face with Him as He shows Himself in the Gospels, and in His presence they have been able to trust the Father's mercy and begin life again. To them He has become the "Word" of God, not in a philosophic sense, but as the living and loving announcement to their troubled hearts that the Father will be at peace with them. They now know that the essence of God's nature is just such compassion as Christ's. To look at Jesus is to know how God would have us think of Himself; the three short years recorded in the Gospels were His self-interpretation; and a sinful man soon discovers that they contain all he needs to know. This is personal relationship at last; it is God dealing with men as the foolish and wandering members of His family, and giving them in pure love a place beside Him.

Thus to receive pardon in the presence of Jesus is an experience which revolutionises our natural thoughts of God. The full truth cannot be expressed by saying that Christ simply corroborates an idea of God long familiar to the average man; rather it is in Christ that for the first time we perceive the true character of God and know, without reasoning, that nothing other or less than this could satisfy. And when we have seen in Christ what we know is God, we are then able to call Christ Divine with some complete reality of meaning. Athanasius, a great man if ever there was one, appears to have supposed that *ab initio* he could give an account of God in agreed and tolerably simple conceptions, since it was quite possible to formulate a statement of His chief attributes which Greek philosophy would have had no difficulty in countersigning. People who take their religion from the New Testament discover that we have first to let Jesus show us what the Father is like, and that forgiveness, about which philosophy as such does not concern itself, is His characteristic gift. As we contemplate Jesus presented in the Gospels, we discern not merely that God is love, but what *kind* of love this is. On that crucial point our true thoughts have all been overheard from Christ. They aid our minds, better perhaps than unverified speculation, to understand what is meant by calling God the Absolute Personality. In no other sort of language can we register precisely the impression He makes on us, as He pardons our sins in Jesus. He is Personality, for only a person can forgive; He is Absolute, for in Him we envisage Love and Holiness invested with boundless and mighty dimensions. The Being whose hand meets ours as we bow before Christ is of a nature infinite and unfathomable.

Hence for the Christian thinker the decisive question must always be: Do we have in the actual career of Jesus—living, dying, risen—a finally trustworthy and religiously satisfying presentation of the supreme Power overshadowing our lives, the "Lord of heaven and earth"? To this the answer of Christian experience, quickened by the New Testament, is wholly confident because based on what actually happens to the sinful. It turns out, invariably, that through trustful knowledge of Jesus we can begin and maintain a forgiven fellowship with God. I am not now asking whether such fellowship is desirable, let alone the one thing needful; I am pointing to the empirical fact, real if anything in the higher spiritual life of mankind is real, that men do attain it under the influence of Jesus, and that in the same sense and with the same perfect inward freedom it is attained nowhere else. Thus there is unveiled to us in Jesus a God whose moral infinitude we cannot measure or rationalise; it *dawns* on us, as He holds our gaze, and bears us down in adoration. The Church as yet has scarcely taken in this disclosure. Quite possibly we are only at the beginning of deciphering the implications of the fact that " God was in Christ reconciling the world to Himself," and have so far done no more than open the vein of meaning they suggest. We must yield our minds to be dilated and reconstituted by the forgiving love embodied in Jesus Christ, and cease to force upon it unnatural and restrictive frameworks of conception drawn from law, or war, or commerce. And even when we pass out beyond these fields in search of worthy interpretative symbols and strive to find them in the highest reaches of human affection and sacrifice, still there is nothing in our narrow and impoverished experience which can do more than faintly indicate what forgiving love can be and do. Here too we have to learn truths we could not produce; and our one hope of learning lies in submitting our minds to the facts spread before us in Jesus. If older thought inclined to say that we can only believe in forgiveness because the Divine Son paid satisfaction to the Father, we preserve the same vital and solemn interest by proclaiming that forgiveness is credible, and is offered, in virtue of the fact that God is personally present in One who stood in with sinners to the last, and, refusing to abandon them, went for their sake to the Cross.

This conviction, however, that forgiveness is fully credible only in view of Jesus, while no doubt universal or all but universal in Christian minds, may strike some people as an irresponsible fancy, for which there is no substantial ground. We are of course bound to admit that no genuinely religious belief can be furnished with irresistible demonstration. At the same time, it can be shown from Christ's own words and practice that in His view also the forgiveness of God was perfectly and uniquely present in Himself. So, for a few moments, I will ask the reader to look on with me at the spectacle of Jesus amongst the sinful. We shall see Him face to face with the guilty, who need pardon and somehow receive it at His hands.

It must not be forgotten that, in some true sense, Jesus continued a religious work inaugurated by the Baptist. The forerunner is pictured as "baptising in the desert and preaching a baptism of repentance for the remission of sins."[2] We encounter here the conviction that all men are sinners, that no one can go into the Kingdom whose sins are not forgiven, and that penitence is the requisite path to forgiveness.

[2] Mark 1.4.

It is in this atmosphere of belief that Jesus began His public work. He does not appear ever to have doubted that such belief was essentially true.

There were, however, other contemporary opinions which He definitely repudiated as misleading. Thus He rejected the habit into which good people had fallen of construing their relations with God in terms of law. There were 613 precepts, none of which must be infringed. The correctest view of God is that He is man's Judge. His righteousness is that of the magistrate. Grace was not denied, but its place was secondary and therefore highly uncertain. The worshipper must accordingly bestir himself to win God's favour and make his own position secure by doing extra works he might have left undone. Looking ahead, he saw at the end of all things a Divine assize where the Jew should receive all that his deeds entitled him to in the heavenly record. There is nothing ignoble in all this, which by no means exhausts the Pharisaic creed. But to Jesus it was profoundly unsatisfying. And one reason why it is well to fix this Jewish background in our view is that thereby we realise the fact more vividly that Jesus' wonderful message of forgiveness was not uttered casually but with strong and deliberate intention, in opposition to a rival doctrine which He desired to expel from human faith. He sought to make it redeemingly clear to the sinful that Law was not His own last word to them, or His Father's.

In Jesus' company, men became aware by degrees that He was reading their nature to the depths, probing motives, discerning wishes, catching unspoken prayers; not, however, with the cruel penetration of steely intelligence but by a new intensity of love. He was indeed altogether open-eyed about low and base things in their lives. His judgment could be of a dreadful severity. His holiness burned in white flame near which foulness could not live. In spite of this uncompromising rightness—or rather, on account of it—men were able to place the utmost confidence in His affection; and in case after case they seem to have flung themselves upon His strength for protection from themselves and against the power of evil. Along with this went the insight that He was worthy of trust. He was such that sinners could depend on Him. They saw Him live in the tempting, defiling world—facing allurements, enduring hardship, ignoring flattery. Plainly there was a struggle; to keep His integrity was a real conflict. More than once they caught His agonised voice as He prayed concerning His difficulties, and at such times they could do little more than stand far off, guessing at the pain. Eventually they reached the irreversible conclusion that His soul had never once been touched with evil. They said to each other that this Man was not, like them, a sinner. He had never felt an evil conscience or had to speak the bitter words of self-accusation due from all the rest.

Thus our Lord produced in His associates the profound sense that morally they were failures. No doubt they came to perceive that God and Jesus were indistinguishable in character, but this, it appeared, could only make matters worse. If what they felt in Jesus shamed them, must not the meaning be that they all were too unworthy for the Holy One to bear them in His presence? Yet just here is the amazing thing. Precisely when their shame grew intolerable, His treatment of them removed their sad despair. He would not send them away, or say that He could make nothing of them. Instead, He somehow let them know that He and they were friends for life. His attitude was at once so stern and so understanding, so holy and so merciful, that in Him God seemed to be standing by their side, and their eyes opened to the truth that what through Jesus' love they were receiving was the forgiveness of God Himself. They did not as yet know that Jesus' attitude to the sinful would one day cost His life, but they quite well understood that He was doing for them the greatest of all services. To speak the word of pardon, to blot out the past and open up the future, to give peace of conscience, to impart hope to the broken and launch them in the career of loving their neighbour as themselves—nothing else could be so great. And this is what He *was* doing, because in reality He was leading them into fellowship with God.

Let us now turn to examine one or two characteristic incidents in which Jesus' mind about forgiveness is made clear, as well as the principles (to use too cold and doctrinaire a word) on which He dealt with the sinful who had sought Him out or had been guided to Him. We may first consider an episode which casts an extraordinarily suggestive light on Christ's view of spiritual facts—the healing of the paralytic.[3] His question to the onlookers, as given in Dr. Moffatt's rendering, is this: "Which is the easier thing, to tell the paralytic, 'Your sins are forgiven,' or to tell him, 'Rise, lift your pallet, and go away'?" This was probably meant not so much to rebuke the murmurers as to make them think. They disbelieved in Christ's power to pardon sin by a word, and when they heard Him say to the invalid, "Your sins are forgiven,"[4] they called it blasphemy, on the ground that no one *can* forgive except God. They were right, of course; God alone is the author of forgiveness, and no declaration of pardon which mediately or immediately does not come from God has any value. In any ordinary case this would have been final. But now it missed the mark, for all that Jesus did or said was revelation. His tears are God's mercy, His wrath God's anger. And just so, to the sin-tormented soul before Him, His absolution is God's forgiveness.

Hence our Lord replied to the objectors by showing them His power in another way. To forgive sin or cure disease by a word is for common men impossible; in their case it is as simple and as vain to speak of the first as of the second. But when the sick man rose and carried out his bed, that was ocular demonstration how very far from vain it was for Jesus to speak words of healing, and, as He proceeds to show, the physical has a counterpart in the spiritual. If His word can quicken helpless limbs, His word also can cleanse the guilty conscience. Salvation—that comprehensive miracle— consisted for Him in admission to a Divine family in which

[3] Mark 2.3-12.

[4] It is important to note the exact words of Jesus as they are reported. He does not say: "I forgive thy sins," but "thy sins are forgiven." And here the familiar distinction between declaring forgiveness and imparting it is not quite relevant. What Jesus really did, so far as can be seen, was at once to declare forgiveness and guarantee the declaration by being what He was. He came in the power of God to pronounce pardon, but it was a power manifest in humility, brotherhood, sacrificial pain.

men were the children of a Father who both forgave all their
iniquities and healed all their diseases. Now the scribes in
all likelihood would have kept quiet had Christ simply
healed the man, but they could not bear to have Him act on
the higher plane; they resented fiercely His touching the soul.
But what Jesus presents to them is an instance in which the
two halves of life are indivisibly one. Body and soul are but
abstractions; together, in the inseparable unity of experience, they make up the world which God has made and will
redeem. Thus to the question, whether asked in the first
century or the twentieth: Which is easier, to forgive or heal?
we must still give Jesus' answer, that both are impossible
for men but wholly possible for God.

Thus one truth shining out of this wonderful interview
is that for the mind of Jesus pardon is supernatural. He and
the sick man knew that something had happened which
nothing but the illimitable power of the Eternal could
account for. We cannot forgive ourselves. No comrade,
with the best will in the world, can do it for us. If we avert
our eyes from God, the order of things is dead against the
thought of forgiveness, for there is not a hint of it in Nature,
or at all events the half-decipherable hints which Nature
may contain are illegible by any mind not already enlightened
by the experience of being pardoned. It has been truly said
that to the first question of personal religion: What must I
do to be saved? Nature, in its regular and majestic sequence,
makes no reply. Sun, moon and stars cannot answer it, nor
can earth and sea.

Moreover, from Jesus' treatment of the paralytic we learn
that in forgiveness the initiative is with God. Jesus spoke
first; before the man had time to ask for it, He placed the
boon in the needy hand, with anticipating love. Very possibly healing and pardon had an altogether different importance for Jesus' mind and the other's. To the patient health
was the one thing needful, and Jesus counted mainly if not
exclusively as the great Worker of cures; to the Healer, God
and pardon were the greatest things in the world. In His
judgment the bad conscience ranks as the sorest of all
troubles, and deliverance wrought by pardon is the divinest

gift in His power. He therefore gave it first. Become right with God, He says implicitly, and trust Me for the rest; or, as He expressed it elsewhere, Seek first the Kingdom and the righteousness of God, and all other things shall be added.

The scene also contains suggestive indications of Jesus' view of His own part in the mediation of forgiveness. And this we might expect, for the episode on the surface of it is peculiar in this point, that our Lord's right to pronounce pardon to the sinful had been openly challenged, and although the Pharisees had on other occasions taken umbrage at His persistent grace to sinners, no other instance can be found in the Gospels where He is represented as deliberately, and as it were by argument, justifying His action in the bestowal of pardon.[5] If therefore we search the story for proofs that Jesus regarded Himself as having a special relation to the imparting of forgiveness, we do so with the feeling that in the words spoken He is consciously and intentionally putting the case for Himself. Now He does not take pardon to be a matter of course; we have indeed seen that He felt it to be supernatural. Why, then, if the thing were so amazing, did He expect the paralytic to believe there and then that his sins were blotted out? Surely the announcement of pardon, to convince, must be uttered by One whose personality is of itself convincing. And here that condition is satisfied. Jesus knew His own unshared power to represent God to men; He knew that at the very moment this power was taking effect in the man's soul: therefore He could speak as He does speak. There is no doubt a real sense in which we also impart forgiveness, as when in preaching or private words of friendship we declare the pardoning love of God. The difference, however, is that when we proffer pardon to men, we do it in view of Jesus, the surety and guarantee of grace to all the guilty; when in the Gospels Jesus does it, it is in

---

[5] Except in so far as the parables recorded in Luke 15, particularly that of the Prodigal Son, constitute implicitly an argumentative reply to the grievance which found vent in the words, "This man receiveth sinners." The number of passages in which this grievance is expressed is curiously large (Mark 2.16, Matt. 9.11, 11.19, Luke 5.30, 15.2, 19.7).

virtue of Himself. Not as though He insisted that men should believe it apart from what they knew of *Him*. As Herrmann puts it: "Jesus did not write the story of the Prodigal Son on a sheet of paper for those who knew nothing of Himself. He told it to men who saw Him, and who, through all that He was, were assured of the Father in heaven, of whom He was speaking."[6] We are plainly bound to give some reasonable account of the acknowledged fact that no one before or after Jesus has ever presented forgiveness in this absolute and personally authoritative way, and the explanation can only lie in the self-consciousness of Jesus as the Bearer of God's salvation. It was in that character that He dealt with men, and, as this incident proves, in that character He could be recognised by others. They found pardon really present in Him: they were aware that He put forgiveness in their hand; as He stood before them, He embodied for their faith the sufficing mercy of God.

The difficult but interesting question how much or how little acquaintance with Jesus could yield an adequate assurance of pardon, is raised by the story of the sinful woman in Simon's house, who wept over Jesus' feet and wiped them with her hair.[7] Here the word of pardon is spoken not at the beginning of the interview, but at the end. Had the woman met Jesus previously? A recent writer thinks not; she had only heard of Him from others. "Before He had seen her or she Him, He had turned her to God."[8] This is not very convincing, and would not suit Zaccheus either; for he, though almost certainly knowing something about the Messiah previously, does not hail Him with words of personal gratitude. But though we may judge that our Lord and the woman must have been face to face before, this had not had its full effect upon her. Otherwise Jesus would have chosen His words differently. He would not have said in an aside meant only for her, "Your sins are forgiven."

The story is as moving in its omissions as in the elements

[6] *Communion with God,* p. 132.

[7] Luke 7.36-50.

[8] K. Windisch in *Zeitschrift für Theologie und Kirche* (*Festgabe für W. Herrmann*), p. 299.

of which it is actually made up. Thus we are struck by the
absence of explicit condemnation.[9] There is no harping on
the enormities of the past, no probing of the wound, no
denunciation. Not that evil is overlooked; how deep goes
the simple phrase: " Her sins, which are many "! But in its
lack of flaming wrath against the guilty the story only repro-
duces a marked characteristic of Jesus' attitude to every sort
of sinner except Pharisees. To Him the wish for reconciliation was enough. Repentance settled all accounts. He will
not keep her waiting, or put her on probation, nor will He
spoil His gift by cruel reminders of the past. To be sorry
for what is bygone is all He asks. This is a delicacy and
magnanimity which we cannot praise, for it is above all
praise.

Light too is cast on the value for God of simple penitence.
The broken heart, Jesus feels, has no need of thundering
accusations; what is in place is that wounds should be dressed
with balm, and tears dried from off the face that is dimmed
with sorrow. At the touch of penitence all doors fly open,
and the child is at the Father's breast. De Maistre somewhere relates a story he had culled from an old ascetic book,
where the same point is made by contrast. " A saint," he
writes, " whose name escapes me at the moment, had a vision
in which he beheld Satan standing before the throne of God.
And as he listened, he heard the evil spirit say: ' Why hast
Thou damned me, who offended Thee but once, whereas
Thou art saving thousands whose offences were so many?'
And God made answer: ' Hast thou but once asked
pardon?'"

Again, we cannot but observe how Jesus represents God to
the woman's aching heart;[10] the name of God is not mentioned anywhere in the story, yet He is everywhere. He in
fact is present in Jesus, and of this Jesus is aware. Is it not

[9] It was not needed: as Herrmann puts it, " She shows herself
deeply agitated even before Jesus speaks to her. The mere nearness
of Jesus, the impression of His moral purity and life which His
appearance gave must have made her feel that she was standing before
her judge " (*Dogmatik*, p. 76).

[10] As also to St. Paul, who says at times that God, at other times
that Christ, has forgiven our sins.

the first promise of escape for the imprisoned soul, always, that some loving hand should be felt leading the guilty one into the open air of heaven? There are steps in the experience of being forgiven, and at the outset we must encounter someone better than we who cares for us and has a personal concern in the question whether we rise or fall. Faith in God's mercy flows from the touch of human kindness. Of this principle Jesus is the last and highest instance. His attitude to the woman was her sheet-anchor in the world of goodness; had He turned from her, she would have sunk instantly like a stone. She could have held out no longer against such evidence that she was beyond hope. But in Jesus' demeanour there was that which weighed the balance against despair. What is more, this aspect of Jesus we cannot be content to describe simply by the word " mystery "; it was the essential, distinctive and most fundamental quality of God which the New Testament calls love. Jesus was this woman's Saviour because through His attitude she once for all knew that God was on her side, and was there and then receiving her as His child. Thus there was laid down at the foundations of her life that initial certainty of His pardoning love which opened to her the gates of righteousness.

We further gain from the story a significant indication of what Jesus believed to be the unfailing consequence of receiving forgiveness. In His view it is inconceivable that the pardoned should not begin to love. Where love is absent, there has been no reception of forgiveness. Our Lord does not hesitate to bring out this truth by a sharp contrast between the passion of gratitude shown by the fallen woman and the frigid reserve of His Pharisaic host. It was as much as saying to Simon: " You have never gained from Me or any other the wonderful conviction that in spite of all you are the Father's child, otherwise how could your heart be so cold?" The sense of infinite debt, the uncontrollable impulse to give outlet to that sense in loving and contrite act—all this He welcomes in the woman as the natural utterance of a changed heart. To know oneself forgiven is to have the spring of love unsealed.

Finally, let us take the incident that marks the commencement of St. Peter's discipleship. In the narrative of the draught of fishes we find the words: "When Simon Peter saw it, he fell at Jesus' knees and said, ' Depart from me, I am a sinful man, Lord.' . . . And Jesus said to Simon, Fear not; henceforth thou shalt be a fisher of men."[11] From these words we learn new things about the impression made by Jesus on a sinner, as also about a sinner's experience in Jesus' company. It makes little difference to the meaning whether we do or do not hold that the story has got out of its right place.

Some points of similarity to the call of Isaiah[12] are fairly clear. In both cases, a sudden realisation of the Divine calls forth an overwhelming sense of creaturely nothingness and unworthiness. The man has abruptly become aware of the greatness of the Unseen, felt somehow as close beside him in Jesus' person. It is a usual comment on the incident that at this stage Peter's ideas were more or less primitive, and that his oppressed feeling of weakness and nullity had in it nothing or almost nothing ethical; what we see is just the reaction of a tolerably superstitious nature upon what seemed to him at the time an extraordinary manifestation of Divine knowledge and power. There is truth in this, but by no means the whole truth. It is inconceivable that St. Peter's experience should have been completely devoid of moral and spiritual elements. After all, what had so deeply impressed him had not been due to any chance passer-by; it had been due to Jesus. Besides, he had been in the Worker's company; he knew something of His spirit; he had heard Him teach as well as do this thing. Hence, as an explanation, superstition will not take us far. The man did not say, " Leave me, for I am as nothing in Thy sight," but " leave me, for I am sinful." His emotion may have been as much owing to astounded gratitude as to a sense of frailty, for there is nothing which so humbles us as to gain a great gift of which we feel ourselves altogether unworthy. But anyhow Peter's words and act reveal one of the most ineradicable constituents of religious feeling, on a par with that evidenced by the words of Abraham: " I have taken upon me

11 Luke 5.8-10.　　　　12 Isa. 6.

to speak unto the Lord, who am but dust and ashes."[13] Here there appears a quality of authentic religion for which there can never be any real substitute, and it is no merit in a man to have discarded it. In the presence of the Eternal we go on our knees; we do not stand erect thanking whatever gods there be for our unconquerable soul. The experience of taking forgiveness from God's hand, when true to type, includes this strain of overpowering awe. He has a poor nature who cannot understand it, or would wish it away.

But is this really an instance of forgiveness, since of that there is not a word? True, but Jesus' words are full of pardoning significance. "Have no fear; from now thou shalt catch men." In this reply to the stricken man Jesus first bids him have courage and stay on beside Him, next He entrusts him with the service of winning men for God. In the sense of being pardoned these two certainties are contained. We are given to know that God has not thrust us away, but in spite of our ill desert will have us by Him; He gives us a place, to be consciously realised, in His fellowship and Kingdom. We were prepared to take the lowest room, or not even that; yet He will neither depart nor have us depart from Him, but conveys instead the certainty that we are not forsaken. Not only so; we are made aware that God is bidding us share with Him in His redeeming work. He trusts the forgiven man;[14] He sends him out with the ennobling consciousness that he is held worthy to be the Father's servant. It is often through these certainties, gradually suffusing the mind till they form part of our very selves, that the complete assurance of pardon reaches the mind. But the chronology of forgiveness as an experience matters little; what is of importance is that immediately or by degrees a man should know that, in Luther's words, he " has a gracious God "—should be certain that he has God and that God has him.

If we look back over these characteristic scenes, one out-

---

[13] Gen. 18.27.
[14] Cf. the memorable treatment of this in Sir George Adam Smith's title sermon in his book, *The Forgiveness of Sins*.

standing feature is vital to all three. It is that Jesus meets the natural hesitation of sinners to believe in God's forgiveness, by His own attitude to them of loving friendliness and good-will. He does not pour out words either about sin's horror or the Father's love, for in a tragic situation we need most not words but the silent touch of a friend's hand. He persisted in this attitude notwithstanding the shocked protests of Pharisees. But He does not act thus in lax indulgence, as though the sins were of no account. He sought the company of the sinful habitually and with open eyes, and did so not for subtle reasons, or as an example to anyone, but because by nature He could do no otherwise, because it was the only possible outcome of His intimacy with the Father. This is not conjecture but certainty, for it was as a result of complaints made on this very ground that He told the story of the Prodigal. The unforgettable picture of a father who made merry over a wandering son's return, and was gentle even to the elder brother, was Jesus' illustration of His own thrilling word: "There is joy in heaven over a single sinner who repents." He expressly justified His intercourse with outcasts by pointing out that to act so is a reflection of God's own mind.

The same principle must go with us when we try to explain how the Cross mediates to the sinful an assurance that their sins are pardoned.[15] For Jesus to keep beside Him the stained and the covetous doubtless was an expression of love like to God's, but also it meant such pain as *we* can barely understand. It is an agony to see vileness eating into the life of those we love. Of this willingness to suffer in prolonged and faithful proximity to sinners the Cross is the last and highest manifestation. Calvary is the pain, felt in unison with God's mind, whereby the Divine readiness to forgive is sealed.

This leads on to a second reflection. All will agree that forgiveness is invariably presented in the New Testament as a free gift of the Father. It is without money and without price. The heathen sense of propitiation has here nothing

[15] This is a topic to which fuller treatment must be given, and it is considered in chapter ix.

to say: pardon is not wrung from God by any sacrifice that persuades Him to put away anger and be friends. But these obviously true thoughts may easily hinder us from raising a cardinal question; the question, namely, whether Divine sacrifice, visible and implemented in Jesus, may not have none the less been present in the impartation of forgiveness, not as a precondition but as an element. On any showing, Jesus assigned to Himself a central part. He was not merely the reporter or spectator of pardon; He was, in this sphere, mediator or agent. But He could not do His share in the conveyance of pardon to men except at a cost. It was not with a heart of stone that He stayed on beside the fallen, to lift them up. And the Cross, borne in vicarious participation of human shame, is the climax of this fraternal sympathetic agony. Jesus, in other words, could not convey the Father's pardon to the guilty in absolute fulness except by carrying His identification with them to the uttermost point; at that point He gave Himself in death. The Bearer of forgiveness perishes in giving complete expression to the mercy and judgment which in their unity constitute the pardon of God. It is tragedy, it is that inscrutable and catastrophic collision of good and evil of which in its measure human life is full. But, if the phrase be permissible, it is not pessimistic but optimistic tragedy; Jesus does not fall along with His cause, He falls that in Him the cause may live.

The Gospels show us Jesus imparting forgiveness to particular individuals not by mere speech but chiefly by the co-efficient of His personality which infinitely magnifies the power of His explicit words; and, in principle, it is the same in the Apostolic Age and ever since. From that day till now faith in Him has been preached as the sure way to peace with God. And yet there is a difference. His human voice, His look, His touch, the deep and holy kindness of His mien —all those traits which had enabled doubting men in Palestine to believe themselves forgiven—these now are gone. No longer does He move amongst us in His habit as He lived. Are we then worse off than His contemporaries? Not so; for now the Cross is there, and upon it the Crucified, to whom we can turn our longing gaze, and find in the sight all and more than all the persuasiveness which before used to look out of His eyes and bear the knowledge of pardon into the contrite heart. The Cross, as the guarantee of God's forgiving love, has replaced the old actual touch with Jesus in the days of His flesh. Its efficacy to this end has been proved by long centuries. Some replacement there had to be. If even we see this, it was still more clear to Jesus Christ; and this is one of the many reasons why every theory which scouts the notion that He regarded His own death as the pledge of forgiveness must fail to satisfy.

CHAPTER V

ST. PAUL AND JUSTIFICATION

Justification by faith alone is the famous title given in a great period of the Church's history to the doctrine that the sinful are received into sonship and peace with God, not because of any good works or holiness on their part—as though they could deserve so great salvation—but only and altogether because of His infinite mercy, freely granted to all who in repentant faith cast themselves on His forgiving love in Jesus Christ. At a later point we shall see that the formal statement of this doctrine, or rather this gospel, in Protestant theology left something to be desired. For the moment, however, we are only concerned to bring out the central and vitally religious import of the doctrine, and to inquire whether it can be exhibited as authentically Christian. It is no part of our task to vindicate every accretion of re-vived scholasticism which came to adhere, in the age of post-Reformation orthodoxy, to a tenet always felt to be funda-mental. The spirit of law and formula can fasten upon any truth, even the noblest, and obscure its glory. But this has little to do with the question, presumably the only one in which serious men will take interest, whether the truth itself, its essential features disengaged, is or is not in harmony with the mind of Christ, and with the believing witness offered to Him by the writers of the New Testament. If it is, if justification solely by faith is part of Jesus' message and of St. Paul's, we are entitled to regard it as essentially bound up with the Christian religion. To this question we now turn.

The idea of justification by faith has often been interpreted as an idiosyncracy of St. Paul, but in fact it is quite familiar to Old Testament religion,[1] as the apostle shows. And if Hebrew faith formed a worthy preparation for Christianity,

[1] Cf. especially the teaching of Hosea.

this is what we should expect. Obviously there can never have been two entirely different ways of being saved, of entering, that is, into fellowship with God—the way of self-renouncing faith and the way of meritorious achievement. Every prayer for pardon and cleansing in the Psalter takes for granted that it is God who freely puts men right with Himself: "Have mercy upon me, O God, according to Thy loving-kindness: according to the multitude of Thy tender mercies blot out my transgressions";[2] "I said, I will confess my transgressions unto the Lord, and Thou forgavest the iniquity of my sin."[3] Similarly, in Romans 3 and 4 St. Paul appeals to the fact that representative saints under the old covenant, such as Abraham, were justified by faith. Abraham's faith, he means, agrees with Christian faith in not being a work, yielding merit; and God's relation to Abraham is not a relation of debt, but of grace. The patriarch had nothing to boast of, nor have we. He utterly abandoned himself to God; in him we see "the spiritual attitude of a man, who is conscious that in himself he has no strength, and no hope of a future, and who nevertheless casts himself upon, and lives by, the word of God which assures him of a future."[4] This attitude, which is faith, is an attitude which everywhere and always is credited to men as righteousness. In other words, it represents to God the quality of soul which His fatherly heart longs to find in man, and which satisfies Him.

St. Paul might also have pointed, had he chosen, to the main teaching of Jeremiah.[5] The prophet comes preaching righteousness, but is met by the difficulty that men cannot repent, cannot set themselves right with God. In consequence his thought takes a new direction. He finds refuge in the sure hope of a new covenant in which God *bestows* righteousness, and does so by way of pardon. "I will forgive their iniquity, and their sin I will remember no more" (31.34). But indeed, to the God-possessed mind of the prophets, the notion of reward or merit was wholly alien.

[2] Ps. 51.1.
[3] Ps. 32.5.
[4] See Denney's Commentary on Romans (*Expositor's Greek Testament*), *in loc.*
[5] Cf. A. B. Davidson, *Theol. of the Old Testament*, p. 282.

Salvation, the great boon, was like all good things the absolute and merciful gift of the Lord.

Still it is of course St. Paul who made the thought of justification by faith his own, so that we associate it familiarly with his name. In recent work on Paulinism it became fashionable for a time to seek the kernel of the apostle's thinking anywhere but in justification. Mystical elements, the operations of the Spirit, cosmic ideas of redemption, sacramental realism, even speculations about angels—each has by one scholar or another been given a higher place. If justification has not been totally ignored, at least it has been consigned to obscurity. And even in this subordinate rôle it has been disparaged as a beggarly relic of Pharisaism, a weapon snatched up hastily in the throes of controversy, but no organic part of the apostle's real body of conviction. It now looks as if good sense were reasserting itself, and as if the gospel of justification by faith were going to be replaced at the heart of Pauline thought. So far from needing an apology, this doctrine is St. Paul's evangelical message not in part but as a living whole; it is his chosen expression, and no unworthy one, for what God's redeeming love in Christ has meant for him. It forms indeed a statement of the Gospel drawn from the nature of the Gospel itself, prolonging the good news announced by Jesus.

This is not to say that the details of St. Paul's view of justifying faith are present in the teaching of Jesus Himself. No apostle ever repeated Jesus: and this mainly for two reasons, first, that the energising of the Spirit within the apostolic mind brought out new truth, implied in Christ but not before expressed, and secondly, that the faith even of an apostle is as it were a resultant issuing from living contact between his special needs or qualities and the salvation which Jesus brings. St. Paul's doctrine is testimony; it is his reading of the Gospel, in an attempt which he would have been the last to call absolute in quality (1 Cor. 13.12) to set forth what he had found in Christ. But although no verbal identity exists between what Jesus said and what was said by St. Paul, identity of meaning is easy to recognise. If the core of justification is this, that salvation begins wholly on God's side, that it begins with an exhibition in Jesus of God's love to the sinful which man has done and can do nothing to merit, and that the assurance of forgiveness is "not the goal to be reached by our own efforts, but the only point from which any human effort can start," then we have a right to say that this comes in a straight line of descent from our Lord.[6]

There is a familiar way of stating the message of Jesus about salvation which may easily hide from us this substantial identity, and breed only confusion. It rests, broadly speaking, on the contention that the Gospel of Jesus is represented by the Sermon on the Mount. On this view salvation consists in a life of obedience to God, a life answering to the character of the Father. That such phrases have a deep and solemn meaning no one will deny; but, as a little reflection proves, they leave a great initial difficulty entirely out of sight. They well describe the experience of living the saved life, but they shed no light whatever on how access to this life becomes open to guilty men, conscious of their guiltiness. When it is affirmed, for example, that humility, meekness, mercifulness, purity are qualities that constitute "the real righteousness which is the *passport* into the Kingdom of heaven," one can only rub one's eyes in wonder, murmuring "Who then can be saved?" What is this but a new Judaism? What is it but to insist that the best kind of morality must first be attained by the sinful before God will receive them? We pass affectionate judgments on the character of our friends, but is there an honest man anywhere who thinks much of his own, or who believes that if he is saved, it is because his character will pass muster? Such accounts of Jesus' message are full of mental and spiritual thoughtlessness. Not that His words are wrongly quoted, but they are put in a wrong perspective and thus made to bear a wrong meaning. The primary thing in Jesus' presentation of Himself as Saviour does not lie in His requirements, His insistence upon humility and purity, His statement of the law of kindness and love, inex-

[6] Cf. with the following what is much the clearest and most effective argument on this long-debated question, viz. von Dobschütz's article in *Theol. Studien und Kritiken* for 1912, under the title "Die Rechtfertigung bei Paulus, eine Rechtfertigung des Paulus."

pressibly significant as these are; it lies in His forgiving attitude to sinners, and in His wonderful power to convey to their aching hearts the assurance that His loving mind towards them was the mind of God.[7] How otherwise could the publicans and sinners have made a beginning with the good life? They were not humble, or meek, or pure when Jesus met them first, and neither are we. Nor did He say to them, with a new Rabbinism, that to enter the Kingdom present in Him they must antecedently be like the Father in self-giving and love. That would have left them untouched, or touched only with resentment and despair. Instead, simply by being what He was He gave them the pardoning friendship of God; if we may put it so, He brought them to God by bringing God to them, in a power and reality that awed and cleansed the soul. Salvation met them not as a new requirement, more exacting by far than the old; it was a gift, rather, capable of making them new persons in a new world.

This clear distinction between Jesus and the Rabbis is of the religious essence of the matter. Everyone knows that Rabbinism strove for righteousness, of the individual and the nation equally. This, it was held, formed a strict condition of sharing in the blessings of redemption, of the great liberating and gladdening consummation known as the advent of the Kingdom. God was to bring it in, but His action depended on man's behaviour. Let the law be rightly kept even for one Sabbath, and the great event would take place. Salvation waited for an obedient people; on no other could it be bestowed. The heaped-up treasure of the people's merits went to hasten the cataclysm, and he whose account with God showed a surplus of righteousness over sins was safe for a place within the Kingdom. Now St. Paul, who had tried this plan with exhaustive assiduity, confessed in the end that it led nowhere. There was no thoroughfare to God that way. And this was the atmosphere into which Jesus stepped. He was surrounded by men who held, as a deep ancestral conviction, that the achievement of righteousness by good works was the contribution asked of them for the realisation of the Kingdom of God.

[7] Of this we have studied three instances in the preceding chapter.

At first sight, our Lord's main interest appears to be identical with that of Judaism. He too speaks constantly of the Kingdom; He too insists that men must be ready for it. But now everything is said with a difference. And the difference lies in this, that He calls not the righteous to enter, but sinners. Previously those called had been conscientious observers of the Law in its infinite detail; forgiveness or acceptance awaited those who could put something substantial in the scale and who, when summoned, could show a worthy record. The Messiah, it was expected, would condemn and destroy the unworthy. But now Jesus comes, seeking not the whole but the sick, not performers of the Law but publicans and harlots, the outcast, the despised, the sinking, the sunken. Representative as He was of the world's Judge, He yet turned with special tenderness to the guilty. It seemed unnatural, it seemed positively wrong and offensive, that He should bring God to the undeserving, like Zaccheus or the dying thief. To rejoice in a Christ like this was not easy, it is not easy now; for it means a new thought of God. The point clearly is that the offer of the Kingdom has ceased to be conditional on men's attitude,[8] because it comes straight from the sheer compassion of the Father, as unsought and unmerited as the presence of Jesus in the world. Henceforward there can be no question of earning salvation by excellence of character. Why should a man earn what is spontaneously offered to him, namely, the unspeakable love of God? God does everything and gives everything; he puts into men's empty hand what they have never worked for or expected. And it is only because God does everything that man can do something, not as price but in gratitude.

This is the Gospel of Jesus Christ, preached at the ultimate cost to Himself of which the evangelists go on to tell; and only when we take it thus can we say why from the beginning unnumbered needy hearts have grown warm at the sound of Jesus' name. In the encounter of Christ and

[8] The *offer* of the Kingdom, not its possession and enjoyment. This last, of course, Jesus says is dependent on a man's attitude, i.e. on his repentance and trust. Cf. the parable of the Pharisee and the publican, where the publican is received in grace not for his virtues but because he is penitent.

the Pharisees we are conscious of the meeting of two great conceptions of religion—legalism, which rests on and revolves round merit and reward, and evangelicalism, adoring the free grace that calls us sons. As it has been put, " The Rabbis spoke perpetually of the righteousness of men, Jesus exclusively of the Kingdom of God." Let a man understand Jesus' message, and rejoice in it—let him once break through the hedge of immemorial Jewish belief to the life-giving insight that to *seek* the lost is God's very nature—and he could not fail to perceive not merely that the Kingdom was already present in Jesus but that no sin, however dark or heavy, could exclude from it the hungering and thirsting heart. He and his like could listen to the words, " Fear not, little flock, it is your Father's good pleasure to give you the Kingdom," and thus encouraged in spite of ruinous guilt could look up trustfully into God's face, and be comforted. In a word: by winning their trust for Himself, Jesus led the sinful to trust the pardoning love of God. And what is this in essence but justification by faith? That doctrine is a simple declaration to men, in view of Jesus, that at once, and without waiting to be better, they may by faith have God Himself for Saviour and Friend. Come home to God, and come now, and you will find that at your coming there is joy in the presence of the angels. This is the new word of Jesus; and when St. Paul spoke of justifying faith, it was this word he echoed.

St. Paul, that is to say, by his paradox about God justifying the ungodly is carrying on the message (known by Jesus to be true because of His fellowship with the Father, known by St. Paul to be true because of his contact with the living Christ) that the unworthy are received not for the reason that the account of precept and performance has been squared, but out of the Father's mercy. Both trace everything up to the free act of a gracious God. The parable of the Labourers in the Vineyard[9] puts the truth too plainly for mistake. There it is taught once for all that God resembles a master who pays the same reward to his labourers notwithstanding their wholly different hours of work; and it is in this

[9] Matt. 20.1-16.

particular respect that the resemblance holds good, for God opens the Kingdom freely to all who will enter. To the seeking heart He gives in grace all that the most obedient think they can justly claim. "It is not because the last comers have accomplished in one or two hours as much as others in a full day that they receive the same payment; they receive it, although they have accomplished far less. It is not the merit of those who seem to be treated as favourites that is emphasised in reply to murmuring envy; it is the sheer goodness of God, who has the right to bestow without merit that which others have deserved, and will never renounce this right."[10] Thus the idea of reward, which enters as part of the indispensable scenery of the story, is intentionally and triumphantly swallowed up and lost in the thought of grace. We cannot—this is the outcome of the whole—we cannot put God under an obligation or establish a claim against Him which He has no choice but to acknowledge; ultimately, whatever our record, we owe everything to His loving-kindness. Men are not employees, laying before God a bill of wages; they are blessed with good, most of all they are blessed with pardon, because God has love and they have faith. This is the gospel, pledged to sinful men in Christ, which St. Paul sets forth in intellectual forms of his own.

The rise of faith in St. Paul's mind is a familiar story, but we cannot recollect too distinctly that it is of crucial importance for his reading of the Gospel. From himself we learn that he had ardently followed the pathway of legally acquired righteousness to the very end, and that eventually it had brought him out into a wilderness of spiritual unrest and frustration. On the one hand, it filled him with a bitter consciousness of failure; on the other, it inflamed him with a cruel spirit of persecution. Then at Damascus all was changed. Christ appeared to him in living glory; and in Him there somehow broke upon the other's mind such a decisive revelation of God as imparted to him, without money and without price, the inner rest he had sought vainly through struggle and agony. Pharisaic assumptions and prepossessions fell away.

[10] Jülicher, *Die Gleichnisse Jesu,* II, p. 468.

He knew himself " saved." The blessedness and acceptance of a child of God were his.

The account which the apostle presents of this great experience is of a very definite kind. He glorifies God for all that has happened to him; he sees the Divine hand in action at every point. It was not that he had fought his way through to peace; God had interposed and given him salvation " for nothing." Now he understood Jesus and the gospel that bore His name. Now it had grown clear how " salvation is of the Lord," and how a " law of righteousness " that in itself is holy and good may become a " curse " if envisaged as a menacing, statutory code, which may prescribe and threaten but can never help the tempted. But Christ has abolished this law of external commandments in order that He may introduce the better law which is fulfilled, wholly and exclusively, in love. He abolishes it by His cross, that sign and seal of Divine grace supervening upon the failure of men to elaborate a righteousness of their own. The cross is the prevenient act of God's love; it is a deed done irrespective of all man's doing. Judaism has sought by meticulous obedience to call forth the Messiah, to elicit and evoke the Kingdom; now, in the light of " righteousness by faith," St. Paul discerns the vanity of all that, as of something superfluous and antiquated, since God has taken active steps to reconcile the world to Himself. This is Jesus' gospel over again; it is the same declaration that God alone saves, and that when He saves it is not to reward human merit but in virtue of His free and unchanging love.

But now a singular fact emerges: St. Paul does not give detailed expression to all this in the terms used by Jesus, but in terms which in origin are traditional and even Rabbinic. He has little to say about the Kingdom as bestowed in grace, but much about righteousness in God's sight. In short, he recurs to the problem as stated in former Jewish thought, and in his present situation he finds the all-sufficient answer to it. He, like the Rabbis, is still asking how the sinful can be righteous in the Divine judgment; he is still concerned with his status before that awe-inspiring tribunal; but his humble and confident solution, briefly put, is that the righteousness after which he had vainly striven is *bestowed,* once for all, in Christ. This use of older categories to interpret an experience transcending the level at which these categories were in place, constitutes a difficulty for modern Christian thought. At first sight it has the look of a relapse to the plane of legalism. But, as we shall see later, this impression is deceptive after all. Law had brought St. Paul to despair; in Christ's presence he had discovered that there is a Divine righteousness to which legal works contribute nothing; and he would not have been himself had he really fallen a victim to Rabbinic influence at the heart of his theology. As he puts it roundly, he is now satisfied to have " no legal righteousness of my own, but the righteousness of faith in Christ, the divine righteousness that rests on faith."[11] When he speaks of the " righteousness of God," there is nothing legal in his mind. It is rather that he employs the phrase in a verbally elusive and yet religiously quite intelligible double sense: at one time it is an order of salvation brought in by God whereby men have conferred on them a valid righteousness if they believe in Jesus, a sense which looks forwards; while at another we have a sense that looks backwards, " the righteousness of God " being now meant as a righteousness which insists on the expiation in Christ's death of sins previously overlooked by the Divine forbearance. In the former case, " righteousness " is God's gift to men; in the latter, it is the constitutive quality of His own being. But everywhere St. Paul is compelling old terms and categories to convey a new meaning which his own experience, born of contact with Christ, has infused.

At bottom, then, and in whatever inherited thought-forms, St. Paul repeats the gospel brought by Jesus to the sinful. This makes it antecedently more than probable that when the apostle gives justification by faith the prominence he does, it is by no accidental or merely controversial device. It is far more than a defensive weapon, adopted for his mission work, with the intention of repelling attacks on his free evangelism among the Gentiles. To-day we are often invited to think that the heart of piety for him was rather the

[11] Phil. 3.9 (Moffatt).

Christian mysteries. Here, and not in justification, lay the centre of his interest. But we naturally find it difficult to understand how one to whom Christianity was one more mystery-cult, although the greatest, could have come to write the emphatic words that the cross is " to the Greeks foolishness." After all, what is contemplated in the mysteries is the pretended death of a being known to be mythical, but St. Paul beholds in the cross the death of a Man whom many still alive had known. There was little in the mysteries to " offend " a Greek, though much to excite and thrill him, for the incarnation and even the death of a God was no such unfamiliar thought. But St. Paul was a Jew; to him therefore the cross *was* an offence; its misery and shame made Jesus' end a proof of His being accursed by God. Relief came only through the discovery that this death had been divinely ordered for gracious ends, that God had put forward Jesus as the means of propitiation by His blood, to be received by faith.[12] Till he saw it as the act of Divine love, the cross remained a thing of horror. So much by way of proof that we have no cause to dislodge justifying faith from the commanding place it has seemed to hold in the apostle's outlook.

There are psychological reasons which confirm this view. It is of course true that the idea comes to the front in Galatians and Romans, where the Judaistic controversy so much absorbs him; but this fact affords no evidence that it had occurred to him only then. Long before he had met the Judaists in Antioch. Indeed, every reasonable consideration bids us suppose that the great new insight formed part of his personal religion from the first. He had no need to await the outburst of controversy; he had a Judaist in his own heart, with whom from the outset he was bound to reach an understanding. As missionary, too, there was one primary thing he had to do—and every preacher finds he has to do it still—viz. clear the ground of the last vestige of the belief that salvation comes as a result of moral excellence, of noble character, and replace this by the revolutionising certainty that character comes rather from the trustful acceptance of

12 Rom. 3.25.

God's love. All along he had to put the case of gospel against law; and this of itself transports his whole argument, in principle, far above all casual emergencies, and makes it vital not for Jews or Judaisers merely, but for man. There are instincts in human nature, everywhere, which constitute St. Paul's message of justification by faith—in essence drawn from his Master—the only possible gospel for a sinner.

All this, however, is entirely compatible with the fact, not to be slurred, that in the statement of his problem, and to some degree in its solution, St. Paul (as we have seen) dressed new ideas in old vestures. It was still for him a self-evident assumption that righteousness must attach to those who are to obtain salvation. He made it his business, therefore, to show that the old order of Divine requirement was still fulfilled through Christ, but in a higher sense. Under the pressure of controversy, his original Christian intuition of the terms on which alone the sinful become right with God took formulated shape. Man, he taught, is not justified by the works of the law but by faith. When we scrutinise such a statement, we can see that it owes something to a specific theological tradition. When, for example, St. Paul declares that "Abraham believed God, and it was reckoned to him for righteousness" (Rom. 4.3), clearly he is using the armour of his foes. The phrase "was reckoned to him," which St. Paul means to indicate that Abraham had no good works to put forward, might be taken by a not wholly obtuse reader to signify that faith in Abraham's case is to be conceived simply as a different type of good works that went into the Divine scale as in its own way meritorious. But although the citation was in a sense equivocal, and could bear this construction, any such interpretation would have been that of the Rabbis, not St. Paul. On the very ground selected by his adversaries, and with their instruments, he would demonstrate the untenability of the doctrine on which they staked all.

The word we customarily translate "justify" strictly means to "make righteous," as "sanctify" means to make holy, but long before St. Paul's time it had been used familiarly in the sense of "declare righteous." That is, its common signification was either a judicial verdict on one accused of a particular crime (in which case to "justify" is to acquit), or a more general pronouncement on his moral worth (in which case to "justify" is to declare righteous, pure or innocent). This is its significance in the Pauline writings. God alone knows the heart, so that He alone can justify in this sense; and in St. Paul none but God is ever said to justify. But since all have sinned, it looks as if justification as such were out of the question. Here the Gospel interposes, with its new light. It proclaims that God now *offers* justification to the sinful, in pure grace, provided they have faith. Had He insisted on good works, it would have been all over with our hopes; none is or can be "just" before God on that score. But faith is so precious to Him that on the ground of it He will justify even the ungodly, as St. Paul explicitly says.[13] His point is that in a world like this justification always is utterly undeserved, and this he reiterates constantly. The sinfulness and weakness of men leave them without the slightest claim to mercy. But God in His love accepts the unacceptable. We shall see how this Pauline gospel was announced freshly by the Reformers.

There are certain misapprehensions of St. Paul's teaching in this matter against which we must be on our guard. As we have noted, he does not regard faith as a well-deserving performance, only of a new sort, on the ground of which righteousness is imputed. He does not mean that God takes something imperfect and accounts it perfect by grace; or that He takes, as we say colloquially, the will for the deed. St. Paul, the Christian, could not have formed the idea that man's performances held any place whatever as securing for him access to God. Nor, again, is it his teaching that the righteousness of Christ is imputed to the believer, by what may be styled a legal fiction. Even in Rom. 5.19 there is no suggestion of this, and the idea is not otherwise characteristic of the New Testament. Nor, finally, is St. Paul to be interpreted as falling back simply on God's sovereign and arbitrary grace as the source of justification. It is God who justifies, but there is no question of His justifying men at random. We are told, indeed, that He justifies "the ungodly,"

13 Rom. 4.5.

but the objects of grace here are unmistakably described as *the ungodly who have faith.* The presence of faith makes possible a justification which before was impossible. Anything else would be to import into the apostle's mind a false and unwholesome element which he must have indignantly rejected.

A pathway can, however, be found through the intricacies of the subject if we recognise frankly that any scheme of ideas that clusters round a legal or rabbinical conception of God's relation to man—and it is the *terminology,* though not the convictions, of such a scheme that St. Paul employs —must fail to do justice to the spiritual fact of forgiveness through Christ as it is actually experienced. Any such terminology could only be a partially opaque medium for St. Paul's real message. He is telling us simply that the man who has faith is now in the right relationship to God; where enmity was, there is peace. To believe in God from the heart is to be pleasing to Him, to satisfy Him, to be right with Him. And so, when St. Paul describes the position of a sinful man who in that sense trusts God by saying that he is "declared righteous," we recognise that the phrase has its own importance and value as a repudiation of "work-righteousness," yet also we may feel that we desiderate a more purely personal mode of denoting simple, loving forgiveness. St. Paul does not mean that in forgiving a sinner God says about him the thing that is not; he means, and it is the glory of his message, that God rather is acknowledging an actually established new relationship, which has been produced through the instrumentality of the cross of Jesus. He who has faith, a faith evoked by the Crucified, *is* now in a new relation which is also the one right relation of a sinful man to God. In other words, he is *de facto* right with God, in this purely religious sense. Justification, forgiveness, is not immoral, but it requires more than moral terms for its expression.

After all this, it scarcely needs saying that for the apostle justification as a Divine act, as God's recognition of our new attitude to Himself, is not primarily a judgment on our moral condition. It is not even that the undoubted moral character of faith is brought in as a make-weight of meritorious quality. True, if I present a friend with a gift, he must of course take it if it is to be his; but the taking is not a performance I reward by putting the gift in his hand. Faith itself, St. Paul would rejoin, is itself the gift of God, and can furnish no occasion for boasting. To it also the question is applicable, "What hast thou that thou didst not receive?"

To sum up, we may say: in the Pauline doctrine of justification the forms of legalistic thought have been so employed as to put legalistic thought out of court in a religion of unreserved grace. The case for gospel over against law has been stated, and as far as meaning goes stated finally, through ideas which in part are derived from law itself.

We have just seen that while St. Paul, like the Rabbis, spoke of the acquisition of " righteousness " in God's sight, yet by being " justified " or " declared righteous " he intended something wholly different from what they had in mind. They were thinking of God's verdict on a man's moral state or moral attainment, he of God's acknowledgment of the trusting sinner as now in the right personal attitude or relation to Himself. He who accepts in faith the grace offered him in Christ thereby becomes right with the Father. But obviously a grave problem emerges at this point, for St. Paul and indeed for evangelical religion as such. If it be held that a man is " justified " who thus has simply entered on the right relationship, in spite of his defects of character, what becomes of morality? Has not St. Paul broken the thread of purely ethical religion which goes back through Jesus, becoming perfected in Him, to the prophets of the Old Testament? How is that profound and passionate interest in moral obedience which St. Paul elsewhere reveals to be linked up with his thought of justification, in a fashion that is real and not merely verbal? Or, to put it otherwise, can the Pauline doctrine of justifying faith be successfully defended against the charge of ethical laxity and indifference?

The question is serious; we need have no hesitation in conceding that the Judaists at first sight had something to say for themselves, for St. Paul's gospel does have an anti-nomian look. But must it not always be so, where gospel is really present? Did not the Pharisees bring a charge of antinomianism against Jesus, who received sinners and ate with them? Naturally, for neither St. Paul nor his Master preached a gospel consisting in ethical demands. Yet it is as much a total misapprehension to charge the one as it is to charge the other with indifference to ethical interests. In point of fact, the principle on which both Jesus and St. Paul proceed amounts to this, that the only really good man is the pardoned man, and he is good because he alone has been delivered from the self-centredness which underlies all moral failure, and is henceforward content to owe everything to God. Nay, the goodness which St. Paul believed must by a spiritual necessity flow from the experience of being forgiven is of so lofty and pure a character that, significantly enough, he has actually been supposed, by a not inconsiderable series of writers, to have regarded Christians as having become sinless from the moment of their conversion.[14]

Still, this hardly meets our point. We are inquiring whether in St. Paul these two interests, the religious and the moral, merely lie side by side independently, or whether he has been able to establish between them a connexion which is real and inevitable. And there can be no doubt at all that he exhibits the connexion as necessarily and livingly involved in Christian experience as such. Of course justification is *imprimis* a religious fact, the ethical consequences of which, certain as they are, are not so far in view. Forgiveness is not the same thing as reformation, or we should not need the two words; and when St. Paul says "justification" he is thinking of the first, not the second. Again, he does not join religion and ethics merely by the idea of grace, in the sense that God is gracious in two distinct and successive manners—first to forgive, then to sanctify. That would merely add goodness to pardon; it would not show how goodness springs from pardon by an inward vital impulse. We find the tie rather

[14] See the late Professor Warfield's articles in the *Princeton Theological Review* for 1920.

in the apostle's great conception "in Christ," or "in the Spirit." The sinful, he teaches, are justified in Christ,[15] and in Him they are renewed. It is in virtue of union with Christ, in the unspeakably intimate sense which faith denotes, that they are forgiven; "there is no condemnation for those who are in Christ Jesus."[16] In virtue of the same union they triumph in duty, in temptation, in trial; "I can do all things in Him who strengthens me,"[17] "My grace is sufficient for thee, for My power is perfected in weakness."[18] The matter has been lucidly explained by Professor H. A. A. Kennedy. He points out that for St. Paul faith means "the trustful surrender of his whole being to Christ, as crucified and risen, and the complete identification of himself with Christ's attitude to God and to sin." This union with Christ is the religious, starting-point, which all his doctrines seek to interpret. "When he speaks of God justifying a man because of his faith, receiving him into a new relation, the relation of a child to his Father, his language seems at times unduly to objectify the process, to keep it apart from the experience of the individual. But for Paul the very existence of faith means that the subject of it is 'in Christ.' Hence, all God's dealings with the individual stand on that footing. To quote the apostle himself, God's grace is 'bestowed on us in the Beloved.' That is to say, God comes into touch with men in virtue of their relation to Christ. So too with the nature of the new life. Paul has formulated something of a theory regarding the 'death' of the believer to sin. That theory is implicated in his conceptions of the Flesh and the Law. But when you get behind his logic, you reach the crucial fact that the man who is in intimate connection with Christ, from the nature of the case feels the utter incongruity of sin, and

[15] Too much has been said about justification being for St. Paul a *future* blessing. The balance of thought in Romans suggests nothing of that kind. "We are justified by His blood," we read in 5.9, where justification is past; "they are justified freely by His grace" (3.24) makes it present (cf. Gal. 2.16). The apostle is obviously intent on some great boon which men can experience now.

[16] Rom. 8.1.
[17] Phil. 4.13.
[18] 2 Cor. 12.9.

must break with it if that connection is to endure. In union with Christ he takes Christ's attitude towards sin and Christ's attitude towards holiness."[19]

Thus there is no hiatus, either for St. Paul's mind or in fact, between justification by faith and a good life, no gaping interval which must be filled by the insertion of some additional moral dynamic not vitally involved in the experience of justification itself. One who looks up into the face of a forgiving God is set within a world of new realities, his personal response to which *is* the Christian morality. As pardoned, he is a new man in God's sight and in his own; and this newness of life takes active shape, as life always does, in ways answering to its specific nature. It is through Christ that he has seen utter mercy in God's face; in Christ, therefore, he beholds fully and persuasively revealed that will of God which he is called to know and obey. Can it be seriously contended that ethical impulses are anywhere to be found more profound or fertile than those which thus rise spontaneously out of the experience of being forgiven for Christ's sake? It yields grateful love to God, and, since His faithful love is now assured, it evokes patience under grief, endurance, the hope that never makes ashamed. It yields the subduing consciousness that we belong to Christ, who gave Himself for us, and that as His possession we must keep ourselves pure. It yields the perception that our brother too is Christ's, and for Christ's sake must be served in love. It yields the sacrificial temper, for by confidence in the God who wrought our salvation we know that sacrifice will not be in vain. All these impulses or incentives flow with psychological necessity from that attitude of grateful and obedient apprehension of God's love in Christ which St. Paul means by "faith." Such motives to goodness are the highest conceivable by man; their action on our minds, St. Paul would tell us, is the presence of the Spirit of Christ within.

It is true, "justifying faith" has at times been thought to need supplementing in an ethical interest. But the reason for this is quite plain. Either "faith" has lapsed into "orthodox assent," which certainly is not morally inspiring,

[19] *Theology of the Epistles*, p. 124 f.

or what it has been supposed to lay hold on is the imputed righteousness of Christ, which in turn affords no inward source of personal goodness and by its externality makes it necessary to seek hallowing influences elsewhere. St. Paul is unaffected by these misunderstandings. By faith he means that which on the subjective side covers everything in Christian religion. It unites men to Christ, so putting them right with God; but *eo ipso* it makes them partakers by fellowship in Christ's own life of Divine power.

The foregoing argument appears to prove that the essential meaning of justification by faith goes back to the mind of Jesus Himself, and that when St. Paul gave it larger prominence he was declaring with special emphasis a message of grace for the sinful which had its roots in Jesus' gospel of the Kingdom and His own relation thereto. If this be so, we need not hesitate to affirm that the idea, in its characteristic import, is native to the Christian religion. It is not the peculiarity of any man or any school; it has its home within the New Testament, and can count upon the witness of the Spirit.

In the next chapter we shall find that the same problem with which St. Paul had wrestled, rose once more into vital urgency at the Reformation. That problem is in fact one of perennial moment for all the sinful who have seen God and know something of themselves. All who cast themselves on His mercy in Christ for the forgiveness of their sins are compelled to do homage, joyful or reluctant, to the basal truth for which St. Paul stands. They may reject this or that element in his doctrine as savouring of Rabbinical dialectic, and indeed there are features of his total view which the modern Christian intelligence cannot be forbidden to criticise. But once they have taken pardon from the Father's hand as a free gift, which costs them nothing because it cost God all, their minds involuntarily move, they cannot but move, on the broad religious lines once for all traced by the apostle. The late Mr. F. H. Bradley, a free and discerning spirit if there have been such, took occasion from his argument in an early work to comment upon the doctrine of justification in terms which may perhaps serve to assure us that in pondering it we are occupied, not with obsolete theological futilities, but with the heart of religion. "You must believe," he writes, "that you too really are one with the divine, and must act as if you believed it. In short, you must be justified not by works but solely by faith. This doctrine, which Protestantism, to its eternal glory, has made its own and sealed with its blood, is the very centre of Christianity; and, where you have not this in one form or another, there Christianity is nothing but a name."[20]

[20] *Ethical Studies,* p. 290.

CHAPTER VI

LUTHER AND THE GOSPEL

In order to appreciate the greatness of the step forward taken by the Reformers, it is necessary that we should have clearly before our minds, at least in outline, the positions against which they protested in the name of New Testament religion. There can of course be no question here of sketching, however briefly, the history of the doctrine of justification in the ancient Catholic and mediæval Church. That is too intricate a matter for a chapter, and might confuse rather than clarify our ideas. But we may usefully devote some pages to three cardinal elements or aspects of the older system of belief which growingly aroused the distrust of Luther and sent him back, in a passion of self-torture and despair, to the gospel of Jesus Christ proclaimed by St. Paul. In his quest for the sense of pardon they confronted him with a blank wall, through which there was no way. They are (1) the virtual disappearance from early Catholic religion of something that the mediæval Church never succeeded in recovering, viz. the conviction that God freely pardons the sinful if they will but trust His love in Christ; (2) the entrance of the exceptionally influential idea of human merit; and (3) the conception of grace which gradually came to prevail and to give a fixed colour to men's thoughts of the manner in which God saves. These three things are so intimately bound up together that they may be regarded as but different facets of a single principle. But they can be looked at separately, and it will help us to take them so.[1]

---

[1] It would be unpardonable were I to fail to accentuate the fact that the Roman Church does in a real sense proclaim forgiveness and seek to mediate it to men, notwithstanding the religiously unsatisfying manner in which this mediation is expressed. It is not that great evangelical thoughts are absent, for they are obviously present in the service of the Mass, even if partially obscured by ideas which, as taught by the New Testament, we must call legal.

(1) In the patristic age, the great New Testament idea of justification by faith, although not denied outright, was very imperfectly understood.[2] It can hardly be said to have been understood at all. Beyond question passages can be quoted from almost every Church Father, Greek or Latin, which have a thoroughly apostolic sound and appear to be inspired by the thought of freely forgiving love to the unworthy. So far there is no suggestion that the penitent must in some way so prepare himself as to become fitted to receive God's pardon. But the point to be noted firmly is this: such words are more than obscured, in reality they are cancelled, by statements of an exactly opposite type, to the effect that men can and must render themselves such that the grace which procures salvation may properly be conferred upon them; and this kind of vacillation between gospel and law is the clearest proof that the Pauline message, as one that answers all a sinner's need, has become unintelligible. It is hardly too much to say that, even in its noblest representatives, the motto of the Early Church is "salvation by faith and good conduct," and the predominant point of view is that sins are forgiven on the basis of amendment.[3] At times pardon was

[2] See especially Campbell N. Moody, *The Mind of the Early Converts.*

[3] Mr. Moody points out that for Hermas "the affliction of a pious person could only mean that God had failed him, or that his sins were not yet wholly forgiven. The popular Chinese-Christian view of the subject," he proceeds suggestively, "is almost exactly the same. When a Christian says, ' My sins are very heavy,' he is often thinking not of sins at all, but of troubles, which are a sure sign of guilt. And when he says, ' My sins are a little forgiven, not yet altogether forgiven,' he means that his afflictions are but partially removed, or that he is not rid of all his faults. The intimate association of guilt with suffering makes it difficult to regard forgiveness as a present experience; it is a hope rather than a fact. And this, as we know, is the view not merely of Hermas and of Barnabas, but of early Christians in general, notwithstanding their doctrine that through faith and by baptism previous sins have been washed away. With such thoughts in their minds the early Christians cast about for some means of hastening the process of forgiveness. There must be more thorough repentance, and more visible signs of it in almsgiving, fasting, and self-abasement. Hermas suggests also that self-punishment may be employed to abbreviate the penalties inflicted by God. The inference that by such means God may be propitiated for post-baptismal sins is

thrust into the background by the boon of higher spiritual knowledge; but even when importance was attached to this, preachers and writers using the language that came to them most naturally urged the moralistic idea, very imperfectly related to the other, that salvation is the prize and recompense of a perfect moral life, to be achieved out of one's own resources. A mistaken ethical compunction, an anxious feeling that before God pardons a man He must first take from him guarantees for morality, deterred great Christian minds from doing justice to the heights and depths of the New Testament proclamation.

It might seem as if the pure grace of God were suggested in the sacrament of baptism, for it is common ground with patristic writers that baptism secures a complete forgiveness of the past, sins being somehow washed away and the baptised cleared of all guilt. But to a large extent baptism itself was understood vaguely and magically; sin was often thought of as a quasi-physical stain or defilement, which could be removed in unspiritual ways. Even so, the need for pardon in their post-baptismal life came home to earnest men painfully, as day by day they experienced their own weakness in temptation. As they deal with this problem, we can perceive in the mind of Church writers a strange mixture of legal and evangelical ideas, for which no one in particular was to blame, but which none the less obscured the glory of Christ as Saviour. It is with these legal ideas we are specially concerned now.

Speaking broadly, we may say that in the early centuries pardon is for those who are, or have made themselves, worthy to obtain it. Thus Clement of Rome says that "we are not justified through ourselves, or our works which we have wrought in holiness of heart," but through faith; yet elsewhere he can speak of our sins being taken away "by love." Barnabas and Hermas scarcely do more than hint at forgiveness through faith as a present experience. Justification is

---

not very far away" (*op. cit.* p. 98 f.). This revealing passage indicates one persistent strain in Catholicism which the Reformers felt to be contrary to the Gospel.

often referred to the future, and pardon seems to be conceived mainly as a thing of degrees, instalments being granted in proportion to repentance and moral improvement. It was assumed that affliction meant that God had not yet pardoned or only in a slight degree, and that by lowly resignation the process of forgiveness could be accelerated. Later Church teachers held that the only completely forgiven person was the martyr. In most quarters we find men tending to confuse pardon with purification, making one the index of the other or identical with it. Irenaeus, though he has far finer things to say, can refer to " the natural things of the law by which a man is justified." We may read some writers from end to end without feeling that the difference between salvation by faith and salvation by works had any place in their minds. " Clear thoughts of the principles on which the Lord deals with men about sins, especially after baptism, never were attained. Out of this perplexity arose, after a long time, the Romish sacrament of penance."[4]

Tertullian, here as everywhere, is both significant and influential.[5] He taught that baptism gives the penitent forgiveness for previous offences and takes him bound, on pain of eternal loss, to win the reward of eternal life. The trained jurist urged a legal and moralistic view of the relations between God and man; he expressed it in formulas borrowed from the case of creditor and debtor and of such external rigidity that the truth that God deals with us as with sons slips wholly out of sight. The convert's penitence buys his first pardon in baptism; and if he needs a second pardon, the Father will insist on satisfactions first. These are rendered through the sacrifices of self-abasement and asceticism. Sin is purged by self-castigation; " the affliction of the flesh is the victim that placates the Lord by means of the sacrifice of humiliation."[6] " The way that leads to life becomes even narrower as Tertullian advances in years. The only sins that are freely forgiven are those committed before baptism, and,

[4] Rainy, *Ancient Catholic Church,* p. 81.
[5] Loofs, *Dogmengeschichte,* p. 165 f.
[6] *de patientia,* 13.

as these are sins of ignorance, grace is reduced to a minimum."[7] In this region as in others Tertullian had laid down lines on which the thinking of the Western Church was to move.

The theologians of Alexandria share in this inability to appreciate the truth that a merciful God justifies us through faith. For Clement the idea of forgiveness had become so difficult that it is hardly mentioned in his writings; it is the grace not of pardon but of enlightenment that he craves. And Origen makes clear that by his time—the beginning of the third century—the Church had fairly come to foster what has been called a conscious ambiguity on the subject, in other words definitely to give both faith and works a place as grounds of human acceptance with God. He enumerates as means of forgiveness such things as baptism, martyrdom, almsgiving, amendment, great love, tearful repentance. In an exposition of Psalm 32 he marks three stages in the process of pardon. " The beginning of conversion," he says, " is to forsake the evils of the soul; by this means the remission of sins is procured. When good begins to be done, and there is more abundance of good than of preceding evils, then sins are covered. Finally, when perfection is attained, no iniquities are imputed."[8] Elsewhere he writes that we are justified by our faith, by our works of righteousness, but most of all by the blood of Christ. So hard did even great Christian minds find it to retain hold of the apostolic thought of a gracious God made ours freely in Christ, and to state it with consistent clearness.

In Augustine's earliest period, the idea that God for Christ's sake forgives the guilty sinner plays no part at all. Soon, however, he begins to place a growing emphasis on the remission of sin bestowed in baptism, and the bearing on this of Christ's historical work, though the grace that aids and transforms inwardly is rated higher than the forgiving grace that liberates. At the height of his powers he builds everything on the truly evangelical premiss that man's salvation, and justification as part of it, depends in the last resort on

[7] Moody, *op. cit.*, p. 234.   [8] Moody, *op. cit.*, p. 286.

the prevenient grace of God; although it must be noted that even here full and free forgiveness is associated exclusively with baptism, while in the ordinary life of Christians its place is taken by the conception of justification as caused by infused grace and love. Grace is a power that transforms the will, making willing those that were unwilling—as prevenient conferring a will to good, as co-operant unfolding itself in a series of stages concluding with full actual regeneration, whereby a man, filled with love, is enabled to acquire merit. Justification is not an attitude of God towards the sinner, of a Divine judgment regarding him; it is the completion of a process of grace by means of which the sinner is actually made a righteous man. This comes about through the infusion of the spirit of love into his heart. Thus justification, while *sub specie aeternitatis* a finished act, is empirically viewed a never-ending process. Justification, in short, is a change that goes on in man's inward being, as righteousness is inspired; it is not the gracious act of God receiving the unworthy into His fellowship. As the man is renewed, his guilt disappears. Moody brings out the combination of gospel and law in which St. Augustine ends. " He was well aware that grace was not exhausted in baptism, that in baptism the sins which belonged to the past and those which belonged to the future were alike forgiven, that there was daily forgiveness for those who day by day came with the prayer, Forgive us our debts, and a daily supply of grace to enable the Christian to live a life of love. . . . Yet it was not clear even to Augustine that in faith and forgiveness all things were bestowed. . . . When he regarded grace as something that annulled the state of sin, he thought no longer of forgiveness, nor of faith, nor of Christ's death. In some of his writings we find but little of faith in the highest and most religious sense as a trust in Jesus that constitutes reconciliation and holiness. . . . In the end it is not the sinner, joined by faith to the Saviour and reconciled to God, who is acquitted at the Judgment-seat; it is the saint who appears clothed in his own merits, the love and good works which he owes to God's inspiring grace."[9] The inconsequent part as-

[9] *Op. cit.*, p. 297 f.

signed to merit in this mingled outlook upon Christian religion calls for closer scrutiny.

(2) Among the cardinal factors in Roman Catholic thought with which the Reformers came into violent collision is that of merit as a religious concept. It is an idea inextricably woven through the Roman texture of Christianity, and made its appearance early. Not that merit is always indicated by Church writers when good works are mentioned, for good works are our duty, for evangelicals as for others, and have no necessary suggestion of "extra" value. Gradually, however, duty came to be regarded as the minimum required, and alongside of it came to stand the view that we can do more than our duty, and, on the strength of this, claim reward. The relapse to pre-Christian standards is obvious. It was not felt that grace and deserved reward were opposed conceptions. At this stage no theorised doctrine of the subject held the field; legal ideas lived on beside evangelical. But the forgiveness of sins, often, is attached to the performance of the believer, e.g. almsgiving, fasting, prayer. As might have been anticipated, it was in the Western Church especially that the notion struck root. Tertullian is of high importance. He can declare roundly that a good act makes God our debtor and wins merit proportionate to its value: *bonum factum Deum habet debitorem, par factum habet par meritum.* Indeed he does not shrink from the position that by meritorious works man can amass capital with God, which is as it were entered against his name. Thus sin is expiated and God appeased. In such things as tears, fasting, virginity or martyrdom lies a surplus of value, which goes to meet the Divine claim.

Even thinkers whose fundamental assumptions might appear to be wholly inimical to the idea of merit can employ it unconcernedly. Thus in Ambrose we read: "Without our work, not by works but by faith through His grace, He has forgiven our sins," yet elsewhere he surprises us by recurring to merit in the old way. So it is in all later Catholic thought. On the one hand, there is a denial of merit in the absolute sense, with a clear recognition, as in Augus-

tine, of the grace of God as the sole ground of salvation; on
the other, a firm conviction that through this grace merits
become obtainable by which, in accordance with the just rule
of recompense, we can and ought to earn eternal life.
Augustine, who rejects the popular notion that at any
moment the Christian can acquire merit by exerting free
will, and denies outright that in this sense the will is free,
because apart from God we can only sin, might have been
expected in consistency to bar our merit as such. And in
fact he does begin with absolute negation; grace, he declares,
is not grace save as it is wholly free. None the less the
older view counted for too much to be quite discarded. It is
carried on, but with the significant Augustinian qualifica-
tion, that grace alone renders merit possible. Merit becomes
possible when the supernatural grace of love has been
breathed into the soul; and, since this love is God's bestowal,
Augustine can say, in a famous phrase, that when God
rewards our merits He but crowns His own gifts.[10] Thus he
has no difficulty in viewing the real attainment of salvation
as a Divine compensation of the believer's merits made
possible by grace. The saved man is by grace given power
to merit or earn salvation. Augustine agrees with the
Pelagians in holding that eternal life is conferred as reward
to antecedent merits; what he misses in them is the perception that even our merits are the gift of God.[11]

Thus Augustine stamped on the thought of the Roman
Church an impression which it has never lost. Faith itself
cannot strictly be merited, but it lays down a basis for all the
merits that follow. Prayer, almsgiving, maceration put God
in our debt; works done out of the infused "habit" of grace,
i.e. the operation of Divine grace which gives man's will a
habitual tendency to love for God and man, are such that
in justice God must recompense them; by meritorious good
works, as tasks imposed by a priest in the sacrament of
penance, we can make satisfaction for sins committed after
baptism. As Gregory the Great puts it, quantity of merits is

[10] See R. S. Franks, in Hastings' *Encyclopædia of Religion and
Ethics,* vol. viii, p. 564.
[11] Schultz, in *Studien und Kritiken* (1894), p. 40 f.

the one point examined in men's lives, and merit proper is gained when we do more than God commands. By the Middle Ages, however, it has come to be taught that *all* works done in the state of grace are meritorious, not merely those which exceed duty, or (as they are usually called) works of supererogation. Mediæval theologians also introduced the distinction between *meritum de congruo* and *meritum de condigno,* or, as we may roughly say, between constructive and intrinsic merit. These are two degrees which depend on two degrees of grace. Merit "of congruity" belongs to a good effort made by man when unaided by anything more than general grace, and is assigned to it not of debt but in fitness; merit "of condignity" attaches to good works done by the help of saving grace, and to such works God owes reward in strict justice. By this time, merit had become a conception covering and embracing the whole of life; apart from it there could be no increase of grace, and the new grace was its recompense.

In the Middle Ages such teaching did not pass wholly without protest. St. Bernard of Clairvaux has uncompromising things to say in his sermons about our incapacity to win salvation, since even our good works are stained with sin. There is no such thing, he holds, as merit of condignity; concupiscence remains in us to the last and rises in revolt against the law. "He is foolish and mad, whoever he be that trusts in any merits of his life, who trusts in any religion or wisdom but only in humility." Yet he can recommend the practice of fasting as a means of averting eternal punishment.

Luther first broke conclusively with this whole tradition. It is not merely that he was able to describe the entire religious and moral attitude of the Christian without drawing upon the idea of merit; he sought positively to expel that idea from true evangelical piety. He goes back to the Biblical insight that man can never do more than he is bound to do, and that he is ceaselessly dependent on the mercy of God which judges and uplifts him. The sinner becomes pleasing to God not through the infusion of any interior gracious quality, which constitutes a new "habit" of soul, but solely in virtue of the Divine compassion which pardons. Between God and man there is no place for merits, or for a grace that apportions salvation to the merit acquired. In Catholic doctrine, a record of performances is steadily in view. Human reason can understand and even demonstrate the relations between justice (always the dominant conception) and the grace which renders men " just " in God's sight by transforming their nature and their character. " In Luther's view, grace passes all understanding. It is above reason, it is mysterious. The perfectly holy God envelopes in His love a humanity that is irreparably sunk in the state of sin. The religion of Luther is that of man conscious of being befouled with stains indelible, but of a man also who has experienced a Divine love the reason for which he cannot understand, of which he never ceases to feel unworthy, to which he can make no claim, for which he can only offer a gratitude that to the end is imperfect."[12] Faith alone produces good works, which issue from it in the nature of the case; and it is faith not in facts or doctrines but in a Person, the God of mercy unspeakable whom we meet in Christ.

At the Council of Trent the Roman Church reaffirmed in essentials the mediæval view of merit, thus giving permanence to that tendency to dwell upon the need for accumulating merit by good works which seems to be inseparable from its ordinary teaching and practice.[13] The Council declared that while the good works done by a justified man are the gifts of God, they are also the good merits of the doer, and that such good works truly merit eternal life and an increase of glory.[14] Bellarmine writes concisely: " The common opinion of all Catholics is that good works are truly and properly meritorious, and that not merely of some particular reward, but of eternal life itself."[15] And the position now taken by Roman teachers, in spite of balanced formulas, is that by the aid of supernatural grace in the case of the

[12] Strohl, *L'Evolution religieuse de Luther jusqu'en* 1515, p. 153.
[13] Bicknell, *Theological Introduction to the* 39 *Articles*, p. 275.
[14] Sess. vi, Can. 32.
[15] *De justificatione*, v. i (quoted by Franks, *ut. sup.*, p. 564).

regenerate, human works can become so good as to obtain or earn salvation, and that even the natural man by good works can deserve reward from God.

The theory of merit, as the Roman Church elaborates it, is plainly traceable to a very old assumption that the relation of God to man is, permanently and decisively, legal. Eternal life is conferred as the prize of achievement. Whether He saves or excludes from salvation, God is properly a remunerator; the last and truest thing we can say of Him is that He recompenses both obedience and rebellion as they deserve. A merit is a good action which He rewards. As we have seen, it is held that this is in no way incongruous with the fact that grace to do such action comes from God Himself; rather in virtue of His very goodness He has decreed that what are His own gifts should be the merits of the justified. In the lines attributed to Albertus Magnus:

> *Quicquid habes meriti, præventrix gratia donat,*
> *Nil deus in nobis præter sua dona coronat.*

Still, merit *is* merit, and has its rights. And obviously if there be a debtor and creditor account with God, the range of possible merits may attain wide dimensions. Each religious virtue is potentially a mine of good works. A wholly indifferent act becomes meritorious if done with a good intention; if the act be good in itself, it is doubly meritorious. Roman thinkers, it is true, frequently use the word "meritorious" as indicating simply the moral goodness of an act, but it seems impossible for them to escape from the notion that this moral goodness establishes a claim which God is obliged to recognise. A further consequence of the legal or commercial nature of this system of ideas is that merit can be transferred. After providing what is needful to make satisfaction for sin and for the attainment of eternal life, there may be an overplus. Thus arises the treasury of merits, primarily of Christ but also of the saints, from which the Church may rightly derive indulgences.

The objections to which this comprehensive view of merit is exposed may be stated as follows.

It is foreign to the New Testament; for while the idea of reward occurs freely in Jesus' teaching, it has there nothing to do with merit. Indeed, the Parable of the Labourers so employs the conception of reward as explicitly to abrogate it as a measure of the relations between God and man. The Father who causes His sun to rise on the evil and the good acts from some higher principle, nor can we do more than fulfil our duty to Him. The thought of meriting a reward is unimaginable for the minds of those placed on the Judge's right hand in Matt. 25; it is in fact absolutely excluded as a motive by the simple consideration that love to God and man is declared the foundation of all true morality, for we cannot act simultaneously from love and from an egoistic desire for compensation. For Jesus there can be no question of rewards men have a right to claim; we should fare ill if God dealt with us according to our deserts. Thus to the child of the Father reward is not a motive to action so much as a symbol of the certainty that his work for the Kingdom is never in vain; it is, in view of God's character, the necessary sequel to labour in His cause; in unbought love He gives our work a place in the eternal consummation. Reward is real, but it is not external or fortuitous; it is God's acknowledgment of the worth of personality. He who has been faithful over a few things is made ruler over many things; yet he has done no more than his duty.

Students of ethical thought will have noted that the concept in question is now virtually absent from the best work in that field. " The idea of merit," it has been said roundly, " is foreign to the genuinely moral consciousness."[16] More

[16] Pringle-Pattison, *The Idea of Immortality*, p. 179. Is it possible that the Roman view is in part a generalisation of what is instinctively held by many an " anxious inquirer "? Cf. the words of David Brainerd : " Hundreds of times I renounced all pretenses of any worth in my duties, as I thought, even while performing them; and often confessed to God that I deserved nothing for the best of them but eternal condemnation; yet still I had a secret hope of *recommending* myself to God by religious duties " (quoted by Pratt, *The Religious Consciousness*, p. 146). Men are naturally as inclined to regard virtue as having a right to reward from God as they are to regard prosperity as a proof of God's love.

and more it is felt that the notion is at home only in a morality of utilitarian and eudæmonistic character, and that it naturally implies a casuistical outlook on the facts and opportunities of the moral life. Merit, in short, is an idea derived from the heteronomous ethics, i.e. ethics for which the law of conduct is something externally imposed and therefore obeyed without that intrinsic freedom which forms the true self-expression of personality. It is obeyed, rather, for the sake of considerations—the hope of reward or the fear of punishment—which have only a loose relation to the content of the "good" act. All true morality, on the other hand, is based on intrinsic reasons, at the challenge of an obligation felt to be unconditioned and absolute. If this be so, action inspired by the thought of one's own ultimate profit must be regarded as imperfectly moral. Thus so far from the term "meritorious" pointing to that which is dutiful *and more,* it suggests an attitude of mind that has positively failed to rise to the level of true obedience. But when the idea is carried over into religion and stretched to cover our personal relations with God, the result must be to induce a temper of "bargaining" which is indirectly anta-gonistic to humility.

The idea of merit belongs not to our highest experience but to the level of our everyday legal and semi-moral notions. So far from being absolutely valid, it is relative to some artificial system of relations. When dealing for example with children, or conducting a competition, or where there is a number of laws or regulations the fulfilment of which can be exactly measured, we naturally speak of an "order of merit." Or again, we say colloquially that well-doing deserves happi-ness and ill-doing sorrow and misery, and that prosperity and adversity ought to be distributed in proportion to the merits of the agents. But the slightest reflection will prove that this manner of thought, if pressed, comes into flagrant contradic-tion with deeper certainties, and that when confronted with some end or object of absolute value, we cannot bring our-selves to apply it. Thus, what honest man ever believed that he had merited the love of a good woman? Is not his immediate reaction to the discovery that his love is returned a feeling of utter unworthiness, and a confession that he is receiving more by far than his deserts? So, when we rise to the highest plane of all, to affirm that we can merit forgiveness or eternal life or fellowship with God is, to the truly religious mind, a contradiction in terms. Even on the level at which we familiarly speak of "merit," we are well aware that praiseworthy action merits just so much as it is worth, and no more; but what can merit God's gift of Himself in pardon? There we face the perfect, the absolute; at once our calculus wholly fails, and is cast aside as irrelevant. There, desert is no more applicable than to the finest things in the life of home and family, for what wholesome child would argue that he *deserves* his parents' care? Thus the range of the concept "merit" in life is curiously and narrowly restricted. We know that we are right in treating men *better* than they deserve. And the idea that by doing so we acquire merit is one that will not bear reflection.

In any case, we imperfect men can possess no merit before God. Jesus has formulated the supreme obligation in the words that we must love God with all our heart, and our neighbour as ourselves. To be *worthy* of fellowship with Him we should have to exhibit, what He must demand, a wholly selfless love; we should have to accomplish the good He commands from an utterly pure motive. To fail here is to fail altogether, since failure breaks the ideal relationship between God and man. In such a situation there can be no distinction between mortal and venial sins; every sin strikes at God and His supremacy. Now in sober fact this is an obligation we are unable to fulfil.[17] To say that we are able is to accommodate Christ's perfect law of love to our inability, bringing it down to a point where we can more than satisfy it. It follows with a transparent and terrible

---

[17] Cf. Hooker: "The little fruit we have in holiness, God knoweth, corrupt and unsound: we put no confidence at all in it: we challenge nothing in the world for it, we dare not call God to a reckoning, as if we had Him in our debt-books: our continual suit to Him is, and must be, to bear with our infirmities, to pardon our offences" (*Works*, Keble's edition, vol. iii, p. 614).

clarity that we can never deserve fellowship with God, or extract it from Him by our most righteous conduct. His acceptance of us must be a pure gift of grace. Augustine and Thomas Aquinas, conscious as these great thinkers could hardly fail to be of certain religious disadvantages in the notion of merit as a whole, had yet retained it as an estimate allowable for the man conscious of his own freedom, while yet from the Divine point of view good action could only be the product of grace. But—apart from the fact that if merit enters at all, claiming a place alongside of grace, it inevitably in practice becomes the more important of the two—the Divine point of view is in religion the only admissible one. God's judgment is the truth, and in His light we know ourselves unworthy.

The evangelical view of faith (*fiducia*) keeps the mind at a level at which the thought of merit becomes unmeaning and even repulsive. Wherever a relationship of confidence has been established between moral beings, gifts can pass without any consciousness of desert on either side. To speak of it is to lapse from the footing of love to that of legality. So, too, when God is receiving us, we cannot put our trust wholly in His mercy, if with one half of our mind we are prudentially intent upon our deserts. To think of our own obediences may be positively noxious if it betrays us to the delusion that we can thereby commend ourselves to God, that He is flexible by our sacrifice, or beholden to us for service beyond what is needful. The presence of a self-conscious or computing temper is incongruous with a relation of trust in which self is utterly abandoned and boundless gratitude fills the soul.

In official Catholicism, then, the Reformers were confronted with a system of ideas concerning the method by which we are put and kept right with God, that rested on and revolved round the assumption of merit. The foreground was occupied by the belief that man was free to acquire merits by the aid of infused grace, and that God, in His distributive justice, fixes His acceptance or rejection of men in accordance with the scale of their spiritual attainment.

Men are gradually put right with God.[18] When the Reformers preached to men their revived gospel of forgiveness for Christ's sake, they did so in view of this established theory of salvation.

(3) We have seen that ability to win merit derives, on the usual Catholic view, from infused supernatural grace; and in order to understand why the Reformers shrank from long-received opinions on the question how a sinner becomes pleasing to God, we must scrutinize more closely the prevailing thought of "grace." As early as Tertullian, we find current and even predominating a view of grace in action which takes it to be the inspiration of a Divine quasi-physical energy or force, changing men substantially; and this is a strain of thought which is developed but not fundamentally altered in later times. Augustine has better conceptions; but even he is prevented by an uneradicated vein of Neo-platonic mysticism from linking salvation vitally to the historic Christ, so that the religious dynamic (grace as infused love) consists more in a secret, wonderful and ineffable Divine energy, operating on the soul-substance, than in the personal influence of God, an influence whose quality is seen in Jesus Christ. To have imparted grace is to be impregnated, as it were, with the Divine essence. Naturally

[18] As this general view has occasionally been questioned, even by Protestant scholarship, I am glad to support it by these sentences from a letter written me by the late Professor Karl Holl, of Berlin, whose recent death is one of the heaviest losses theology has had to sustain. "Justification, for the Schoolmen," he says, "is really *both* an event *and* a process. It is the first in its character as the infusion of supernatural grace at baptism. But this infusion of *gratia habitualis* is not the final thing; there follows the task of employing this 'supernatural' power for the performance of supernaturally good works, for the acquisition of *merita*. Only when these are present in sufficient measure is real *iustitia* there—the *iustitia* which later is acknowledged at the Last Judgment. As such, however, as ever-increasing *iustitia*, justification is a process; hence the Schoolmen, as also the Tridentine Decrees, speak of a *magis iustificari*. It was precisely this aspect of Catholic justification, in which it is conceived as a process, that formed one of the grounds that forced Luther out of the Catholic Church. The Catholic scarcely knows on what terms he stands with God; Luther feels that he *must* know."

of such grace sacraments are *in sensu eminenti* the appropriate vehicle. For Aquinas "created grace," by which men are justified, is a supernatural "habit" or habitual tendency infused into the soul's essence, and constituting the new nature. After the soul has regained through grace the capability of self-movement, it can acquire merit. He fails to bring out any clear connexion between grace and Christ except this, that He alone merits for us its initial impartation. It is a Divine force impinging on the soul, the psychological mediation of which is far to seek.

Luther, breaking once for all with the idea of grace as a communicated quality of the soul, or Divinely induced "habit," identified it rather with the personal mercy of God which we encounter in Christ, or in those whom Christ has changed, and which comes home to us primarily and essentially as forgiveness. To have faith is to have grace; *wer glaubt, der hat*. In the gospel God Himself deals with us and gives Himself in Christ to be our own.

This means that we must form our idea of grace from the felt redeeming influence of Christ, the embodied love of God. So far from being a mere supernatural force emitted by Deity and acting upon us in ways which disregard the fact of moral personality—a more or less physical energy, stored within the Church, and applied to the soul-essence in its unconscious depths—it is the Father's saving will, reaching us through means which appeal to a rational and spiritual nature. Taught by the impression of Jesus, we see it to be no coercive force, for which the will is only a medium of transmission, and which can never fulfil itself in our volition, but the free active love of God to sinners. Religion begins when we meet with a Power or Reality which subdues us by its spiritual content, not destroying freedom, but creating it and raising it to its highest power. As I have sought to express it elsewhere : " Grace, as seen in Christ, does not cause faith by any *vis a tergo*; it evokes faith by means of the felt significance of the Redeemer, working upon us through ethically qualified motives. All ideas of law or reward drop away. The needed moral dynamic, rich in all true and triumphant morality, flows from the transforming apprehension of the fatherly grace held forth to us in Christ."[19]

Thus to the Reformers grace, which is God's love flowing down to the unworthy, excludes all merit and displaces the order of precisely adjusted rewards by an order in which forgiving mercy reigns. The anxious efforts by which men seek to deserve and prepare themselves for it are swept away by the great persuasion that God gives what we cannot claim. Grace, in Melanchthon's classic phrase, is not medicine but good-will. Through it we have that firm assurance (sprung from the believing apprehension of Christ's reconciling death) of the pardon of sinners, of those who still are sinful though pardoned, which gives and is a new attitude of soul, enabling us to obey joyously.

It is to Luther[20] that we owe the recovery for the modern world of this gospel of the New Testament. Neither friend nor foe requires to be told that for him the kernel and test of all Christian preaching lay in justification by faith. In his agony he had learned this from St. Paul, and so become a new man. In the Schmalcald Articles he declares that "we cannot in any wise depart from this article, or yield it up, though heaven and earth and all perishable things should fail; on this article stands firm and fast all that in teaching or in life we have against pope, devil and world." At times he made no difficulty about using "justification" in the traditional sense—as old as Augustine—according to which to justify signifies to transform a sinful man into a man just or righteous. But the one point, and it was crucial, at which he parted irreconcilably with the Roman Church lay in the conviction that justification takes place through faith, and through faith alone, not through works or merits in any

[19] Cf. article, "Grace," in Hastings' *Encyclopædia of Religion and Ethics,* vol. vi, pp. 364-367, from which one or two phrases in this section are drawn.

[20] See among quite recent literature Holl, *Gesammelte Aufsätze,* vol. i, 'Luther'; Loofs in *Studien und Kritiken* for 1917 and 1922; Kattenbusch's article, "Protestantismus," in Hauck's *Real-Encyclopädie;* Mackinnon, *Luther and the Reformation,* vol. i. But the subject has a library to itself.

sense. His passionate message amounted to this, that faith apprehends the grace proffered to sinners in Christ and grasps firmly the assurance there contained that our sins are forgiven, while *eo ipso* and simultaneously this same faith becomes the gateway by which the Spirit of God finds entrance into the heart, to change and renew it. Faith lays hold of pardon, the same faith regenerates; not, however, a faith groping vaguely in the inane, but one directed to the limitless Divine mercy unveiled and realised in Christ.

Justification is exclusively God's work; man cannot contribute to it but only put hindrances in the way. Not at the beginning of the Christian life merely but during its whole course, grace is the absolutely free and sovereign will of God. As he puts it, " the glory of God appears in all its splendour when sinners are received in grace, for it is God's glory to load us with benefits." Such transcendent kindness on God's part is wholly unintelligible to the mind that beholds in Him nothing but a passionless or forbidding holiness; it is Christ alone who enables us to believe in it. In this forgiving grace God treats man as if already he were just. He will not impute to him the sin which he has but imputes to him a righteousness which in himself he does not have. The Christian remains a sinner to the end; in spite of all, God in compassion takes his sin away and for Christ's sake and in Christ grants him fellowship with Himself. Law can furnish no true notion of God's relation to men. The natural mind is haunted by the idea that a legal principle exists to which the Eternal has to conform in His treatment of the sinful, and by which man in his turn is able to compute the degree of Divine favour or disfavour that rests upon him. But law in this sense is abolished by the reign of grace.

These revolutionising thoughts came in upon Luther with ever greater force as he contemplated the sacrament of penance. There the one great question at issue is: How can I be made free in God's sight from the guilt of my sin? and it is a noble trait in the Catholic Church of the West that from century to century she imprinted this question on the human conscience. But her answer to it inevitably shut the believer up to suspense and uncertainty. Only at one point did the

Church offer him full and unconditioned forgiveness, viz. in baptism. Later, forgiveness is still offered, but only under conditions that must sustain the mood of uncertainty, and may deepen it. Now the sin must be repented of, confessed to a priest, and made amends for by penances. When in his monastery Luther turned with agonizing eagerness to ecclesiastical means of absolution, both the severe conditions under which absolution was promised and the easy fashion in which the Church, exerting its supreme power through a priest, could alter and mitigate these conditions, left him a prey to doubt and discouragement. His conscience forbade the softening of the absolutely stringent demands of God (for he took the Divine law more seriously than any Churchman before his time), and warned him against resting upon the consolatory assurances of a priest. Yet to him it was a matter of life and death to know how he stood with God. In demanding that he should know, he had already broken with the Catholic system, for he had asked for something which the mediæval Church refused to grant. He found no peace till he had learned from St. Paul that God attaches no " conditions " such as penance to His forgiveness, but grants pardon without merit to the simple faith that casts itself upon His word. " The faith which is the gift of God makes the believer see in the Christ who is there before him a revelation of God's Fatherly love which gives him the sense of pardon, and at the same time excites in him the desire to do all manner of loving service. He is like the forgiven child who is met with tenderness when punishment was expected, and in glad wonder resolves never to be naughty again—so natural and simple is the Reformation thought."[21] It is a view which by its fearlessness seemed to invite the charge of antinomianism, just as St. Paul's gospel did, or our Lord Himself amid the publicans and sinners.

One fact upon which Luther perpetually insists is that the justification or forgiveness so received is a continuous or permanent one. It is no longer intermittent, having to be done over and over again like priestly absolution. It comes through faith in a Christ ever available; hence the believer can be

[21] Lindsay, *History of the Reformation,* vol. i, p. 451.

steadily sure of the Father's grace. Indeed, we cannot be too sure of it; the presumption is in him who doubts. Of course it is only in theory that justification by faith is easy to believe in; the Christian's abiding consciousness of guilt makes it difficult enough in practice. None the less Luther always considered it a Christian duty to be assured of the truth that God will not cast us out. When God forgives a man, He says to him " Thou art Mine"; and He says it constantly, as often as we need and ask for it in trust. In an exquisite passage he writes: " Just as the sun shines and enlightens none the less brightly when I close my eyes, so this throne of grace, this forgiveness of sins, is always there, even though I fall. Just as I see the sun again when I open my eyes, so I have forgiveness and the sense of it once more when I look up and return to Christ. We are not to measure forgiveness as narrowly as fools dream."

There are features of this great conception which deserve special emphasis. Luther expressed his new insight by saying (with St. Paul) that the believer is for Christ's sake regarded by God as righteous: *justi reputamur*. In virtue of his faith God views and deals with him as righteous; and this, not his being made righteous by moral renovation, not the process by which he is gradually turned into a righteous man and thoroughly and substantially changed, was always for Luther the basal thing in justification. But this does not at all mean that the justified man is not *ipso facto* made righteous; on the contrary. He certainly is not made righteous by any grace that acts magically on the soul's substance; but none the less justification, in the Lutheran sense, is effective as well as declaratory. Proof of this is supplied by the fact that Luther frequently uses the phrases " being justified" and " being regenerated" as equivalent; and he undoubtedly means by " being regenerated" that fundamental change whereby the natural man, who is incapable of good, is put in a condition in which he can do good spontaneously. For the presence of faith is the presence of a new heart. What hinders the natural man from doing good acts is that his relations to God are wrong, so that he cannot fear and love Him; faith, from the first moment of its existence, is the incipient manifestation of real goodness, towards God and man alike. True, it is an incipient manifestation only, not a full or completed accomplishment; hence we must never forget the cardinal distinction between God's putting us right with Himself in forgiveness (which He does once for all, though He repeats the assurance of it as often as we sin and ask pardon) and the progressive renewal which is never finished in this life. All this progressiveness and incompleteness, however, leaves quite unaltered the fact that in pardon we receive from God an initial assurance of His grace to us personally, which goes deeper than all our sin. "The righteous man," said Luther, "is not made so by acting righteously, but being made righteous he acts righteously and well, and, *before* he acts justly and well, is and remains a person righteous, holy, and pious solely by faith in Christ."

A second matter of importance is this, that faith for Luther is not correctly to be described as but a *condition* of being justified or accounted right with God; for a condition might be separated in time from that which it conditions. Faith itself *is* righteousness. From the Divine point of view, for God to give faith and to justify are one thing. The gift of faith, moreover, is identical with the gift of the Spirit, for faith is the Spirit's work and cannot be dissociated from His presence. The Spirit is God's giving effectively; faith is what He gives. Luther's view as a whole may be summarised in the conviction that faith, as heartfelt trust in Christ who is God personally present to save, is the fruitful secret and germ of all that can rightly be called Christian religion. "We daily sin much and deserve nothing but punishment," he says; our one hope, which suffices, is the loving promise made ours in Christ. Faith mediates everything, both forgiveness and personal goodness, because through it we are in living touch with God Himself. It is by faith we possess a pardoning God; it is by faith, the same faith, that we daily overcome sin.

Again, faith is for Luther naturally and inevitably productive of good works. Since it renews the heart, we say far too little when we talk of obedience *following* from it, as if by an interval; obedience is as vitally and indissolubly united to faith as breathing to life, or body to soul. How could it be otherwise when faith is the realisation of God's boundless love to us in Christ Jesus? This is a point at which later Protestantism fell into confused psychology as a result of a mechanically forensic idea of justification, so that the Westminster Confession *e.g.* at the crucial point can say no more than that "faith is not alone in the person justified, but is ever *accompanied* with all saving graces." But to put good works alongside of faith, and assert merely that they go together, is gravely inadequate; faith must be so exhibited that we see it welling up of itself in obedient character. Luther did not work out the subject into a full or systematic exposition, but his intuitions went to the heart of things. In his Preface to Romans he breaks out: "O it is a living, busy, active, mighty thing, this faith. It is impossible for it not to do good perpetually. It never asks whether good works are to be done, but before the question can be put it has done them, and is always doing them. . . . Hence without constraint the man is joyously willing to do good to everyone, to serve everyone, to suffer all things, for the love and praise of God who has shown him such grace. So that it is impossible to separate work from faith, yes, just as impossible as to separate heat and light from fire."

In the foregoing pages we have made Luther the chief spokesman of the Reformation faith, not only because he alone uttered it with the living tongue of religious genius, but because he first gave it to the world in a form that changed the religion of half Europe. But though the greatest of the early Reformers, he did not stand by himself. There was a common Reformation gospel which produced revival in country after country. It may therefore be useful to state in summarising fashion three cardinal points in the new conception of justification, which mark it off clearly from the leading and characteristic ideas of mediæval theology.[22] What Luther, Calvin and Zwingli did, as guides of the new movement, was

[22] See Haering, *The Christian Faith,* p. 809 ff.

to set forth in Scriptural and experimental terms, as well as weave into creeds, a simple evangelical faith; a faith which, though often obscured by theologians, had never died out of the Church.

Justification at bottom is deliverance from guilt; it is forgiveness. Doubtless forgiveness may have a negative sound, but what it denotes is positive in the most absolute sense. God forgives no man except as He takes him into the relation of a reconciled son; and He takes him altogether into this relation, for God does nothing by halves. This entirely new fact means for the pardoned an ethically changed attitude to his neighbour, to his own nature, to the world; not only, that is to say, is guilt removed but by simultaneous implication the power of sin is broken. Forgiveness regenerates; justification is at the same time renewal. In fixing upon this great experience and calling it *justification*, the Reformers were bent on signalising the truth that God's liberating mercy comes to those who have no claim upon it, and who would not dare to make their assurance of its reality hang upon its ethical reactions or consequences in their own character. It is primarily in this experimental side of the matter that the Reformers were interested.

Justification confronts us as objective, for it is the act or pronouncement of God; but this is not to say that it happens far away in an abstract heavenly tribunal. If it is an act of God, it is also an experience of man. It registers itself in such things as our assurance of God's love, peace of conscience, joy in the Holy Spirit. These are no mere fruits of justification, detached in time from the reality itself; they are the actual experience of being justified. As it may be put, they are the side of justification that is turned towards us, or the form in which the Divine forgiveness reports and registers itself in our consciousness.

Justification, far from being a passing act of God, ushers the sinner into a new, permanent relation to the Father. The Reformers felt an aversion to statements of the truth that corresponded only to one type of experience. Now there are those to whom conversion comes abruptly, others in whom the Divine life unfolds by imperceptible degrees; and what men like Luther desired was to bring out the ground of assurance for all, without distinction. No matter what the past history of the anxious, they must be furnished with trustworthy means of knowing how they stood with God. To the question about assurance the Romanist had his own answer; assurance, of a kind, is given him in the voice of the Church speaking through the absolving priest. And the worst evil here is not that the priest becomes an indispensable intermediary between the soul and God, or even that absolution is made dependent on the performance of various satisfactions. It is rather the doctrine implicit in the system as a whole that with every new mortal sin the Christian forfeits his standing with the Father, that with each fall into intentional transgression he ceases to be God's accepted child and must work his way back into grace by way of penance. This obviously encourages and maintains a mood of precarious uncertainty; for, since he is constantly falling into sin, and may lack immediate facilities for priestly counsel and absolution, he may spend the greater part of his religious life in a condition of suspense. Hence the saying popular in some parts of Germany, that Romanists become Lutherans when they are dying; they come to God then, not as One who calculates nicely the less or more of a sinner's merit but as One who receives him, if only he be willing, in simple grace.

It is notorious that in later Protestant theology, justification was more and more interpreted as consisting in a nakedly juristic imputation of Christ's merits. Forgiveness became an external acquittal at the bar of heaven (*in foro cœli*) and thereby lost living touch with experience; if it was merely God's judicial decision outside a man, it could not change him inwardly. A second Divine act must occur, viz. the gift of the Holy Spirit, if the justified were to be made good. The fact was almost completely overlooked that forgiveness is the Father's taking us into a new relation of fellowship with Himself, and that the ethical effects of this change are of a wonderful and creative kind. In protest against barely forensic notions, a tendency arose to turn the moral quality and effects of justifying faith into the *ground* of pardon. But in view of the imperfections and vacillations of our moral life, this could have no result but to undermine the inward certainty of God's love. On these things, however, we need not dwell. Men alike in the Roman and the Protestant Church are often better and even wiser than their creed; and the legalities of post-Reformation orthodoxy did not wholly succeed in obscuring the supreme fact that the foundation of new life with God and man lies in the objective Divine will to save which anticipates all our need—that unreckoning love which meets us in Christ, in whose life and death the Father gives Himself pardoningly, despite their sin, to the sinful and the lost.

CHAPTER VII

THE DIVINE REACTION AGAINST SIN

In treating of sin and its forgiveness we have need constantly to remind ourselves that we are engaged in the discussion of a religious problem, not one that is simply moral. To raise the question of pardon is itself to enter a sphere in which religious experience insists on being recognised as having a quality and implication of its own. Stoicism, to take one example, is chiefly a high type of philosophical ethics; hence the Stoic is not particularly troubled by our problem. But where specific religion has lived and moved, the reality of Divine pardon has become a matter of life and death.

Otto's remarkable book, *The Idea of the Holy,* whatever its exaggerations of emphasis, brings this out in an original and arresting way, with varied illustration from the wide field of the history of religions. He points out that in religion God has always been felt to have the first and last word. Awe is a cardinal element in the pious mood. The devotee bows before the object of worship with a sense of creaturely self-abandonment. God is felt to be a Reality not so much unknowable as unfathomable, the alone sublime and great; it is not so much that men have religion as that religion has and claims them. In Otto's vocabulary, the Divine or numinous is directly apprehended as possessing two indissociable aspects; it is at once more formidable and lovable; it is fitted to evoke both reverent fear and trustful surrender. The believer, conscious of sin, is aware of the two voices " Depart from Me " and " Come unto Me." A sense of *obligation* to Deity is never absent. Hence the feeling of guilt and spiritual uncleanness, so far from being incidental, is a constitutive element in every great religious worship known to history. Conscience is awake and active to tell men something of the truth about themselves. Thus while religion is not morality, and every attempt to reduce it to purely moral terms must fail, it is never apart from morality, and the higher a faith is the more completely do these two sides of experience merge in each other.

However far back we trace the religious tradition, this sense of obligation to Deity is found to have beside it a penitent or foreboding awareness that the obligation has been imperfectly fulfilled. None has been able to render the whole debt of worship or service; and this consciousness of defect commonly induces, more or less intensely, "a certain fearful looking for of judgment." Sin is believed to entail punishment, and the sole agency by which punishment can be averted is the mercy of heaven. Wherever men have appealed to have trespass overlooked, guilt covered, fear removed, it is to Divine compassion and forbearance that the appeal has been made.

In the field of moral religion, where Christianity predominates, the absolute distinction of right and wrong takes on a Divine and ultimate significance. The distinction, it is felt, is one not so much established or acknowledged by God as rather involved by necessity in His being what He is; at each point the Divine action is determined by inviolable moral principles. God, for the Christian mind, is more than the moral law alive, but we cannot conceive of Him at all except as subsisting in a moral universe and acting under moral conditions. When He forgives sin, accordingly, the thing is not done by leaving moral realities behind. He would not be more Divine if He dealt with sin as a trifle, merely letting the sinner off; He would cease to be God. The consciousness of being forgiven is unmeaning apart from the assumption that in the forgiven life there existed something at war with the Divine nature which could not be ignored. The holiness of God must react against it with a gravity echoed, not always faintly, by the man's own conscience. In the moment when the scales fall from our eyes and, seeing Him, we know what we are, the hostility of sin, *our* sin, to His perfectly righteous love becomes overwhelmingly manifest, and in part the meaning of that word comes home to us: "It is a fearful thing to fall into the hands of the living God." At such a time, nothing but the reassurance of the Gospel can sustain us.

The inconceivable evil of sin, the infinite need for a higher interposition if it is ever to be removed, is indicated by the fact that no one has ever gained the sense of pardon by thinking hard about it. The great religious biographies contain no record of men who argued themselves out of the consciousness of guilt. Sin is so unworthy that logic can see no way out. The problem it exhibits cannot even be formulated, let alone resolved, by means of dialectic. Logic applied to such a situation can do no more than set Divine purity and human evil over against each other and argue that almighty righteousness must prevail and obliterate the life which has become identified with wrong. None the less, as Christians know, the very thing which the sinner's conscience, and his logic too, have declared to be unthinkable, does in fact occur. Sinful as he is, he is pardoned. The barriers fall, and the man who had seen no gate of admission anywhere passes into the fellowship of God, and has the witness in himself that he is the Father's accepted child. But the wondering gratitude with which Christian men, unloading their hearts, speak of the grace of pardon is itself an indirect testimony to the magnitude of the obstacles to its realisation, which had like to have proved insurmountable. When the apostle writes, in adoring praise: " Behold what manner of love the Father has bestowed upon us, that we should be called the children of God," in the background of his intense thought we catch sight of sin's receding shadow, that awful power with which God Himself grapples in strife and pain. How deep were the waters crossed by Him who conveyed deliverance, none of the ransomed can ever know; but the elusive greatness of the Divine sacrifice is the measure of the danger that threatened once but threatens no longer. There is in forgiven men a shuddering thankfulness, as they look back and draw breath in the peace of reconciliation, which seals the horror of the darkness in which we should have sunk but for the dearly paid mercy of God. *Nondum considerasti quanti ponderis sit peccatum,* said Anselm in his dialogue; and the words have repeated themselves ever since, judging facile theories.

If sin be of this grave character, and if God be truth itself, it follows that in forgiving sin God must condemn what He forgives. It is the very God of grace who reacts strongly against sin, as One with whom evil cannot dwell. Pardon does not consist in excusing the transgressor. It is the aim of love, indeed, to make excuses where it can, and not to impute responsibility on any wider or more crushing scale than truth demands. But nothing which can rightly be covered by excuse requires pardon of any kind. Beyond all that lie the failures and open trespasses for which, when we deal honestly, we make no self-exculpating apology because they are inexcusable. And when we thus condemn ourselves, we are reproducing, however dimly, the condemnation of God our Father. His judgment, which too often we merely throw forward into the distant future and imagine at times as a problematical element in what comes after death, has moved out of the future into the actual present and become a searching experience.

The intense reaction of God against moral evil is designated in the Bible as His wrath; and it is well known that certain modern thinkers, of whom Ritschl is perhaps the most distinguished, have sought to disparage the idea of Divine wrath as from the ethical point of view not only puzzling but unworthy. To them it connotes mere caprice and wilful passion. But the writers of Scripture would not have allowed this for a moment. "To them the 'Wrath' of God, so far from being a diminution of His Godhead, appears as a natural expression of it, an element of 'holiness' itself, and a quite indispensable one."[1]

According to Ritschl, the wrath of God is not a present fact; it is only an eschatological possibility. It stands for His fixed purpose to destroy at last those who unchangeably set themselves against His saving powers; but that is reserved for the future, and in strictness there are *now* no objects of the Divine anger. Those whom God has appointed to eternal life can never, at any stage of their history, be such objects.

[1] Otto, *Idea of the Holy*, p. 18.

No doubt they themselves often declare that they feel, or have felt, the wrath of God resting on them; but this is no more than an illusion which it is possible to account for by the forms of human thought being unavoidably determined by time and the experience of time. It may look as if God successively were angry with the sinner, and later, on his repentance, at peace with him; but this corresponds to no reality. The change is not in God but in our point of view. Such anger would be incongruous with God's nature as love.

It is significant that Ritschl should own that his theory is, at least *prima facie,* out of touch with Christian feeling. Of course he should have been the last person in the world to argue on those lines, for much of his energy was spent in turning speculative rationalism out of theology and replacing it by the Christian consciousness, fed by the Gospel; and his contention about love and wrath is a plain infidelity to that principle or criterion. He appeals to what is really a metaphysical theory against the clear dicta of faith. Christians feel that both things are real in God, the love and the wrath. It would hardly be an exaggeration to say that it is only when we are not very indignant with our own sins that the indignation of God becomes either doubtful or incredible. He is the enemy of cruelty, falsehood, uncleanness; He repudiates such things with a feeling absolutely pure and holy which registers itself unfailingly in the living conscience; and every philosophical argument used to deny this, on the ground that it implies excessive anthropomorphism, is an equally good argument for denying even His love. We have only to persist in this line of thought and we shall totally dissipate strong faith in the Living God, whose relations to men are active and personal. As a minor point, it may be noted that if wrath in God is inconsistent with love now, it can never cease to be inconsistent with it. On his assumptions, therefore, Ritschl ought to have denied even the eschatological validity of the idea, for in such a region times and seasons count for nothing.

But *is* wrath incongruous with love? Plainly if their incongruity be axiomatic, the Christian mind will be under the strongest temptation to negate the reality of wrath, since at all costs we must cling to the love revealed in Jesus. The modern prevalence of the notion that love and anger exclude each other may be subterraneously connected with the altered view of parental authority now defended in many quarters, a further symptom of the same temper revealing itself in the popular sympathy with the law-breaker to which writers on criminal statistics have recently called attention. But should we dream of describing as good or loving one whom we believe to be incapable of anger at wrong-doing? Just here is found one of the difficulties of which earnest but not very clear-headed people are conscious when they are being urged to forgive an injury. They hesitate, because to pardon looks like confessing that their anger was reprehensible; whereas they know, without reasoning, that in the circumstances anger was not only permissible but obligatory. Lack of indignation at wickedness is a sign, not of a poor nature only, but of positive unlikeness to Jesus Christ.[2] As it has been put: "There are evil things against which our first and surest safeguard is the instinctive reaction of the soul in righteous resentment. The man in whom they evoke no quick repulsion, who is not moved to a sudden heat by them, is dead while he lives. It is not his virtue, but his vice, that he is superior to passion." Unless we sophisticate ourselves, we all feel this. Intentional discourtesy, the calculated ruin of purity, an act of savagery to a child—he is not to be envied who can look on calmly when such things are done. For beings like us, doubtless, it is hard to be angry and not sin, but we must not turn this frailty into a proof that wrath is inconsistent with Holy Love.

Occasionally the flank of our difficulty seems to be turned by the phrase that God is angry not with sinners but with their sin. And it would be pedantry to cavil at such an expression when used colloquially or in poetry:

[2] It is a fundamental conviction of the best modern theology that God must be conceived as like Jesus. But the wrath of Jesus is made incontestably plain in the Synoptic Gospels.

Thou judge us: Thy purity
Doth all our lusts condemn;
The love that draws us nearer Thee
Is hot with wrath to them.

None the less, the phrase when insisted on is a misleading catchword. There is no such thing as sin apart from a sinner, any more than pleasure could be real, in pure abstraction, irrespectively of a pleased consciousness. The one fact in the case is the sinful life to which God's attitude invariably is personal. To be angry with a thing—and sin abstracted from sinner is no more—ranks as a moral absurdity. The man who spitefully kicks the stool over which he has tripped in the dark has for the moment become irrational. Anger, the anger of moral love, can only be directed upon moral beings. If therefore it is permissible to speak of God's wrath, it is with sinners—with ourselves when we defy love —that His wrath has to do.

Further, if we acknowledge that in God indignant antagonism to the sinner and his ways may co-exist with love, as its essential manifestation under certain conditions, there is no particular difficulty (except for theories which deny all change in God) in understanding that His anger may pass into other manifestations, such as forgiveness, if the conditions have been modified. Feeling rightly changes with the nature of its object; and a penitent is different in fact, and hence for God's active thought, from an obstinate transgressor. A mechanical conception of the Divine personality must of course put all such statements aside as unbelievably fantastic; but at all events they are true to the type of faith characteristic of the prophets and of Jesus.

The reaction of God against sin is evidenced, as we have seen, by loving wrath; and this wrath, it now appears, finds expression in punishment. The indignant mind can preserve its inner truth only as it becomes manifest in action which stamps sin as reprehensible and brings its evilness home to the sinner. Such counteraction of sin, unveiling its true character and repelling it in righteousness, is penalty. This holds true of every sin, not merely of sins within a certain class. All sins are punished by God, and they are punished with a view to their being forgiven. The punishment is an essential in the very grace that effects reconciliation at its own cost, and when this is denied it can only be on the ground of an external or hedonistic conception of punishment as such.

We are nowadays familiar with the contention that it is radically unworthy of God to inflict penalty, no matter what the guilt of the transgression. This, it is held, would amount to making rewards and punishments a controlling principle in the Christian view of the relationship of God to man, with a consequent legalising of its quality both as a religion and an ethic. Evil automatically is its own nemesis. In reply, it must be pointed out that Christian opinion is now fairly unanimous in conceiving this life not, in older language, as a probationary experience but as a scene of education. The world, in Keats' phrase, is "a vale of soul-making." But the educational value of punishment may be, and actually is, enormous. Plenty of educationalists have protested that children ought not to be punished physically; there can be few serious teachers who believe they ought not to be punished at all. "What parent or schoolmaster," Rashdall has argued, "would say to a child, 'My good child, enlightened Philosophers are agreed that conduct motived by fear of punishment and hope of reward is worthless: therefore henceforth I shall leave you to be guided by your own innate sense of right and wrong. I will not corrupt the purity of your will by threats or promises. Your virtues shall be their own reward: your misdeeds shall never interfere with your pleasures or cause the withdrawal of my favour.' What child would flourish morally under such treatment as this? And yet," he continues, "it would be a very cynical view of human nature to suppose that the average schoolboy is actuated by no motive higher than selfish hope or fear. He has higher motives, but he requires to be aided in his efforts at self-conquest by lower ones. And after all most of us are a great deal more like children than it is fashionable among Philosophers to suppose—at least in our moments of weakness and strong temptation."[3] Punishment, in short, is a part of kindness in dealing with immature or undisciplined characters (which we all of us are), and it is difficult to imagine a religious man quietly contemplating his own past without the reflection that the fatherly chastisements of God had frequently gone to school him in adhesion to righteousness for its own sake. The whole conception of divinely inflicted punishment, it is true, has been scouted in the name of Jesus' teaching that from suffering we must not infer the sufferer's sin as its necessary pre-condition. But the same Jesus who said: "Neither hath this man sinned nor his parents, that he is born blind," said also "Sin no more, lest a worse thing come upon thee." To impute vindictive fury to God is pagan; to believe that His love corrects our faults by pain is part of Christianity.

The objection just considered, however, is in its own way a disclaimer of the notion that punishment can be based on utility. If penalty were merely the repulsion of an assault upon a useful moral system, a counter-attack upon the attempted violation of beneficent convention, but one which left the evil will untouched, no result could follow but a heightening of the moral loss. Nothing in the moral world can be useful in the long run which is not in itself right and good. A similar line of reflection goes to show that the purely reformatory view of punishment leaves the essence of the matter unexplained. It ignores the crucial fact that penalties simply demoralise and infuriate the victim when they are seen to be unjust; and thinkers who deny the retributive character of punishment never seem to ask themselves why this should be so. They overlook the fact, which is surely obvious once it has been pointed out, that if the sinner's punishment is to do him any good, it must be felt to be his sin coming home to its author—the moral reaction of things which he has no option but to recognise as his due.

Older writers were accustomed to divide the punishments of God into the two types or classes of natural and positive; and this classification still counts for much in popular thinking. Natural penalties were defined as those which flow

[3] *Theory of Good and Evil*, vol. ii, p. 261 f.

from sin by natural causation—disease, for example, due to habitual profligacy, or loss of reputation owing to a known act of fraud. Positive penalties, on the other hand, were such as by their striking and abnormal character led the sufferer or the observer to trace them to the direct action of God. The distinction, however, is unreal. All chastisements of sin are positive in the sense that God wills them; and the fact that their incidence has been mediated by natural causes does not alter this in the least. The system of causation is itself a Divine appointment. It is an order, as has been said, "which, while it is the completest example of law, is never, in any part or at any moment, separated from the living will of God." Men are often tempted to dissociate the penalties of sin from Divine volition because in ordinary circumstances they seem to arrive with automatic regularity. We miss God's voice because, in certain spheres, He speaks with a uniformity that makes no distinctions. But this does not mean that He is ever indifferent to evil, or inactive with regard to it; it means that His opposition to evil is so intense that He has actually formed the world on such lines that it infallibly reacts against the wrong-doer.

But we stop short on the fringe of experience if we consider merely those penalties which affect our natural or outward situation. The final truth lies deeper. Sin registers its proper punishment in our own soul, in our social relationships, supremely in our relationship with God. To begin with the first of these, there is at the outset a self-stultification of the evil will. In sinning we aim at objects that promise happiness, yet by the path of sin can never reach it; indeed, after each fresh effort, we are further from the goal than ever. Sin, in McTaggart's phrase, is like drinking sea-water to quench thirst. Again, there is punishment in the accumulating strength of wrong desire. Each bad choice graves deeper the path of tendency; each fall imposes an added weakness with which we face the next temptation. Once more, there is punishment in the loss of self-respect. After sin, we are under the necessity of despising ourselves; and not least among the reprisals of a moral universe is the wound left in memory and in the estimate we form, in hours of clear self-knowledge, of our own being. It is significant that in the Parable of the Prodigal Son, when He is picturing unreserved forgiveness and acceptance, Jesus touches for a moment on the point that the wanderer's self-respect is restored. "But the father said to his servants, Bring forth the best robe, and put it on him."

Yet the sorest punishment of sin lies in the sinner's isolation alike from God and man. To sin and to break up fellowship are one thing. Whether it be pride or lust, sin essentially involves the shutting up of our life within the limits of our own ego. We banish ourselves from the presence of the Father and of our fellows. All is contracted into the narrow sphere of self, even the natural and needful self-affirmation of the individual being perverted into an absolute standard of value. And just because this self-worship is constitutive of all sin, it follows that, in proportion as he comes under its power, the sinner loses the capacity to transcend self and share the life of others. All consequences of sin are minor in comparison with this; those affecting the body scarcely count when put beside the penalty of alienation from God and neighbour.

This loss of a living connexion with God is *par excellence* the punishment of sin, the standard of reference by which all other penalties are measurable and which imparts to them their sting. For Christian faith recognises eternal life in God and His kingdom as the highest good and ultimately the only true good. Conversely, the greatest evil, ultimately the only real evil, is eternal death, i.e. definitive separation from the living God. Of this, as of eternal life, there may be foretastes or preliminary stages in our present existence; neither is reserved exclusively for the destiny that supervenes beyond the grave. In its temporal form it is known as "spiritual death," the absence of all that makes existence worth having, and consisting in exclusion from fellowship with God; an exclusion which reveals itself in inward dispeace and bitter self-dissatisfaction. It is no objection to this view that there may be hardened or frivolous minds, lost to self-discipline, who are unconscious of any judgment of God within themselves. That such men may exist is undeniable. But the

Christian certainty of Divine reaction against sin as an inevitable expression of the very nature of God is only confirmed by such a fact. Their insensibility is the last sad proof that souls may fall into utter isolation from the living God. This paralysis of the personal self *is* the death which separation from Him means.

That the forfeiture of communion with God is the punishment of sin which includes and interprets all others, that we cannot think this state without using the terrible word " death," is proved by a simple fact. When a man faces God in Christ, apprehending the love manifest in the cross, he is willing to say: Give me fellowship with Thee and with my brother at my side, and other chastisements I can endure.

The foregoing argument forbids us, it is clear, to turn the grace and (in a true sense) unconditional freeness of Divine pardon into an argument for the comparative unimportance of sin. This has occasionally been done. It is sometimes contended that the fact that God deems it possible to forgive sin at all nullifies, in the last resort, its real gravity. The reality of pardon is thus utilised to dissolve and abrogate the reality of sin itself. If this were sound, it would mean that to proclaim the forgiveness of sins is to do something which at bottom is unmeaning or self-contradictory, since what *can* be forgiven needs in fact no forgiveness. Sin, on these terms, is a purely relative thing, and when God is said to forgive it what is really meant is that He can and does regard it as an intelligible stage on the way to perfection, the unavoidable manifestation of human finitude and error. And we do not require to be pardoned for defects which are the natural, indeed the appointed elements of finite imperfection.

Clearly then the ideas of forgiveness and sin vary together; if we grant the validity of the conception of Divine pardon, we must own that the pardon was necessary and that the pardoned sin was rightly the object of condemnation. It is condemnable in and by itself; it is not so merely in our mistaken view, still less is it conceivable, as in Schleiermacher's curious theory, that this mistake on our part is encouraged, not to say produced, by God in order to intensify our desire for reconciliation. If we are not to trust our penitential intuition that our sin deservedly lies under the Father's judgment, there seems no reason why we should ever trust our minds at all. In the hour of repentance we know that we can only be forgiven in so far as we own our sin *as* sin and not simply misfortune, and that this self-pronounced verdict is the echo or counterpart of the verdict of God. To be offered pardon for an act or abstention which, after honest thought, we regarded as wholly innocent would not pacify conscience, but mystify and offend it. By His Gospel of forgiveness, therefore, the Father implicitly declares to us not only that sin rests under His condemnation, but that nothing achievable by the sinner can ever make it good. It is something so real and dark that only three modes of Divine treatment are possible—to judge it, to bear it in sacrificial love, to forgive it freely. All these are present in the great act and experience of God which we call the Atonement.

CHAPTER VIII

THE PARDONING GOD

Reflection on the forgiveness of sins, as we observe it in the Bible, passes at its highest level through three stages, which may broadly be described as that of the prophets, of Jesus, and of the apostles. Prophets and psalmists indubitably grasped the fact of pardon, but in their consciousness of it we can detect an element which it is not unfair to call precarious. The index of its reality for their minds was apt to lie, at least partly, in outward felicity, and the man in whose experience calamity had been replaced by well-being was *eo ipso* convinced that his transgression had been taken away. But a great personal misfortune shook his confidence again. It seemed to be clear proof that God had cast him off. As it has been put: "God's external treatment of men was held to reflect His true relation to them. Chastisements were indications of His anger. A distinction was not yet drawn between God's external providence and God's true mind towards men."[1] This is not to say that a higher view did not struggle to the surface in the Book of Job and was not disclosed, in principle, by the experience of the Servant of the Lord in the second half of Isaiah, where suffering is pictured as being borne for the sins of the guilty. Yet the Old Testament as a whole exhibits the problem of evil as oppressive to the devout mind, largely because pain seemed to prove the withdrawal of God's favour. He had forgotten or rejected the victims of disaster.

It is unreasonable to charge this kind of religion with hedonism or superficiality. Old Testament believers were the least utilitarian of men. Doubtless they did wrong to find the mark of Divine favour in individual or national prosperity, but in the deepest sense were they merely wrong? Jesus Himself conceived the Kingdom as a universal order

[1] A. B. Davidson, *Theology of the Old Testament*, p. 284.

of things, a world-dispensation, in which the omnipotent love of the Father has free course, and the realms of spirit and nature are one in absolute perfection. When we use the word "heaven," we are thinking of the same thing. We are thinking of a "changeless prime of body and of soul," a perfect society in a perfect environment, with God over all. And when Old Testament believers felt in the hour of agony that suffering had cast a shadow over pardon and acceptance, when with suffering faith they claimed that grace must express itself in bliss, they were but antedating that ideal.

Somehow this problem of theodicy has ceased to torment the apostolic writers; the New Testament contains nothing like the Book of Job. For reason the problem is still insoluble, but it has been solved for faith. In Christ they have gained a view of God which is conclusive; suffering no longer disturbs their certainty of pardon. This can only mean that the fact round which thought concerning forgiveness must revolve, and on which it must rest, is the known character of God. When men rejoice over pardon with joy unspeakable and full of glory, it is because of what they have found God to be. And, on the other hand, the experience of being pardoned brings into singular relief some great aspects of God's nature and ways. One or two of these must be examined now.

It is worth noting that certain questions which may be raised about God's nature, as revealed by or involved in forgiveness, can only be answered experimentally. We can make nothing of them by the method of *a priori* analysis of what we think *must* be the Divine plan. The question whether a necessity existed that God should forgive is not one to which any answer can be given, and the same is true of the question which scholastic minds have canvassed, whether He could have conveyed forgiveness to men in any other way than that in which He has actually conveyed it. But, with our eyes upon Christ, we *can* reply to the inquiry why He has chosen to forgive and has carried out the work of redemption to which we owe all our hopes: it was because of His free, unbought grace, out of a mercy that passes all understanding, and for which no reason can be given which lies outside itself. The point of departure for Christian thought in this region is the great and absorbing fact that forgiveness has been made ours in Christ; we start from the reality as given, and only seek to know its implications. If the reality of a fact be perceived by direct acquaintance, that is something which can never again be rendered dubious by any problems that may be raised about its possibility or necessity; even for the metaphysician the category " real " is more fundamental, more logically satisfying, than either " possible " or " necessary," for they are based on it, not it on them. This holds good also for the declared pardon of God in Jesus. Why God should have taken away men's sins in Christ will never be more than partially intelligible to the sinful; the incomplete success of theories of Atonement prove how impossible it is to find a logical or juridical solution of the mystery; but while the world stands, grateful hearts, taught by Jesus, will give thanks that the Holy One can and does receive sinners. And the character of Him who is thus receiving them leaves most definite impressions of itself upon the mind of the received.

To begin with, the forgiven man is acutely conscious of the personality of God. This at least is true of the Biblical type of believer, and in proof we might quote one-half of the Psalter. Unless God be a personal spirit, who hears and understands and answers prayer, the man who comes craving for reconciliation would of necessity be as amazed and disconcerted as if, to use Newman's famous illustration, he were to look into a mirror and not see his own face.

This is a point which, if it has any importance at all, is quite obviously of crucial importance. In the strict sense of the term it is fundamental; that is, we have no alternative but to lay it down as the foundation of all significant or profitable thought upon the subject. If I am engaged in a discussion of the possibility of forgiveness, or its meaning, with one who denies that God is personal in the sense that He can have personal relations with men, I can tell from the start that our arguments and counter-arguments can never meet. They move in different planes; they have no common and decisive major premise; and unless we both are out for purely logical exercise, the debate might just as well be called off. Argument about constitutional government with an avowed anarchist, to whom all government is anathema, could not be more vain than reasoning about forgiveness with one to whom God is other than a self-conscious spirit.

Is not this one reason why books of philosophy so seldom prepare the mind for insight into an idea like the pardon of sins? We search vainly in works of metaphysics or even of moral philosophy for any serious approach to those issues of life and death which chiefly concern the passionately religious man—the hearing of prayer, for example, or forgiveness, or the acquisition of power to be good. And this, perhaps, admits of a simple explanation. Taken as a whole, the preponderant stream of philosophical tradition has relatively little positive teaching to offer with regard to the personal being of God. Plato himself hesitates. Aristotle, the Stoics, Scotus Erigena, Bruno, Spinoza, Hegel—they are all of them more interested in what can much more justly be described as the Absolute than as God. Now you may speculate on the Divine, dream of the Divine, aspire to the Divine, lose yourself in the Divine without ever raising the question of pardon, or even after having put it aside as unmeaning; but you can only ask for pardon if the Divine, ultimately, is a free, loving conscious spirit. It is as a Spirit, a personal Spirit, that God claims us, rebukes us, comforts us; above all, it is in that character that He forgives our sin. What has to be forgiven is relative to such a Being. The religious mind nourished on Christianity instinctively assents to the words of Mr. Webb: " I can only declare my conviction that to regard sin as an offence against a personal authority, and still more to regard it as an affront to a loving Father, is a more intelligible and a more ethically significant way of thinking about it than it is to conceive it after the analogy of a physical defilement or an automatic mechanism."[2] The love of God will lose meaning for the heart in proportion as He ceases to be a Person for the mind. And it is love we need, and at all costs must have, when we come with the burden of our sins.

[2] *God and Personality*, p. 250.

Hence there is no cure for Pantheism like a sharp fit of penitence. As Amiel puts it in his *Journal*: "What tears us away from the enchantment of Maya, is conscience." The man who has faced his own badness is in small danger of confusing himself with God. He knows, if anything is knowable, that God and he are not identical, and that he must stifle plain conviction before he can adopt as his own the claim:

> "I am the eye with which the Universe
> Beholds itself, and knows itself divine."

Ignore conscience, and nothing is easier than to attain a metaphysical point of view for which Pantheism is perfectly simple and satisfactory. Everything, then, is God, and nothing but God exists anywhere—not the intellect or heart of man, not the difference between truth and falsehood or between right and wrong. One pang of contrition breaks the spell. Instantly the personal distinction between God and man stands forth commandingly; we awake to the fact that the moral law is the will of God, and that in violating it we have lost touch with the Father. And unless on analysis "Father" connotes or includes the idea of personality, does it have any reality which our minds can apprehend?

Again, He who pardons is intuitively known as—to use the great Biblical phrase—the living God. He is perceived to be One who wills and acts; in forgiving, He produces a change in our relation to Himself. What the unsophisticated Christian is thinking of when he speaks about forgiveness is not primarily an alteration in his own mind; it is something that primarily concerns God's attitude to him as a sinful man, a Divine act to which his inward experience of being reconciled is a response. In religion, interest centres in what God does, and it is He who initiates pardon and gives it reality. In forgiving our sin, He acts toward us, He acts upon us.

Antagonism to the idea of a God who is veritably and effectually active within the believer's experience has arisen in two quarters otherwise keenly opposed to each other. On the one hand, traditional theology from very early times gave prominence to a conception of God as the one unchanging Substance, strictly devoid of attributes and out of positive or direct relation to the events of time. This conception can be traced down the centuries in parallel to the warmer and more living New Testament thought of the Father whose gracious action on our behalf is the source of all human hope; and much of the interest of historical theology lies in watching the varied fortunes of the struggle between these two interpretations. On the other hand, even that convinced foe of speculative rationalism, Ritschl, as we have seen, was guided more by speculation than by faith when he taught that it is a mere subjective illusion, though an inevitable one, when the pardoned man feels that the expression of God's love towards him has undergone, in forgiveness, a change from condemnation to gracious acceptance. He surely is on firmer ground when he asserts, as he does with emphasis, that the Divine act or judgment of forgiveness is synthetic or creative in character. But if creative, it must produce a new situation. It is the Father opening the door of communion with Himself and placing the sinner in the position of a reconciled son. It is the victorious love of God for good reasons depriving our sins of their power to exclude us from His fellowship. The man who has passed through this regenerating experience will be very hard to persuade that God was not the real agent in causing light to arise for him, or that the only thing which has really happened is his awaking from a bad dream to the new insight that God and he had never been estranged at all.

Moreover, the living God is known to be such because He acts supernaturally. And it is of His supernatural action that we are made specially aware in forgiveness. Consciously to receive pardon (whether the consciousness of it springs from intuition or from inference need not be considered now) is to know that a change has taken place in our relation to the Father which can only be accounted for by His direct interposition. If it be said, as doubtless it may be said with point, that in the world of love forgiveness is a matter of course, this only throws us back on the marvellous character of a love to which utter forgiveness is natural.

That the view just stated is that of our Lord, can hardly be questioned. Not that it originated with Him, though He countersigned it. The conviction that at bottom forgiveness is supernatural really goes back, like so many great religious ideas, to the Hebrew prophets. They took the personality of God seriously; they took the personality of man seriously; and as a result they took seriously the contact between God and man which forgiveness is. Because God is what they knew Him to be, He can recreate a man's soul by taking him decisively into communion with Himself—an event which no immanent categories like law or evolution can ever explain but which is miracle proper. This, I say, is the thought of Jesus, and a thought on which He laid stress. To recur to a Gospel incident already referred to, by His behaviour to the paralytic, recorded in Mark 2, He explicitly calls attention to the fact that pardon is as supernatural as cure. "That ye may know that the Son of man hath power on earth to forgive sins (He saith to the sick of the palsy), I say unto thee, Arise, take up thy bed." His judgment has been echoed by the Christian mind. In the pardoned soul, as all pardoned men feel, something has been brought to pass which merely psychical forces moving exclusively within the mind itself could not have effected, something so great that it demands a transcendent cause. It is the Lord's doing, and it is marvellous in our eyes. Life has been given a new start. It is not merely that in principle the tendencies of character have been reversed; that, true as it is, is the consequence of something else. The antecedent condition of moral renewal is the fact that the burden of past sin—sin that cleaves to us with the dark warning that it is ours for ever—has been lifted away by Him against whom all sin is done, and by revolutionising mercy the sinner has been drawn back to the heart of God. Who but He can thus open to us the gates of righteousness? Who but He can so knit up the cords of union, or say to the aching heart, "I am thy salvation"? Thus in pardon, understood in the only sense commensurate with the mind of Jesus, God does an act which is conclusively supernatural and impossible for any being other than Himself—He separates between the sinner and his sins. He cancels the significance for personal relationship to Himself of the guilt which previously had barred men from His enjoyed presence; and He does so, not by declaring sin not to be sinful, not by forgetting it or letting the sinner off, but by countervailing its power to estrange the Father and the child. It is true, the man who comes to God with a load of felt unworthiness may be tempted fiercely to deny the possibility of its removal, especially if in any degree he has yielded to that sombre naturalistic pessimism which tells broken men that things must always be with them as they now are, and bids them endure their fate as they best may, with brave dumb stoicism. But in countless instances, as Christians know, these misgivings have vanished like smoke in Jesus' presence. At first glance it is unbelievable that anywhere in a universe like this forgiveness should occur, yet it occurs every day. It occurs simply because within and above cosmic law there is a Father. In the last resort we confront not impersonal tendencies of things but the living God, who in Christ puts forth His hand to grasp ours, and through forgiveness ushers the contrite into a boundless world of good.

In the proper sense of the term this event is supernatural. It is a transcendent act to which the normal operations and processes of phenomenal reality are inadequate. Such an act cannot at all be described by formulas indicative of mechanical or immutable sequences; for, unless the experience of being pardoned has been wholly misconstrued, it represents the immediate entrance of God into our life to inaugurate a new attitude in which He and we shall henceforth stand to each other. Of course the psychologist will have his own account to give. He will have much that is important to say about diverse ways in which the assurance of pardon captures the focus of consciousness and instals in the mind a new dominant system of ideas. But what most concerns the believer lies in a different plane. What chiefly interests him is the direct action of God in blotting out his sin. It is in fact part of the definition of forgiveness that nothing but God in His grace can effect it, as conversely it is part of the Christian thought of God that He, and none other, is the Being who can do this thing. He alone can rescue us from the necessities and fatalities of evil in which nature and history appear to entangle us, as if to make free personal life an impossibility. Forgiveness, imparted by God's love, is indeed the act by which we are constituted persons in the full sense—not things, or links in a chain, but free men.

Is it not advisable that our working conception of what miracle is, should be formed upon this model? There is a moral order of things, as there is an order which we describe as physical. We are to-day the creatures of yesterday, and we are shaping now the to-morrow that will be. "Whatsoever a man soweth, that shall he also reap" is a text from which imaginative literature has often preached with a terrible power. Yet this adamantine moral order can be entered remedially by God's love, and the experience of being forgiven is there to prove it. By His mercy men do *not* invariably reap all they have sown. He is above as well as within those ordinances of moral causation. He can use them, acting along their lines. He uses them perpetually, but His love in its sovereign power can transcend and overflow their narrow range, intervening to make all things new. He can come close to deal with us personally, approaching so near that His hand and our hand meet. And for God thus to enter and effect a transforming change in our relation to Himself is a supernatural kind of event, the amazing character of which is only concealed from us by that deadening familiarity which too often has turned the Gospel into commonplace.

How God forgives, i.e. by what precise kind of action He imparts forgiveness, what precise thoughts or volitions are in His mind (to speak humanly) when the forgiving act is done —these are questions to which no reply is possible, and which it is difficult even to clothe in words without an appearance of folly. We possess no psychology of God. We can no more solve such problems than we can explain how God creates the world, or how His being can at once be transcendent and immanent. The *form* of the Divine existence or the Divine activity remains mysterious to finite thought, and this not by accident but essentially. This is far from saying that from the Divine point of view there is ultimate mystery, and that in the light of that infinite love which Christ has disclosed pardon may not show as perfectly natural and transparent. But from our standpoint it is otherwise. On the one hand we are assured in Jesus of a Divine mercy to which all—even the wonder of forgiveness—is possible; on the other, we have as believers the inward certainty that our sins *are* pardoned. But how the gap between these two is bridged, how God makes our forgiveness real, is hidden from us, and no enlargement of human faculty is conceivable for which the mystery would be resolved. But the emergence at this point of an element in our problem which is inherently incalculable need not disturb us or awaken the suspicion that we are altogether on the wrong track. Events of vast spiritual significance—and every instance of Divine pardon, if it occurs at all, is such an event—cannot be wholly judged by narrowly rational canons which appear sufficient for simpler cases. Thinkers are less sure to-day than formerly of the universal jurisdiction of the understanding. On the whole problem of forgiveness, as a miraculous Divine act, we may reasonably cast the light of F. H. Bradley's words: " A lingering scruple still forbids us to believe that reality can ever be purely rational. . . . Though I am willing to believe that my metaphysics may be wrong, there is, I think, nothing that would convince me that my instinct is not right."

Some there are in our time who might well discover in an adequate analysis of their personal experience of forgiveness, a decisive aid towards a more joyous faith in a free and living God who is perpetually present in His world, and perpetually at work. Let them inquire more closely into the meaning of what happens when, by God's act, their sins are blotted out, and it is possible that new vistas may open before their thought. They may realise that what actually confronts them is, in sober truth, a miracle not in the far-off distances of antiquity but in their present lives. God, it appears, has invaded their being in a fashion which neither nature nor human nature can account for, in a power which transcends nature, and for ends that lie beyond it. This is the supernatural in the form that lies nearest, for it belongs to experience; and, apart from experience, religious beliefs are hypotheses and no more. It is better to start our thinking about miracle here than with the swimming of the axe-head. Why should we hesitate to say that forgiveness, in the sense Christians give the term, is an event in which there is illustrated in a uniquely verifiable manner that direct, personal and infinitely varied activity of God to which religious men, and amongst them those who have drunk deepest of Jesus' spring, give the name "supernatural"? On the spiritual side of reality, it may be manifested in the reconciliation of a sinful man to the Father; on the physical side, just because the universe is one and there is one Lord of heaven and earth, it may also be manifested in equally unpredictable ways, as by the resurrection of Jesus from the dead. These are works which only God can do. They are works declaratory of the fact that Almighty Love is immediately active in history and throughout the world as a whole; and to the objection that as events they are isolated or sporadic we may answer, with Ruskin, that "an energy may be natural without being normal, and Divine without being constant."

Our aim is to elucidate those qualities in God which are revealed to the forgiven man, the man who has had this experience of the living God working the wonder of wonders in his own life. We have found that to such a man God is disclosed as Personal, and as the Doer of miracle. To this we may now add the insight also reached by way of pardon that His very nature is sacrificial love.

In other words, like the apostles we are unable eventually to separate the question of Divine forgiveness from the question of atonement, i.e. the act and experience of God in reconciling the world to Himself. Not that in theory the two problems cannot be distinguished and treated so far in abstraction from each other; the thing often has been done. But while a man may receive forgiveness without raising the issue, in what sense Christ is involved in its mediation, or even without feeling that to understand this is for him a matter of vital importance, almost certainly it will be very different if he should go on to make forgiveness the subject of reflection and specifically to ask what are its implications for the love of God, on whom the strain of pardon falls. In the New Testament, the grace of God makes on the contrite an impression of absolute and unreserved personal sacrifice; the pardoned feel that they owe everything to Him. Once we have taken this in, and in addition have learnt from life the lesson that the best things are of dearest price, we shall be unable to refrain from putting atonement and forgiveness in a close and vital connexion.

Who first described the doctrine of atonement as the doctrine of the cost of forgiveness to God? I have not succeeded in tracing the idea further back than Horace Bushnell, and his was an intelligence so free and rich that the phrase may well have been of his own minting. No one was ever readier to lift the anchor and steer his own way. In *Forgiveness and Law* he writes, with a curious turn of expression: "Our human instinct puts us always on making cost when we undertake to forgive."[3] At an earlier point, explaining how atonement is reached between a good man and an offender, he lays down that true forgiveness requires two things antecedently: "first, such a sympathy with the wrong-doing party as virtually takes his nature; and secondly, a making cost in that nature by suffering, or expense, or pains-taking sacrifice and labour."[4] This is followed up by two or three affecting and credible examples of the truth that one man can really pardon another only in so far as he takes the other's sin upon himself in the cost he personally bears on his behalf. It looks as if this were an exceptionally attractive and rewarding path of approach, with collateral advantages of various kinds. If it be true, as has been said in only too familiar words, that the higher man of to-day is not worrying about his sins, there is point in the rejoinder that "in that case, somebody else has got to worry about them all the more." There is a principle here not unworthy to interpret even the relationships of God and man. I could understand a preacher who told his hearers—though the phrasing might be beneath the solemn dignities of official theology—that atonement was a learned word which meant that Christ, in whom God came to men, had so worried about our sins that it

[3] P. 48.　　　　　[4] P. 40.

brought Him to His death. It is no poor or cheap forgiveness He imparts, but one flowing from unmeasured expenditures of spirit and will. And He is no changeless Absolute, but One who shares our grief and shame.

We may therefore find a key to God's experience in forgiving the sinful if we endeavour to realise, even if only imaginatively, what happens when a man forgives a great wrong done to himself. As so often occurs, the best things in human intercourse turn out to be windows, as it were, into the life of God. It is evident we must choose an instance of deep gravity, with something hideous to be pardoned—say, the treachery of a friend, bringing disgrace to the injured man and a loss of happiness never quite to be made good in this life. Such a case, though not common, is by no means unfamiliar. It has occasionally been studied in theology and in preaching, but technical moral philosophy has been curiously silent about it. The present writer asked two of the most eminent philosophers in the country to name any passage in works treating of moral psychology where this precise question is discussed, the question what in such a case goes on in the forgiver's mind and again in the mind of the person forgiven. Yet, although the inquiry concerns what is undoubtedly one of the most tragic and shattering moral experiences open to man, not a single reference could be given.[5] It is possible that Shakespeare has some light to cast, and that a sufficiently profound study of the greater Russian novelists, Dostoievsky in particular, might help us at just this point.

Denney writes, in his piercing way, that " there is no such experience in the relations of human beings as a real forgiveness which is painless, cheap, or easy. There is always passion in it on both sides : a passion of penitence on the one side, and the more profound passion of love on the other, bearing the sin of the guilty to win him, through reconciliation, to goodness again." It is on the second of these two

[5] Aristotle's words in *Eth. Nic,* xi, 11 (Peters' translation): " The equitable man is thought to be especially ready to forgive " become in Mr. W. D. Ross's later and better rendering: " The equitable man is above all others a man of sympathetic judgment "; which is not quite the same thing.

aspects that we must fasten our thoughts. When by self-conquest which even by-standers can see to be noble the injured man (or, as it may be, woman), refusing to ignore moral realities, yet reaching over and beyond the wrong to knit up the old ties of communion, attains to the act of deep pure pardon, the act presupposes and is mediated by costly suffering.

It is an exacting thing to pardon a great wrong; assuredly it is not with a heart of stone that an act so brave and free and loving can be carried through. A man engaged in it is conscious of wrench and agony in proportion as on the one hand he feels the shame of his friend's evil and as on the other sympathy brings him close to the guilty life, actually by intense feeling putting him where the other is. To enter by passionate imagination and self-projection into the other's conflict, to hold by intercession his faltering hand, to weep with his sorrow, actually to think self still at the other's side in the misery and loneliness of guilt—all this is requisite; and how true it is that in heart and mind the forgiver must set out on "voyages of anguish"! It is an experience of sacrificial pain, of vicarious suffering. It is the state of a soul under great stress. To the onlooker it may appear as if the suffering were the offspring of wounded pride, of reluctance to bear burdens at war with memories of old, unclouded friendship; but the truth is not so. The man is not pardoning merely because he cannot but acknowledge pardon to be his duty, though an abhorrent one, whereas were a chance to offer he would speedily wash his hands of the offender. Such suffering is due merely to the resented invasion of personality; but this is sacrificial agony. When he moves out to find and claim his friend again the other's evil, as never before, comes in upon him freshly in its indescribable repulsiveness and need of cleansing; yet he takes it on himself redemptively as by creative and substitutionary fellow-feeling, submerging it in love.

If justifying reasons be demanded for what, at first sight, appears the daring plan of taking all this as in some real sense an analogy of Divine forgiveness, its method and its intrinsic cost, we answer that the parallel is in fact natural and convincing. Certainly it is an analogy drawn from " the most sure and sacred things in human experience."[6] But in addition two considerations have weight. First of all, in the Gospels we do see Jesus entering, in just this way, into the lives of sinners by loving communion with their misery. He placed Himself beside the guilty; conscious of the gulf fixed between God and sinners, He crossed in spirit to our side of the breach and numbered Himself with the transgressors. And secondly, face to face with Jesus we become aware, by intuition, that the love in virtue of which He does this amazing and redeeming thing is positively the love of God Himself. What touches and blesses us in the Redeemer's sympathy is the Divine grace breaking and beating through it upon our life. Thus he who has learnt of Jesus will be apt to construe the mediation of the forgiveness of God as something parallel and kindred to what takes place amongst ourselves when a good man pardons wrong.

In other words, if in a profound and intense case of human pardon there is tragedy for both sides—pain forming the necessary vehicle of forgiveness, in an experience in which nature is rent asunder—it may well be so likewise between God and man. To us pardon is free because for Him its realisation came through agony. The cross presents and represents God's anguish, an awful grief answering to the greatness of the remitted sin. In Him eternally that mind towards the sinful has existence which we behold in the dying Christ. What holy love in God required as a condition of pardon, more correctly as a living element *in* pardon, was not reparation from the guilty, which can never be, but rather such a sacrificial manifestation of His own nature as must, if God and man be of one moral order, form the only conceivable medium of forgiveness. Thus, at Gethsemane and Calvary most of all, faith discerns such an exhibition of Divine reconciling passion, such a tragic tension in which God spares Himself nothing, as makes our heart faint within us and stops every mouth before God. In this wholly direct (and surely, in so far as we know the inmost being of love, not

[6] The analogy goes back to the unforgettable experience and teaching of Hosea.

unintelligible) sense, atonement is what it cost God to forgive the sin of the world. It is the cardinal point at which we stand confronted with the ultimate and recurrent paradox of religious thought—that the God who stands infinitely above human life is yet deeply and decisively implicated in our most inward experience, and that to see into the unchanging heart of things we must gaze upon the travail of a cross. The forgiveness of God rises up through the depths of a self-abandoning passion that sinners can never fathom.

In the next chapter we shall attempt a fuller and more detailed interpretation of the mediation of forgiveness through Christ, and supremely through His death. To this, these last pages may serve as an introduction. But one remark may be added. We are constantly under a temptation to suppose that the reason why we fail to understand completely the atonement made by God in Christ is that our minds are not sufficiently profound. And doubtless there is truth in the reflection that for final insight into the meaning of the cross we are not able or perspicacious enough. But there is a deeper reason still. It is that we are not good enough; we have never forgiven a deadly injury at a price like this, at such cost to ourselves as came upon God in Jesus' death. We fail to comprehend such sacrificial love because it far outstrips our shrunken conceptions of what love is and can endure. Let the man be found who has undergone the shattering experience of pardoning, nobly and tenderly, some awful wrong to himself, still more to one beloved by him, and he will understand the meaning of Calvary better than all the theologians in the world.[7]

[7] The idea that the atonement represents the cost to God of forgiveness is to be found in many passages of Luther. In his suggestive book, *Christus Victor* (1931), p. 133, Aulén goes so far as to write: " Luther's chief interest is to show how much the atoning work (if the phrase may be permitted) *costs* God."

CHAPTER IX

THE ATONEMENT

It is impossible to think out the meaning of forgiveness in the experience of sinful men—which is the side of things nearest to us—without realising that it must have meant something great and costly in the life of God. Not only so, but its meaning as an act or experience of God, as His paying of the price apart from which forgiveness could not be, is the *prius* and the evoking cause of what we know as the sense of pardon received. We have peace, because He loved and suffered first. At the close of the preceding chapter we reflected in a general and introductory manner on atonement as the cost of forgiveness to God, arguing that a true analogy may be drawn, in this tragic matter, between man's life and God's. In the one case as in the other, the sin which is pardoned must in a real and profound sense be borne by the pardoner. We have now to elucidate this truth more fully by reference to the career of Jesus Christ. For apart from the actualities of Jesus' doings and sufferings, all that we might say respecting the significance of forgiveness as costly to God would be no more than speculative and precarious opinion.

We do well, indeed, to remind ourselves at each point that *a priori* thoughts about God's way of realising and conveying forgiveness are for us impossible. Here we are simply thrown back upon fact. The fact, in the first place, that the man who in God's presence has discovered the dark truth about himself and has awakened to the appalling danger he is in of being irretrievably shut out from the fellowship of God, knows by simple intuition in his despair that if help should come, it can come from God only. With God even the impossible is possible, but with Him alone. None but He can creatively change the relation we the sinful are in to His holiness. But in the second place, we can do no other than bow our heads before the fact that He *has* interposed in Jesus, and through

168

Jesus has accomplished reconciliation in the chosen way of which the New Testament tells. We are confronted with the plain fact that God has taken a mode of redeeming the world which could never have entered the heart of man to conceive. " It pleased God," as one has said, " to select one nation from the rest as a priestly nation, and for all time to give one Person from its midst the power to speak the liberating word, the word of reconciliation, and to seal this word with His passion and death."[1] All who in their desperate need have lifted their eyes to Christ and caught at the promise for the guilty with which His cross is laden, can bear witness to the sufficiency of His mediation. They, and they only, can tell whether in Him there is or is not pardon.

Hence in what follows no attempt is made to reason out atonement beforehand, as though by way of postulate we could determine how God must help us, if help should come. The truth about atonement, like all truth in Christianity, is discoverable and verifiable only through submission to Jesus' power to set us right with God. And in formulating what we call doctrine, we simply interpret what comes home to us as we let the living and dying Redeemer bring us to the Father.

Our thinking about atonement, to be real, must be our own. God has not dictated to us, even in the New Testament, any final theory of His reconciling work. We must search it out in the light He gives. Of course in that quest the Bible is our indispensable inspiration. But we learn to use the Bible, here as elsewhere, in the light of its own deepest principles. We have to take the truths about God which Scripture brings us, and which the best thought of the Church has selected for emphasis, and try, not to collect authoritative passages, but to move in the spirit of the Bible towards apprehension of what God in Christ has done to convey to us His pardoning love.

Again, argument concerning reconciliation, if it is to lead anywhere, must move within the field of Christian experience. Only there do the wheels, as we say, bite the rails. The man to whom Jesus means nothing will inevitably find the cross a

[1] Karl Heim, *Das Wesen des evangelischen Christentums*, p. 82.

superfluous mystery; he cannot see what it is for. And his first duty is not to excogitate a theory of atonement, but to make up his mind for God. When he has begun to take the specifically Christian attitude to Jesus, some of the necessary assumptions will be present in his thought for appreciating Jesus' work. There will be a sense of unworthiness; there will be a consciousness of infinite debt to Christ; there will be a settled conviction of the power Christ actually has of mediating between God and man; and these are among the indispensable presuppositions of valid thinking here. We ought to fix it in our mind that the atonement is only relevant to the guilty and alarmed conscience, that we must look at it with penitent eyes. Anselm begins his great work by professing to put the actual Christ aside (as if He had never been) and to prove by irrefutable logic that it is impossible for anyone to be saved except through the God-man; and he ends by claiming that his argumentation ought to convince even a Jew or a pagan. It cannot be too emphatically said that this is hopeless. How could we know that *Christ* is necessary, if we did not know by acquaintance the person called "Christ"? It is true that apart from the knowledge of the Christian facts we might feel sure that we needed what would cleanse conscience and break sin's power, but except through having conscience cleansed by contact with Christ how could we tell that Christ is the person capable of doing this needed thing? Unless we have stood before Jesus and felt the impression of His holy love, the meaning of what He anticipated in Gethsemane and underwent on Calvary is necessarily hidden from us.

Again, the wise man will look with suspicion on theories of atonement which are only too complete. There is in the Christian mind an instinctive revolt from easy and shallow views. We rightly suspect all interpretations of a simplicity so transparent as to render it an insoluble problem why great minds in every age should have pondered over the *mysterium crucis*. If atonement be the act of God, it has in it the unfathomable quality of God Himself. Whatever the meaning of the cross, at least it evokes awe and wonder. We perceive that it brings salvation, and we thank God for it, but we cannot measure it or reduce it without remainder to conventional and manageable terms. As Otto suggests, the cross is the supreme instance in which we confront that fusion and interpenetration, so profoundly characteristic of religion, of elements which for our mind are paradoxical and unreconciled; it presents a mingling of rational aspects with those which are other than rational, of the revealed with the unrevealed, the open with the merely surmised and divined, the last and highest love with the most awe-inspiring judgment of sin. It is the central and decisive manifestation of the great enigma—the innocent suffering of the just for the unjust.

Once more, the death of Jesus has significance for reconciliation only when considered in the light, and as the expression, of His life. It is impossible to proclaim salvation through the death of an Unknown; and if men are to understand who the Christ is to whose cross they are invited, some real impression must be afforded of His words, His inner life, His mind concerning God and man, and the influence He exerted on those who associated with Him. Not only so; at point after point in His career we seem to observe the gathering intensification of His reconciling work. His entire experience can be described as a continuous and ever-deepening self-identification with the sinful. More and more He was numbering Himself with the transgressors. In His baptism, for example, He took His place beside sinners and made their dark responsibilities His own. It was not for Him a baptism of repentance; yet it was an act of experience in which He refused to be reckoned apart from the other members of God's family and stood at their side before the Divine holiness. And in that hour the cross cast its shadow before. Already it is clear that Jesus feels " socially involved in the iniquities and frailties of all His brethren." The same willed unity with sinners is evident in His learning obedience, His sharing the human struggle to do and endure God's will; supremely, perhaps, in His practice of faith and His inward knowledge of temptation. The culmination and full expression of all this is death. It came to this, that if Jesus was to stand in with sinners to the last, death in their service and God's must be not merely accepted but chosen and spontaneously affirmed. Thus the cross is significant only as the full and definitive self-expression of all He had already been. We err when we lose that perspective.

None the less, the uniqueness of the cross will not bear denial. In the New Testament it occupies a place of its own, indicated by the (at first glance) disproportionate length of the narratives of the Passion and the constant preoccupation of the Epistles with the glorious meanings of Christ's " exodus "; and the Church, in turn, had no option but to fall into line with this, on experimental grounds, as may be gathered from its celebration of the Lord's Supper. For Jesus above all, the cross though inseparable from His life was distinct in intensity of meaning. He unquestionably conceived of His own death as inaugurating a new relation between God and man; and in that character, especially near the end, it was never out of His mind. There are passages in the Gospels which do more than suggest that in His death Jesus anticipatively saw something that at heart made Him shudder. It was continuous with His life, yet it was by itself, lonely in its import of shadowed anguish. This too must be allowed for in our reflections.

The interpreter of atonement needs most of all, I think, to recapture that attitude of penitent trust and grateful adoration in which, if God will, we find ourselves at the Lord's Table. Whatever theory we rest in, must do justice to the intuitive convictions which there arise within us. It is vain to choose a doctrine of atonement which in the main overlooks the greatest things that come home to us as we take in our hands the bread and wine. Now in that posture, that consciousness of inestimable reception from Christ and of self-abandonment to Him, two predominant impressions appear to be registered on the mind.

In Jesus' death, we behold the absolute judgment and condemnation of sin.

Very probably such a phrase may appear more than tinged with unreality. What does it mean, except as a reiteration of familiar dogma, to say that in the cross sin is judged, and judged with absolute finality? How is it possible to think of God as attaching His censure of sin, His infliction upon sinners, to what happened at Calvary? At first sight this looks, or may look, as theatrical and arbitrary as old-fashioned pictures of the Last Judgment. We must therefore try for a point of view at which it becomes evident that in moral fact the cross *is* the irreversible condemnation of sin, and a condemnation which is God's act. Three considerations may be adduced.

(1) In the first place, sin is condemned in the cross because it there is permitted fully to expose its true nature. Once for all it is forced into the light. What sin really is—its rebellion, malignancy and horror—could never be completely detected or revealed while it was being committed merely against those who themselves shared the imperfection of the sinner. The sinfulness of sin varies with the character of those against whom it is done, with the clear-eyed acceptance of hostility to those who, in lesser degree or greater, are good and represent the good. And in Jesus men for the first time were up against pure goodness. Never before had sinners confronted unflinching and perfect love; never before, accordingly, had it been possible for sin's malevolent antagonism to perfect love to declare itself without reserve. Hence, by its treatment of Jesus Christ, man's sinfulness was exposed: its sheer evil was laid bare to the bone, reprobated, doomed, sentenced without appeal. What we are as sinners was lit up by a flash that told the whole and left nothing to be said.

For the sin manifest at Calvary is ours. We all are in it together; no separating lines can be drawn anywhere, between individuals or generations; we cannot any of us disown a part in the sin that rejected and slew the Son of God. The same kind of selfishness and suspicion and grudging envy and callous neglect and hard cruel injustice as we perceive, mixed with nobler things, in the Jewish leaders are poisoning our hearts also when in sinning we take sides against love. There are movements within us that vibrate in sympathy with the hatred poured on the dying Jesus. As it has been put, " we seem to see the face of a rigorous Pharisee or a lax

Sadducee or a false Judas staring out at us from our own thoughts and impulses." The fact that God gave Christ to men, and they could do no better than crucify Him, casts a terrible light upon our nature. That light of exposure has fallen full upon its object, and it has not been totally ignored. Since Jesus, the world has known a new kind of self-reproach and compunction.

(2) Sin is judged in the cross by Jesus' attitude to its intrinsic evil. Now this attitude of His goes much beyond the *words* in which He habitually declared His antagonism to wrong, which were words of anger in the deepest sense. It was because He loved that He recoiled from evil with abhorrence and scourged it with scathing speech. But a profounder expression of antagonism to sin than speech is possible, and in Jesus' case became real. The best men have opposed sin by setting their life against it, by placing themselves in its path, at whatever cost, and constituting their personal being a dedicated obstacle to its progress. This path Christ pre-eminently chose. It was for Him not enough to denounce wrong; He went further and took the last step; He exhibited an utter opposition to sin by dying at the hands of sinners. By letting sinful men vent their utmost hate upon Himself, He revealed and condemned sin as the absolute contrary of love. An apostolic admonition bids Christians remember that " ye have not yet resisted unto blood, striving against sin." There is something you have not done as yet which it is possible to do; and it is this that Christ did. He resisted unto blood; not by shedding blood, for in force, in violent suppression and angry retaliation, no condemnation of sin could emerge which could have left conviction on the sinner's mind—not by shedding blood, but by letting His own blood be shed. As it has been expressed: [2] " There is in the holiness of God a radical opposition to wickedness which cannot express itself adequately in mere punishment, but can express itself only by receiving upon itself the assault of the sinful will. It is Christ Himself Who has enabled us to see that this must be so." And it is because men have in some degree learned this lesson that the type of morality towards which

[2] By Professor A. G. Hogg.

mankind is moving is a type in which evil will be quickly and keenly resented, but in which, instead of visiting fierce and bitter penalty upon the sinner, those sinned against will rather suffer on his behalf. We may therefore say that Jesus disclosed His hostility to sin not merely by probing words in the Sermon on the Mount, or by lifelong efforts to save and restore sin's victims, but supremely by bearing death at sinful hands. The cup He must drink was in part the knowledge that His love had evoked the sin of others to the full.

It is difficult to understand how we could contemplate the dying of Christ, regarding it with penitence, with trust and with a sense of unspeakable indebtedness, and fail to be implicitly aware of what so far has been said. Indeed, the insight that the cross is a final and unalterable testimony against sin, which decisively assigns its place in the world of moral realities, may reasonably be taken as present in the thought of every Christian. But the mind of Jesus at Calvary is the mind of God. This is not an inference of any kind, but a direct transcript of experience. The condemnation of sin uttered whether in language or in silence through Jesus' life and death is in fact uttered by the Eternal—not by a commissioned deputy or prophet merely, but by God. We have a living sense of this as we stand confronting Jesus. Through His eyes there looks out on us, with convicting and humbling power, the dread-inspiring holiness of God with which evil cannot dwell. His oneness with the Father, in unbroken sonship, vouches for it that what He brings home to conscience is the final truth concerning sin.

When therefore we seek to put the truth about atonement in a form that throughout keeps touch with experience, one principle we may with a good conscience set down is this, that the cross reveals in a final and for ever unmistakable way God's mind regarding sin and His active attitude towards it. The cross does this because this is in fact the result it has upon faith. Forgiveness is only possible in so far as all concealments which hide the real nature of sin are torn away and men are convicted of utter and inexcusable unworthiness. It would appear that in Jesus' death God has effectively set His finger on the evil of the world by which it is estranged from the Father. He who has gazed in faith at the Redeemer giving up His life knows, indisputably, that in sin there is something guilty and tragically real to be forgiven, something in which he personally is implicated. That death reveals sin—*our* sin—by making undeniably plain sin's attitude to the holiest life ever seen upon the planet. Hence if forgiveness be conveyed through the cross, it is a forgiveness that includes, or is fused with, judgment.[3]

(3) Sin is judged in the cross of Jesus because the connexion between sin and suffering is there made utterly clear. Transgression entails pain, and He who numbered Himself with the transgressors came in an inevitable way under the sweep of that Divine ordinance.

In all probability it is at this point that the most serious difficulties about atonement are felt. Let us note precisely what the worst difficulty is. We are trying for a point of view at which the cross visibly embodies the Divine judgment of sin. And it may naturally be objected: How can this be true? The judgment of God must be pronounced by God Himself, as His act and decision. But the death of Christ, so far from being produced or occasioned by God, was a crime perpetrated by men; it was sinners, not the Father, to whom the crucifixion of Jesus, as well as His antecedent suffering, was due. How then is it reasonable to characterise this supreme sin of history as *God's* judgment, as in fact the manifestation of *His* righteousness? This is the problem.

The first part of the answer, so far as we can see for the moment, is to underline afresh the cardinal principle that we are living in a moral order, which surrounds and informs human experience; and that one feature of this all-embracing moral order is the fact that sin, everywhere and always, is followed by evil consequences. It would therefore seem that the presence of Jesus in a sinful world, associated with sinners as closely as one personality can be with others—identified with them, indeed, to the very limit—unavoidably implied

---

[3] A recent writer has pointed out that it is a dangerous illusion to suppose that religion makes things easy, in the sense that in religion we can get at God, as it were, " behind the back of the moral law."

for Him a real subjection to the standing appointment of God that sin and condemning pain go together. He could not be amongst us, in loving communion with our bitter need, and fail to be involved in that.

Further, our human life is plainly such that the evil consequences of sin, while they come inexorably, do not always fall most direly on the guilty. The guilty, it is true, are invariably penalised; they are estranged from the Father and injured in character. None the less, the greater part of the resulting evil may light upon the innocent and loving, whose life is entangled with theirs. Not the culprit, but his friends, have to shoulder the burden. The solidarity of men is both a blessed and a poignant fact; it is constitutive of human life, which would be wholly different in nature were this fact absent; and in virtue of it the righteous suffer with and for the sinful of account of their sin, and are capable of this suffering just in proportion to their goodness.

This is a truth which long before Jesus Christ was enunciated in the 53rd chapter of Isaiah. In the Servant of the Lord one is pictured who, innocent as he is, gives up his life as an offering for the sin of those around him. His death, to the prophet's mind, is no mere martyrdom or miscarriage of human justice; rather in God's intent and purpose, as also by the Servant's willed self-oblation, it is a sacrifice mediating forgiveness. It is of course true that for historical exegesis the Servant is Israel the nation, or the righteous within Israel, whose sufferings form a sacrificial offering for the iniquities of the surrounding peoples; the other nations, that is, had imagined the Servant to be punished for his own sin, but now see that these sufferings of Israel should have fallen upon themselves. But this national aspect is hardly central or vital for us here. What is central is the spiritual principle that—as is affirmed in the passage twelve separate times—the sufferings of the Servant are vicarious in character. The Sufferer, though suffering at the hands of the wicked, is bearing the painful consequence of their sins, and bearing them by Divine appointment. For the very reason that he was related to the sinful with such profound intimacy, the judgment of God on their sin struck *him*; but it did so, not by

M

any mechanical or external fiat, but because it is on these lines that human life is built.

In the last resort, however, the prophet's ideal picture is such that its counterpart or fulfilment could not emerge in any ordinary human person; for since all normal men sin, their suffering for sin and on behalf of the sinful could not, by the nature of the case, be wholly vicarious. Perfect fulfilment only came in Jesus. As has recently been demonstrated, we have good reason to believe that Isaiah 53 was steadily in the background of Jesus' mind; it is indeed explicitly referred to in more than one of His important sayings regarding His own career. He seems undoubtedly to have applied to Himself the prophet's thought of One on whom " the Lord has laid the iniquities of us all." The Divine reaction against the sin of man He perceived to be falling upon Him, and in that sense He accepted it in faith.[4] If it be asked how this is possible, two suggestions can be made: first, that the good always are challenged and enabled to bear the consequences of their neighbours' wrong-doing, and in the second place that Jesus in sheer love was unreservedly identified with guilty men. It was because He thus in love made Himself one

---

[4] It has been maintained that for Jesus His passion in no sense constituted a problem, but was a perfectly transparent necessity of redemption. The final sacrifice rose for Him simply and unavoidably out of the thought of service. As the corn of wheat must fall into the ground and die, so self-evidently He must go to the bitter cross. No one will think of denying most of this; but can it be the whole truth? Our Lord walked by faith, with something therefore of that admixture of insight and trusting premonition which make Him, here also, our Leader. Hence the meaning of His death, its full import, the ways in which it would tell for reconciliation, may well have been both known and unknown, illumined and decisive yet shrouded in partial mystery. His words in Gethsemane, " If it be possible, let this cup pass from Me," appear to indicate a consciousness that the Father's will must be accepted, while yet it could be asked whether this way of death was the one conceivable means by which that will might be realised. So the cross beckoned Him, yet at the same time there may have been something in His experience analogous to that feeling of inner compulsion to do things the significance and outcome of which they do not wholly understand, which at times is familiar to His followers. Throughout His life He had followed the path of obedience, content to trust the Father's love and wisdom. Can we be certain that this element of inner thought and feeling was completely absent as He envisaged His death?

with the sinful that He bore their burden. Not by abrupt introduction of some new spiritual principle but as the unique and highest expression of the self-transcending moral order in which we live, His sufferings were the bitter fruit of sin vicariously borne.

"The moral order" we say; but for the religious mind the moral order is of course equivalent to the will of God. Hence we are entitled to affirm that in the cross the *Divine* judgment of sin is manifested, because there, by the normal and appointed self-unfolding of sin and its results, God's attitude to sin was finally and unequivocally revealed as well as actively expressed. It was not that God stretched His hand from the sky, seized the mass of human iniquity, transferred it to Jesus by capricious fiat, then chastised Him for it. God does nothing in that way. But when Jesus entered into our life, took the responsibility of our evil upon Himself, identifying His life with ours to the uttermost and placing Himself where the sinful are by strong sympathy in a fashion so real that the pain and affliction due to us became unspeakable suffering within His soul—*that* was the act of God, that (if we take seriously Jesus' oneness of mind and will with the Father) was indeed the experience of God. In no way other than by letting sinful wills do their worst to Jesus could it be openly demonstrated, and for ever, what sin involves in God's righteous judgment.

If we recur to the attitude of adoring reception from and self-abandonment to Christ which befits us at Communion, it can be laid down, in the second place, that in Jesus' death we behold the absolute disclosure of Divine love to the sinful.

That it *is* the love of God, not merely of Jesus as a figure in history, which meets us there, is no matter of argument or inference, but of direct intuition. In what He undergoes at Calvary, Jesus is not merely reporting or indicating a Divine love beyond and independent of Himself, a love of which He is but the official messenger; rather, by being what He is in circumstances He Himself has chosen, He is bringing in God's love upon us and making it ours. He puts it in our hand as we fix our eyes upon Him; we possess God's love in possessing Him; there is no distinction to be made, of quality or intention, between the grace of the Lord Jesus Christ and the grace of God Himself. I repeat that this is the impression recorded on our heart and thought in the holiest moment of Christian worship, when the fountains of the great deep are broken up; and unless Christian faith as such has been a blunder, it is difficult to understand why an impression so central and self-evidenced should be misleading.

The suggestion is occasionally made that this emphasis upon the revelation of love in the cross (at all events when this aspect is given supreme significance) represents a modern declension from a profounder and more rigorous interpretation preferred by antiquity. But in fact our contention is very old. St. Augustine for example writes: "It was mainly for this purpose that Christ came, to wit, that man might know how much God loves him; and that he might learn this, to the intent that he might be enkindled to the love of Him by whom he was first loved, and might also love his neighbour."[5]

Now it is because what comes home to us in presence of the cross—interfused, that is, with the sense of sin's utter condemnation—is a new apprehension of Divine love acting on an infinite scale, that we are able to surmount what might otherwise be an insuperable difficulty. There is one question we should expect to be asked very frequently, though in point of fact within Christendom it has seldom been heard. It is this: Why does the crucifixion not so horrify and revolt us as to make sceptics by the thousand? In a sense such an effect would be only natural; for at Calvary the holiest of our race, whom we do not praise because He is above all praise, terminates His life in misery, shame, agony and loneliness. It is an event which appears wholly incompatible with a righteous or loving world-government; why then do our minds not flame with indignation against God Himself on that account? The reason plainly is that in the cross what is felt to be both present and presented is God's own

[5] Quoted by Cave, *The Doctrine of the Person of Christ*, p. 126.

love; and it is present as enduring a vicarious burden due to human sin. We cannot call His love in question at the cross if it is precisely in the cross that the greatness of His love is for the first time fully exhibited. God was in Christ reconciling the world unto Himself.

Moreover, from this angle we can discern a patently vital connexion between atonement and the Divinity of Christ. The atonement has neither substance nor efficacy apart from the assurance that in Jesus very God is personally present. Writers of an older day inclined to state the connexion misleadingly by taking the Divinity of Christ as (so to speak) an infinite factor or co-efficient which multiplied His human sufferings to infinity, thus rendering them an exact equivalent for the infinite guilt of sin. Modern Christian feeling recoils from this; but it sympathises, I think, with the ultimate conviction behind such calculations. The two great doctrines do hang together. Unless the passion of Christ in which His life consistently culminated is an index of *God's* love, and not an index merely but also an expression of it in virtue of God's personal presence in Him, so that at Calvary we behold *in sensu eminenti* the sacrifice of the Eternal, neither heart nor conscience is fully satisfied. The power of the cross over the human heart has rested on an intuitive certainty that in its pain and surrender there is more than meets the eye. It has rested on a sense that perfect fulfilment has been given to the thought long ago enshrined in the words: " In all their affliction, He was afflicted."[6]

The history of theology proves to the hilt that the great ideas of Atonement and Incarnation lose the life-blood of meaning when they drift apart from each other. As Denney has put it: " It is a common idea that Socinianism (or Unitarianism) is specially connected with the denial of the Incarnation. It began historically with the denial of the Atonement. It is with the denial of the Atonement that it always begins anew, and it cannot be too clearly pointed out

---

[6] Even if this rendering of the Hebrew is indefensible, the words express a real conviction of Old Testament writers; cf. Jer. 12.7 ff, 31.20, 45, Hos. 11.8 ff.

that to begin here is to end, sooner or later, with putting Christ out of the Christian religion altogether."[7] The reason for the inevitability of such a development is that apart from atonement we have no ground for ascribing to God such chosen self-sacrifice within the life of man as the word Incarnation properly denotes. What confronts us in the dying Christ with heart-subduing power is the sight of God giving up for our sake, God in the act of bearing our sins. This is at the back of everything that can be called Gospel, giving it preciousness and momentum. A great evangelist was accustomed to say that in his first days he spoke most about the sacrifice of Christ, but when he got older he came to speak as much of the sacrifice of the Father. Naturally; the sacrifice of Christ *is* the sacrifice of God, in which He makes our burdens His own and puts away sin by the surrender of Himself; and it is this life-giving apprehension which men declare, rather than define, when they say Incarnation. Nothing else does justice to the deep words of St. Paul, to which believing hearts everywhere beat true: " God commandeth *His own* love towards us in that, while we were yet sinners, Christ died for us." The love could not be His own, in the absolute sense insisted on by religion, were not God veritably present in Jesus, to give Himself for us.

Love is not love 'which confines itself to words. There is no more bitter contrast in man's life than the gaping chasm that may sever fine words from deeds of self-denial. To be itself, to win the soul, love must be clothed upon with costly action. By being what He was and doing what He did Jesus Christ has been able to convince men that this supreme law is submitted to even by the Eternal, and that when God stooped down to bless us in His Son the dream of the prophet, concerning the Holy One who in our afflictions is afflicted, had come true. When we think of this, letting it fill and dilate the mind, the word Incarnation rises unavoidably to our lips. We are not operating here with any general idea of incarnation, which can be fitted to Christianity; we are not engrossed with general ideas of any kind, but with Jesus. And it is the movement of our whole personality in

[7] *The Death of Christ*, p. 320.

His presence, supremely as He takes upon Him in death to deliver man, that impels us to say: " My Lord and my God."

Futhermore, this is the weapon we may and ought to use against all suggestions—which even yet are occasionally made—that God had to be induced to love men, and that what Christ did and suffered provided the inducement. This of course must be false if our direct intuition of God's love in the cross be valid. What older writers, who at least seem to tender these wholly unscriptural and more than half pagan suggestions, were endeavouring to bring out was, I think, in the first place the reality of the Divine wrath against sin. We need not pause upon this again. It has already been argued that in order to assert God's wrath against sin, as you must, you need not question His eternal and essential love. It is because God loves that anger in Him is conceivable and credible; the behaviour of Jesus in the Gospels and our own highest experiences indicate as much. It is love alone that makes wrath pure, sublime, redemptive.

But the second truth that they were intent upon, whatever their success in formulating it, is of importance for our present argument. It is that through the reconciling work of Christ, attaining its climax in the cross, not merely is God's love exhibited on an absolute scale, but a new situation arises for the sinful, as between God and them. To dwell upon this for a moment is worth while.

Let us recur to what we have already found to be the best available analogy of God's forgiveness—human forgiveness, in a noble form, as the spontaneous restoration of fellowship or friendship by the act of the offended person. Now, when we scrutinise such an act closely, we can see that in an important sense it is creative. It not merely registers something that is present irrespectively of the forgiving act; it produces what is decisively new. It affects the course of events positively and remedially, calling a fresh situation into being. "Nothing," it has been said, "is harder for us than to forgive; while we are trying to 'make up our minds to it,' all the laws of our being, the considerations of our reason, and our sense of justice, seem to bar the way. But if the deed is done, and the forgiveness has been offered and accepted—

then we seem to have broken through into a new world of friendship, which our own effort of will has created."

Many people, if they were frank, would confess that so far as they have gone in life, they have never yet been able to understand what forgiveness means. That is not surprising: there *is* in forgiveness something that baffles common thought. It appears to show a conclusion for which the premises do not account; it appears, at first glance, to be both impossible and immoral. "Forgiveness," writes Bernard Shaw, "is a beggar's refuge; we must pay our debts." To undo the past has the look of being beyond the normal resources of mankind. Yet this is but a partial view; we know each of us from our experience of home that forgiveness can and does happen. It cannot ultimately be impossible, for it occurs; it cannot be immoral, for it calls out a new and victorious goodness. The difficulty of understanding lies in the fact that it is creative.

If we carry all this up to God, as a legitimate aid to the interpretation of His presence in the cross, it yields some appreciable light. That the cross should be borne for the ungodly and thankless, for men who wish for nothing of the sort, is a Divine act of the initiatory and creative type. There the love of God invades us, all the fuller of grace because totally unsought; and when those who have become aware of it refuse its appeal, the refusal costs them a real effort: they have the sense of resisting a powerful influence, which they have to exert force to thrust aside. But if the cross be thus God's creative act, in relation to sin, it is impossible that it should leave things between Him and us just as before. And the change produced by it may, I think, be stated thus: All that went to the death of Christ, constituting it the definitive self-expression of God towards the sinful, not merely *reveals* God's antecedently forgiving love; it actually *conveys* forgiveness and renders it effective. The analogy of human experience makes clear that a forgiving disposition obtains no result as long as it is silent, quiescent, inactive; it bears fruit only when the message of reconciliation has been sent and delivered, the word of pardon spoken, the look exchanged, the hand grasped. The point is that such acts are both declaratory and effective; they reveal what already exists, but also by the enacted revelation they call into being what is new and original. So the cross not merely disclosed the Father's eternal attitude of willingness to pardon but produced in addition a new relationship. If we may put it so, the relation between God and man is not unchanging, although its moral basis cannot alter; it may change in the sense of being developed out of an estrangement consciously felt on both sides into a situation—realised at the cost undergone in Christ's spirit and body—in which the forgiveness of the Father is sent home to the guilty conscience and heart.

At this point the question may naturally be put: How could Jesus impart forgiveness to sinful men during His lifetime, if in any important sense His sufferings and death are the creative medium through which the Divine mercy reaches us? I do not know that to this any complete answer can be made, but the problem is not wholly dark. We must recall the life-work to which Jesus had dedicated Himself. This life-work may be briefly described as that of establishing the Kingdom of God as the Father's representative, in a world of sin. And for His mind, as everywhere in Scripture, the Kingdom is built upon the forgiveness of sins. Such a work cannot be done mechanically or from outside, but only through experience. It can only be done from within the sinner's situation, its misery and sense of condemnation. There is a sympathy which does not stand aloof, content with words, but which descends into the depth of need and lays hold upon the other's burden. If we picture Jesus face to face with one of the penitents who encountered Him—the sick of the palsy, the woman that was a sinner—we may ask ourselves precisely what it was in Him that conveyed to them the sense and reality of pardon. What created their assurance? Manifestly not the simple fact that He admitted them to His presence, or that He looked at them, as a spectator of their misery. Rather it was that in spirit He went down to where they were, in their bitter, grief-stricken distance from God; and that thus joining Himself to them inwardly He took hold of their hand, that He might raise them up.

This may be repudiated as fantastic and sentimentally

unreal; but is it actually so? From other quarters we may gather that it is an experience possible for good men. "Do you know," said William Morris the poet, "when I see a poor devil drunk and brutal, I always feel, quite apart from æsthetical perceptions, a sort of shame, as if I myself had some hand in it?" In well-remembered words, too, George Fox tells how he prayed "to be baptised into a sense of all conditions, that I might know the needs and feel the sorrows of all." The true-hearted pastor, coming close to the moral derelict who signals for help, has a consciousness of mediation resembling this; entering into the desperate need, he goes into God's presence with the weight of the other's sin upon his spirit; representatively and intercedingly he takes his hand to lead him in with himself to God. It is impossible not to believe that we approach the true view of Jesus' mediation when we think along such lines to the very uttermost. But for Jesus thus to enter into our condition by strong sympathy implied in the final issue nothing less than death. As it has been put in words that catch the very spirit of reconciliation: "The sinless Sufferer on the cross, in His oneness with His brethren, felt their wrong-doing His own, confessed in His forsakenness that God would have nothing to do with it save destroy it, felt that it separated between men and God, and that He was actually away from God. . . . That He with His recoil and quiver should still have loved us so intensely that, when He felt the gulf fixed between God and sinners, He thought Himself on our side of the breach and numbered Himself with the transgressors—that is the marvel."[8]

Thus in the cross God in Christ links Himself with our sinful spirit in its sorest need, owning for all His omnipotence the reality of righteousness and guilt. For Christ thus to save from within the human experience is the limiting case of that deep principle whereby the higher soul puts itself in the place of the lower.

If, as has been argued, the cross is the supreme manifestation of Divine love, it may seem as if the position we are seeking to occupy may easily be determined. How shall we answer

[8] H. S. Coffin, *Social Aspects of the Cross*, pp. 13, 23.

those who protest that forgiveness has no vital connexion with Christ's death, and that to understand its presuppositions we have only to read the Parable of the Prodigal Son? Now it is true that that parable says nothing of the cross; as indeed for that matter it says nothing of Jesus. Apart from such details, however, and also from the fact that there is something curiously mechanical in the idea that after a certain point no further truth, say, regarding the *cost* of redemption, could reach the believing mind, there are still good grounds for interpreting the cross as the medium of pardon, and this not despite God's love but because of it.

In the first place, everything is relevant here that led us at an earlier point to describe the cross as the condemnation of human sin. The love of God is holy, majestic, awe-inspiring and august; nor can any love possess the respect of moral beings which lacks this self-maintaining stringency. Holiness is the austere element in love, preserving it from wrong. We are able to speak separately of the two things, love and holiness, because in men they often seem distinct; but in God they are indistinguishable. There are principles of righteousness native to the love of God, and in dealing with the sinful He acts in harmony with these principles, not against them. Forgiveness can be taken by the living conscience only as it comes through judgment, and it is part of the Christian conception of God that He forgives in such wise as will not foster the seeds of evil within us. Hence in God's very nature there is what may be called a moral necessity that pardon should be mediated through active condemnation. He so reveals Himself in the cross that His mind about sin is unequivocally disclosed; the world is shown how awful goodness is.

Not only so, but in every great forgiveness there is enshrined a great agony. If God be Father, with the immeasurable access of meaning that name has received through Jesus, we cannot but throw out our minds with conviction towards the truth that He is better than the best earthly fatherhood or motherhood in His anguish over the sin of children, with a pain that flows out in sacrifice. We cannot set limits to the magnitude of suffering which even human affection will undergo in its ministries of care for the estranged and wayward, and in view of Jesus we have still further to dilate our thoughts of what is possible to love. Ideas of the Divine impassibility derived from ages which were very far from humane, and which too often regarded suffering unconcernedly as a mark of the weak and the vanquished, can now make little appeal. The power to forgive, to send forgiveness home to the needy heart, cannot be had for nothing; in God or man it is bought at a price. It is bought only with the suffering of the offended spirit. The electric current that pervades the whole wire flashes into light at its sensitive point; so the timeless pain of God over human evil becomes visible in Christ's passion. I cannot profess to demonstrate such a thought by logic, and we perhaps do well to distrust all pretensions to argumentative cogency in this sphere. But these things, it may be said unhesitatingly, do come home to us in the hour of Communion; in ways to which language will always be inadequate we are there brought in contact with Divine suffering for the guilty, with an unsuspected love that for our sake bears all things.

These considerations impart a substantial meaning to the view that from the Divine side what may be called a spiritual necessity attaches to reconciliation through Christ's suffering and death; in the light of the Divine nature the cross is envisaged as something that had to be, because God is holy and is love. But not less it is necessary for ourselves. We, the sinful, need the cross where Jesus died.

It may indeed be urged that if God is love, then redemption is in any case secure, whether there be a cross or not. Once fix the truth that love is God's very being, and forgiveness becomes self-evident. The fountain implies the stream. But here the objector is met by a formidable prior question: How do we know that God *is* love? It is assumed, perhaps, but on what grounds? Far from being an elementary common-place, the proposition that God is love would be denied at this moment by the vast majority of mankind. That love certainly does not leap to the eye as we observe nature or scrutinise history. Modern literature, filled with the darkest fatalistic pessimism, is being written by able men who deny passionately that all things are ordered by a humane intelligence, and who reject the statement that God is love as the most utter falsehood, and a crime against the human race. Such men point to the desolating facts of life—its injustice, disease and pain—protesting that the universe exhibits not the faintest trace of loving control. Well, their facts are there, visible to all, whatever may be said of their inferences. And in view of the innumerable sorrows which have burdened men's hearts from the outset of time, are we to believe that Divine love is something to be taken for granted, an unimpeachable and self-attesting reality? The truth is that apart from Christ we should in great measure be nonplussed by the cosmic phenomena; we should really not know what to make of the world. But if so, there is something like affectation in the idea that the cross of Jesus merely illustrates a truth we could have discovered for ourselves. It is not the case that belief in Divine love has given credibility to the story of Jesus; it is the other way about. The story alone has made the belief credible in its specifically Christian form. We need the cross, if we are to be fully persuaded that God pardons to the uttermost.

Also we need it to induce penitence. It is vain to argue as though what the New Testament calls "repentance unto life" is the simple product of reasonable or even unanswerable appeals to the understanding. That is a pure hallucination which a single experiment will dispel. There is indeed no point at which the thoughtful observer has the conviction thrust upon him so irresistibly that there must be a Holy Spirit, if the Christian life is ever to be begun. Nothing but the inward energising of a Divine power will bring men to repent in Jesus' sense. But penitence must have a motive. There must be presented to the mind that which will fill it with grief and hatred of sin; and when we examine the past, or look around us, we discover that nothing in thought or experience is comparable to the cross for power to induce penitence in Christian or non-Christian, in old or young, in learned or simple. In the passion of Jesus there is that which breaks men down and melts them in contrition. Not in a remorse that goes out despairingly into darkness, but in a piercing and softening sorrow for all they are and have become; a sorrow which on its other side is an apprehension of the Father's mercy. To repent before Christ crucified and to trust because of Him—these are two aspects of one regenerating experience.

Nor is it to be forgotten that by the evocation of such trustful and purifying penitence, laden with moral impulse, the reconciling work of God—the atonement, in ordinary terms—serves the ends of righteousness more effectively than could have been done by mere punishment. Punishment by itself cannot produce the specifically evangelical kind of repentance. Doubtless it may lead men—it often does—to wish they had let sin alone and not made fools of themselves; but this is at best self-pity, not repentance in the least. When a man from whom nature is exacting the penalty of broken law confesses that he has himself to thank for his misery, that his sin has found him out, such confession by itself will not change him. It will not put him in a new relation to the Father. But precisely this new relationship *is* created by the right kind of response to the solemnising love of God made manifest in Jesus, above all in His death. In other words, the Father's mercy is held forth in an act which persuades men to be done with sin. The assurance that guilt is removed comes in a manner and through a medium which secures the breaking of sin's power. The aim of reconciliation, on any showing, is that in humility we should live with the Father on the footing of pardoned sonship; this aim is realised wherever men apprehend Christ—*vestitum evangelio*—with contrite faith.

The problem still remaining may perhaps be formulated thus: How does the reconciling work of God in Christ take effect for us and in us? The perfect obedience of Christ stands out as a great past fact; how can it benefit or savingly embrace others? How does His homage to the righteous will of God take us in? Assuming that He manifested the holiness and love of God, that He fulfilled all righteousness, echoing the Father's condemnation of sin and sharing the

Father's grief for it—may we come to be involved and have our own share in it? Can His response to God's judgment become ours? What lets us into partnership with it before God, and gives a worthy meaning to the statement that we are forgiven "for Christ's sake"?

I suggest that, so far as may be, we best elucidate this problem by viewing the cross of Christ as a sacrifice, in which by faith we partake.

It has been urged that the conception of sacrifice is sub-Christian in quality, and has no further relevance to what we see in Jesus. But it is difficult to understand why sacrifice alone, among the great and immemorial religious ideas, should be insusceptible of a higher and completely spiritual meaning. Prayer too may take higher and lower forms; yet there may be a perfect sacrifice, as there may be perfect prayer. As a fact, even in the Old Testament it is one of the salient characteristics of sacrifice that as a method or institution it is a Divine gift. The whole conception of sacrifice in reality falls under the category of revelation; this is the way in which Jahweh has made known His desire to be approached; and when it is offered in the right way, the worshipper effectually draws near to God. It is not a device contrived by men, through which God is propitiated in the heathen sense; it is a means to cover sin from His sight which God provides. The initiative is with Him. No one will suggest to-day that Christ's death is interpretable by the light of detailed prescriptions in Leviticus; yet even there a spiritual principle may be struggling into visibility. Often when people speak of Christ's sacrifice, perhaps deriding His death in that character, they appear to suppose that the self-offering of Jesus is being viewed as a tangible inducement requisite to persuade God to forgive. Nothing could be more unlike the New Testament. If Jesus' death is a sacrifice, then the sacrifice originates with God. It is a medium through which a well-grounded assurance of pardon is conveyed to the penitent. In Jesus the self-giving of God to man and the self-giving of man to God meet and absorb each other. "Through eternal Spirit He offered Himself without blemish to God."

Sacrifice, then, as exemplified at its furthest limit in Jesus, is initiated on God's side. Next—still eliciting the principle to which Old Testament thought at its height points forward—we must note that sacrifice consists in the offering to God of what is ultimately identical with our personal being, an offering which can only be made complete in death. In its application to Jesus, this means that *His* sacrifice was primarily inward; it was an unseen self-oblation in mind and will. In Christ's dying there was an absolute surrender of life, of Himself, to that Divine will which made His experience a manifested judgment upon sin. On the other hand, this surrender was not simply mental; it was expressed in act, in accepted destiny, in the appointment of the Father bowed to at whatever cost; it was an inward mind clothing itself with the vesture of suffering up to and including death. It is misleading, as well as altogether unlike the concrete thought of Scripture, to take the artificially refined position that Jesus' actual death was somehow a fortuitous concomitant of a sacrifice already complete within; which is as inept as to say that a poem *is* the thought it embodies. A poem is thought or feeling taking shape in noble words, apart from which there is no poem at all; so the sacrifice of Jesus is obedience vested in that act, at once inward and outward, in which He gave the life needed by the Father's reconciling will. And it is equally misleading to speak exclusively of the shedding of blood at Calvary, as just so much physical torment, in forgetfulness of the fact that it was the spirit underlying and expressed in the sacrifice that gave it all its worth.

Throughout we have sought to understand how the essential mark of Christ was utter self-identification with the sinful whom He forgave. And this chosen oneness with sinners, evinced at His baptism and elsewhere, came to a head in death. But such identification with us on His part involves consequences for Him, and it involves consequences no less for us. It was not as any isolated or separate individual, disowning responsibility for others, that He gave Himself at last. For us, with us, He there bowed under the Father's judgment on sin, confessing the sinfulness of wrong and its utter evil in God's sight. His bowing thus, in perfect love, *was* His sacrifice. And what we do by faith is to conjoin ourselves with Him, before God, in that momentous doing and suffering. Nothing less than this is the implicit meaning of faith. We take His confession as our own, pronouncing our Amen to His utter acceptance of the righteous will of God. By faith we drink of His cup and are baptised in His death for sin. The man who by faith unites himself to Christ upon the cross, numbering himself with the Redeemer in the sacrifice which that death was in God's sight because animated by God's Spirit; the man who submits in Christ to the condemnation of sin there manifested and borne by love, and who with Christ and in Him affirms his self-abandoning homage to God's holy will—this man is right with God. Such a sacrifice or self-giving he could not have made by himself or for himself, but he can identify himself with the perfect sacrifice; for what is original in Jesus may be derivative in us. When he does so, he exhibits the mind and spirit of perfect sonship, which alone is satisfying to the Father's heart.

Thus a true and worthy meaning can be found in the phrase, "forgiven for Christ's sake." It of course does not mean that Christ propitiated God, or by the atonement moved Him to remit our wrong; which would be to use the cross to hide God rather than reveal Him. So long as our thought of God remains imperfectly Christianised, we shall have perpetually to reiterate the truth that the love of the Father is the fount of all redemption. The atonement is the manner, necessary to His love, in which His pardon is given.

There is a partial analogy to God's reception of us for Christ's sake in the fact that one man receives another for the sake of a friend, intimately related to both. The newcomer is admitted to good-will because his connexion with that intermediary vouches for his spirit and temper. This may possibly be hinted at by the words put in Jesus' lips: "The Father Himself loveth you, because ye have loved me."[9] Christ takes us with Him, as it were, into a communion with God. His value to God stretches over and covers those who have become His disciples.

[9] John 16.27.
C.E.F.

None the less we feel such an analogy, even if drawn from the profoundest regions of human intercourse, to be lacking in that ineffable and transcendent element which distinguishes religion from morality. For this we must turn to the great conception of Union with Christ, as it appears in Pauline and Johannine thought. All Christianity resides in the two companion truths: God in Christ for us, we in Christ for God. The second of these concerns us now. It is part of Christian experience, at its highest, that what may perhaps be designated an "organic" connexion is felt to subsist between Christ and His people; the idea is one to which the New Testament constantly returns, and which has gathered round itself the sympathy of many saints. The wisest theological reflection has probably been aware that the conception as a whole will scarcely bear intellectual analysis, but becomes significant and luminous only in the loftiest moments of believing insight. On any other terms Union with Christ may degenerate into a cheap and superficial phrase, which does not so much illumine as obscure and which inevitably provokes a purely negative and desolating criticism. We need not therefore attempt to *prove* that Christ and sinful men can be united in that close and living personal fellowship indicated by the New Testament picture of Christ as Head of His Body the Church, or by St. Paul's unforgettable words: "There is now no condemnation to *those who are in Christ Jesus.*" But that this union is fact appears to be vitally bound up with the plain circumstance that we find ourselves taking to Christ an attitude which is specifically religious, and that in the Christian life, as the saints have lived it, it transpires that Christ is not isolated from Christians, but one with them and they with Him. In the relation to Him created by faith, the supposed isolation of one personality from another is somehow mitigated and overcome; and, without ever a thought of mystical absorption, we are able in living adhesion to transcend ourselves, and, abandoning self, commit our life to Him. Either the Christian religion has been a mistake from the first, or this inexpressible thing is fact. And to be forgiven "for Christ's sake" means, in this light, that we being one with

Christ, God sees us so, and in His great love and righteousness acknowledges us so. He receives, despite their sin, all those who in virtue of being thus in spirit united to His Son are satisfying to His fatherly mind.

This mode of stating what is involved in reconciliation and forgiveness does, I think, fairly meet the common objections to the doctrine of atonement that in quality, and considered as an arrangement, it is thoroughly immoral. How, it is said, can we worthily conceive the transference of ethical responsibilities from one person to another? And it is only too certain that not infrequently the doctrine has been so put, in sermon or hymn-book or theology, as to invite and more than half justify the reproach. If, however, we make Union with Christ, in its profound New Testament sense, our point of departure, there can be no question of our guilt being externally imputed to Christ, and His righteousness as externally to us. It is a case rather of spiritual and willed self-identification with Jesus Christ the righteous, making us by no fiction but in actual will and spirit right with the Father. If it be the truth, as we have seen, that Christ's sacrifice consisted in the perfect surrender of Himself to God, in obedience that merged at last in death, if His self-offering was His dying acquiescence in the loving Divine condemnation of sin present in His pain, this is not a sacrifice which makes our sacrifice needless; it is one, rather, that makes it possible. As united to Him, we can even perceive Christ to have been our Substitute, doing that for us which we could not have done for ourselves, and which, since He has done it, we have no need to do over again. He was the pathfinder for the sinful to the Father, and one pathfinder suffices. But we are saved only as in spirit we join ourselves to His act and suffering. That adherence to Him in faith ushers us into communion with God. Thus atonement construed in the light of Union with Christ, so far from ministering to ethical laxity, means that the sinner who has admitted Christ to heart and life has now within him the living principle of radical goodness. To take Christ for pardon and to take Him for holiness are one thing. The moral resources of life now abide in that Other, the partner of our spirit. This is something we may experience but never can explain; and the counter-assertion of this man or that other that he knows nothing of any such experience avails nothing to disprove its reality.

One thing more may be said. By making Union with Christ central and determinative in this matter of forgiveness and its conditions, we do justice to a spiritual instinct which declares that by no possibility can we be saved outside ourselves. The crucifixion as an event of bygone history does not reconcile. The merely given fact of Jesus' death may leave us untouched and estranged. Somehow the virtue of that sacrifice must come to be within us. There was a spirit in it which must become our spirit if we are to be the sons of God. In His death at the hand of sinners Christ was the complete revelation of the Father's holy love; but the reconciliation thence arising is not, as has often been affirmed, something past and once for all finished. In a perfectly moral and spiritual religion, reconciliation can consist in nothing but the actual effectuation of fellowship between men and God, through seeking, costly Divine love on the one hand and its penitent reception by man on the other. Hence reconciliation, due to Christ's great act of love at Calvary, is still proceeding, as one after another men unite themselves by faith to the Representative who answered in their name. So we are pardoned " for Christ's sake " as being " in Him." Believers know Him as the sole Mediator and Surety of their reconciliation; as the source to which all reconciliation is traceable, and from which unceasingly it flows. His life, His passion, His death are the satisfaction not of incensed Deity, but of our guilty conscience, and of an ultimate necessity based deep in the nature of the Father's holy love.

It is no matter for surprise that at the cross supremely we should become aware of elements in Christianity which pass the limits of human speech and thought. All true religion enfolds that which is unfathomable, and the cross with the saving experiences it engenders is the focus of Christian religion. If we have stood beneath its shadow, if its aspect has touched and changed us, we too can bear witness to its ineffable significance; we now know that the mystery of goodness is greater by far than the mystery of evil. That the abyss between the Holy Father and us the sinful should have been crossed, from the farther side; that in Jesus the guiltless suffering of the righteous, and for us, should have put on its absolute and final form, leaving nothing undone by God that might be done, nothing unendured that might be borne—this is nothing of course, but a strange and unimaginable miracle. We cannot measure it, but we can drink in life from the thought of it; and its wonder, which no mind can compass or define, we can sing.

True, it cannot be assumed that the significance of the cross will be equally manifest, or indeed equally welcome, to all men or even all Christians. There are distinguishable stages in the appreciation of Christ and His achievement. A man may embark on the Christian life by taking Jesus as his example, and may derive from Him in that character an imparted faith and power which in a most real degree give victory over temptation. Christ thus far is in large measure only a new and homogeneous factor in his moral development, bringing his own higher impulses to fruition. But a deeper necessity may emerge. He may well be obliged to face the shattering discovery that all his moral efforts are vain and that, in the light cast by God, he now appears even to himself as one who, guiltily and unconditionally, has failed. In Christ's presence he learns, gradually or suddenly, the final truth about himself; and the revelation breaks him. It is in such hours of inexorable conscience, when in his lonely responsibility and acknowledged impotence a man has bowed his head and fallen on his knees, that "the word of the cross" can find its most effectual entrance. Nor will any message of reconciliation suffice which does not contain a worthy relief for this, our profoundest and sorest need.

CHAPTER X

THE EXPERIENCE OF BEING FORGIVEN

The characteristic faith of the New Testament preached anew by the Reformers, is a faith which sees the demands and accusations of conscience in a clear but dreadful light. The way to God for such beings as we are lies not through æsthetic impressions, or through submissions to authority which ethically are irrelevant; it lies through the sense of right and wrong. It appears indeed to be the will of God that no one can appreciate pardon, in the sense it bears in the Gospel, who is not on the way to recognising himself as a complete moral failure, between whom and the Holy One lies a deep, broad gulf. The inner oracle of man's heart, where there is spiritual sensitiveness, declares him polluted and unclean. And if God be holy, the place of the unclean must be far from God.

To the average man, doubtless, this is scrupulosity in an absurd degree. He sincerely thinks that much ado is being made about next to nothing. The more sensitive man, on the other hand, the man who for a month has tried to keep one single Divine command—say, the command to be wholly pure in thought, or to love God more than all else—cannot but confess that far from being what he ought to be in the sight of God, he is poles asunder even from his own ideal. What comes home to him, in hours of sober, clear-eyed self-scrutiny, is his intrinsic unfitness to live before God. He is evil, and evil cannot dwell with the Eternal. The attempt to live unbrokenly in the presence of God is bound under these conditions to be unendurably painful; something in fact that could not long be sustained but for the hope of better things.

So that to understand forgiveness we must take the relation of religion to morality on its deepest plane. By the creative will of God we have the moral law, the moral consciousness, at the core of our being; and in accordance with this our given constitution, it looks not merely altogether natural but positively obligatory that we should seek to win our place with God on the lines of moral achievement. Yet the harder we try, the more certainly we lapse into despair. Were it not that we have learned that the ways of God are not easy to argue about, we should tend to say that a Divine purpose is manifested here. I mean that if the universal experience of believers is any guide, it looks like God's intention that we should first make trial of our moral independence, and, failing utterly, should learn that righteousness and holiness belong to God only. Certainly it is mysteriously easy for the morally earnest man to grow proud of himself; and if it were to be laid down that the self-approval of a good conscience is never, even in the best men, untainted by worthless pride, I do not suppose that the assertion could be seriously refuted. If we are ever to be in a right—that is, a wholly filial—relationship to God, this self-satisfaction must be torn out by the roots. We must come with empty hands, content to owe everything to God, though it seems more than nature can bear thus to take all and earn nothing. To bring us to this point, the only possible starting-place, a sense of moral unworthiness is the indispensable prerequisite.

Quite simple experiences of the inner life may reveal us to ourselves.[1] It becomes plain that self-love, mixed with better elements, is at the roots of our being. However firm our self-control, the first reaction of which we became aware upon a sudden and cruel blow dealt us by a passer-by would unquestionably be one of hatred; the first emotion that filled our mind at hearing of the success of a rival would unquestionably be one of envy. We should recover ourselves promptly, no doubt; we should suppress the envy or hate; gradually our feeling might even pass into positive compassion or a pleased delight in others' good. But in the meantime, if we faced the truth, we should have seen deeper than before into the terrible make-up of our nature. It is a corrupt nature, the worst ingredients of which are undeniably

[1] Cf. Heim, *Das Wesen des evangelischen Christentums*, chap. vii.

beyond our own power and blaze up in sinful fire before ever we realise what is happening. By strong self-discipline, it is true, we can tame and train ourselves to decent behaviour in the presence of our fellows; but while action may be curbed, the struggle with the first involuntary spurts of feeling is all but unavailing. And as we face God, it becomes clear that in any case such violent and forced self-suppression can never satisfy His fatherly heart. What He asks is that we should love Him and our neighbour with all our heart—freely, gladly, unfeignedly. And this is worlds away from our actual state, it is like the marooned sailor's imagination of wife and child and home. Nothing that can be said, and said truly, of the good that is in a man can change the fact that this evil, so fierce and guilty, is also there.

Not until we have learned these things about our own heart, can we be said to know more than the crust or surface of ourselves. When the truth dawns upon us, it is all over with self-satisfaction; one of two things must ensue—either we must sink in ruin or we must find God.

There is but one way out: we are undone except as there is made good to us the utterly free forgiveness of God. And the state or attitude of thought, feeling and will in which we receive this inestimable gift is that which can only be designated by the two great words, Repentance and Faith.

There must be, that is, at once trust in the merciful goodwill of God and penitent revulsion from our personal evil. In responding to the Father, we both own and disown our past. We cannot reach out towards Christ and not (at least incipiently) hate our sins, any more than we can love candour and not abhor a lie. To see God in a new light is to change our estimate of all that we have been and are. It would be almost superfluous to argue the point, which is agreed among us.

That the attitude is one, although with these two aspects, is made fairly obvious by the teaching of Jesus. Religion for Jesus centred in faith, which He lived as well as taught, and which unceasingly He communicated to others. Little faith, fear, undaring prayer—He condemns these in the sense that

He views them as an unworthy response to the Father, and His call is for unqualified trust in God's adequacy to all man's need, for whole-hearted adhesion to Himself as the Father's representative. Yet it would be correct enough, statistically, to say that Jesus spoke more about Repentance than Faith; the *Logia,* for example, appears to use " faith " only twice. He assumes that there will be pain and shame felt over the evil repented of. But throughout, whether faith or penitence be emphasised, our Lord evidently has one and the same thing in His mind. We may call it " change of heart." The great instance where He exhibits its actual occurrence is the Prodigal Son; and how human a story it is, that of a man in whom repentance began with nothing more exalted than hunger! Also we can watch repentance at work in the parable of the Pharisee and the publican, which it is difficult to think Jesus told without great intensity of feeling.

As we read books about faith and penitence (and good books on that topic are not rare), two reflections are apt to suggest themselves. In the first place, our ideas of the spiritual attitudes so designated tend to be unduly static, insufficiently dynamic. Or, in plain English, we incline to view them as experiences completed as it were at a stroke— things fixed and finished, which can be all seen at a glance and reduced to black and white. Yet in reality they are living dispositions of the soul, to whose essence it belongs to move and grow, as by inherent quality. Their true character and value is discoverable rather from the direction to which they tend than from any transient or emotional manifestation in which they flash out. And again, we are perpetually being tempted to construct a model scheme of Faith and Penitence, even against our better knowledge, and to apply it pedantically by way of standard to each new instance. Thus questions are forced into prominence which gave immense trouble to Christian thinkers of a past age, and which of course *are* highly important once you assume that a certain regular programme of inward experiences has to be gone through. It was debated at great length, for example, which of the two, faith and repentance, comes first; whether repentance issues from apprehension of the Gospel or of the Law;

whether there may not be a preliminary and as it were introductory penitence which the Law evokes, but which is succeeded by a fuller and genuinely evangelical penitence that is the only thing worthy of the name. But the infinite variety of life scouts all such prescriptions. We can hardly venture on anything more than a generalisation such as this— Wherever you find a forgiven man, who, as forgiven, is living in fellowship with God and in reconciliation with men, you may be sure that in the past his spiritual life has come to exhibit two mobile and permanent companion tendencies— the tendency to take humbly from God, which is faith, and the tendency to judge and amend himself, which is penitence. One of the two may predominate at a certain age or under special conditions; but both will invariably be present, and each will feed and intensify the other. As he comes with empty hands to God revealed in Jesus, he will learn ever more profoundly his unworthiness of love so great; and as he judges his own life, the quickened sense of its selfishness and folly will force him back upon God's free love.

Repentance (to take it first), like every religious act, concerns the three cardinal modes of being conscious—knowing, feeling, willing. Sin is recognised, it is disliked, it is disowned. Recognition of sin by itself is not repentance; it may be defiance. Nor is sorrow for sin repentance, if it be alone in the mind; it may be remorse or despair. Abandonment of sin, by itself, may be no more than prudence. The regenerating fact is all three, as a unity, baptised in a sense of God's personal grace to the sinful.

The Shorter Catechism, to which the virtues of Scotsmen have occasionally been ascribed by sanguine natives, offers a noble reply to the question, what repentance is. " Repentance unto life," it answers, " is a saving grace, whereby a sinner, out of a true sense of his sin, and apprehension of the mercy of God in Christ, doth with grief and hatred of his sin turn from it unto God, with full purpose of and endeavour after new obedience." The knowing, the feeling and the willing, of which I have already spoken, are obviously present here. Where the " true sense " of sin comes from—whether it is called forth by acquaintance with Christ, or by a noble friendship, or by the painful or solemnising facts of life—is not stated; what is insisted on is its reality. But it is at least closely associated with "apprehension of the mercy of God in Christ"; which indicates that in all probability the authors would have agreed that the sense of our own badness and ill-desert stimulated by a realisation of God's presence in Jesus is likely to be sharper and more lasting than that due to our conceiving God simply as Moral Governor or Judge. It cannot be forgotten that the character of Jesus itself acts as the most searching of all criteria of sin.

These seventeenth-century thinkers have a look of being all but infallible on questions of what is called "experimental religion." In the present case, they perceived that in describing what goes on in the mind of one who is accepting the Father's forgiveness in Christ, they must on no account set up a narrowly conceived pattern of experience to which each penitent is expected to conform. They did not lay down that the consciousness of sin must be poignantly acute, or duly protracted, or accompanied by quaking terrors of conscience; in a plain manly way they declared that if the man was serious the sense of sin would be real. Nor did they assert that to have peace with God the penitent must believe a special theory of atonement; for them, the one thing needful is to apprehend the mercy of God in Christ. They gave no colour, either, to antinomianism, as though the forgiven were now chartered libertines who after obtaining pardon could act pretty well as they chose, with the certitude that if they should again happen to do wrong, more pardon could easily be had. They simply said that part of the mental content of true repentance is the resolve to stop sinning and serve God with a right intention.

This emphasis on the volitional aspect of repentance is of special value. Stress is laid, not on storms of feeling, but on the act of turning from sin. It is not only that God cannot pardon the man who intends to remain at his old level; such a man cannot take pardon. Hence all great evangelists have insisted strongly on reparation. In reference to the moral stringency of Jesus, which so impressed Zaccheus, Dr. W. M. Macgregor observes: "Preachers are apt in talking of the mercy of Jesus to forget that there is no mercy in allowing a mean and dishonourable man to go on in meanness; mercy to such a man requires that he should get the chance of escaping dishonour." After all, we lay hold upon God by the strongest thing in us, our sense of right; and evangelical religion is poisoned which loses this sense of the moral inexorability of God's claim. Without the abandonment of evil—in predominant desire and intention, that is, I do not say in achieved completeness—penitence may become nothing higher than a disease of feeling, with no more reality in it than the habit of self-disparagement indulged by some peculiarly vain men. The resolve, at whatever cost of humiliation or effort, to set things right, is a part of repentance; and although it is no doubt implied in a penitent's secret transactions with God, it dies out, and the reality of penitence with it, unless it is given practical embodiment and made explicit.

Two difficulties are often felt at this point. First it may be said: Why contend that repentant faith is a precondition of our being forgiven? Can there be conditions of any kind? Does true love wait on repentance, and especially love like that of God in Christ? Surely mercy on that scale transcends the offence, anticipating all movement on the transgressor's part, even that of compunction, and heaping its gifts on the unworthy without reserve. Anything else (it is argued) would be a timid and calculating love, very unlike the love of Jesus. The self-giving of love in pardon with unqualified generosity is itself the most powerful incentive for the evocation of penitence such as makes a repetition of the offence impossible.

With the intention usually in the mind of this objector there will, I think, be widespread sympathy; but he does not greatly help matters by his indiscrimnate use of terms. In reality, the objection rests of a confusion between love as a feeling or attitude, and forgiveness as an act. Certainly no one who had learnt religion from the New Testament would affirm that before *loving* an offender, you should first wait and see whether he is penitent. But loving and pardoning are not, as such, identical. Love is the creative capacity of pardoning, and the mainspring of its effluence; but it is not, simply and by itself, the decisive concrete act of restoring peace between estranged hearts. Love, just because it is love, and is the very nature of the living God, is affected by the entrance of sin; not in the least that it has ceased to be, but that, personal relationships having been affected the activity of love is affected too, and its activity is (so far) interrupted. A moral love, in short, must take the form of active antagonism to the sinful life, even though the personal affection is still there, constant and waiting. Now pardon is the establishment of right mutual relations; and mutual relations, of a personal kind, *cannot* be restored in absence of a willingness on both sides to have them rectified. As it has been put: "Forgiveness, like any other gift, may be refused; the will to forgive must meet the will to be forgiven."[2] Thus while love is the fount of all, pardon does not flow forth automatically but by free spiritual action. It is a specific application of love to a certain situation, and the kind of situation is determined not arbitrarily but by love's intrinsic nature. It is for this reason that pardon without penitence (if for the moment we assume its psychological possibility) demoralises, like indiscriminate charity. Even the offender feels it to be an instance of moral levity, too plainly signifying that the injured man has not really pardoned the fault at all, but merely tolerated it. And how far is toleration of evil from indifference? The effect on an unformed character of the repeated assurance of forgiveness without regard to penitence is undoubtedly to foster egotism and its bevy of attendant vices; and a single case of the enfeebled ruin consequent on such facile condonation affords a more damaging refutation of its claim to high virtue than all the arguments in the world.

It is however unnecessary to labour the point that forgiveness in the absence of repentance would demoralise; such forgiveness is by the nature of the case impossible. Pardon is not a thing, like money, which can be bestowed or withheld at random. As between God and the spirits He had made pardon is not a thing at all; it is His taking us back

2 White, *Forgiveness and Suffering*, p. 60.

into full, unhampered communion with Himself; it is His inauguration of a relationship between Him and us in which the perplexity and confusion of the bad conscience have vanished, and which in His purpose is characterised by mutual trust; for not only do we trust His loving good-will, but with incomprehensible grace He trusts even us to go out and be His representatives among His other children. And can it be thought that the existence of such communion of Spirit with spirit is independent of the inward attitude of either? Personality has been defined as "capacity for fellowship"; if sinful men are ever to enter upon fellowship with God they must acknowledge their unworthiness of love so great; and this truthfulness of mind is penitence.

It is of course this direct bearing of repentance upon God that gives rise to its specifically religious character. There may be a turning from sin which is in no sense turning to God. For the preacher, very specially, it is not enough by satire or invective to persuade his hearers that they have made fools of themselves and missed the happiness they might have had. Such handling of their need may produce a sense of degradation which is almost wholly self-regarding, or at best æsthetic. Repentance then becomes no more than an apology to ourselves. Men only repent as Jesus would have them do when their experience has an immediate relation to the Father, when it constitutes a fitness for a new relation to Him, when it opens the heart in the direction of His reconciling love and melts something of the hardness within. In the absence of this, not even the moral import of sin is appreciated. Sin does outrage our own nature; it does estrange self and neighbours; but even these truths are in part missed when we overlook its antagonism to the love of God. It is actually possible to conceive of a man who measures his own life by the moral beauty of Jesus and laments its deformity, who yet is not repenting "unto life" because of his complete unconsciousness of the fact that in this Jesus the Father is coming near to him in mercy. Penitence, in a word, is a reaction toward God produced at its highest by the demonstration afforded in Jesus of what sin is to God, and of the unimaginable lengths His love will go to reach and win the guilty.

Repentance unto life, moving as it must between conscience and God, is as lonely a business as dying. We sinners come face to face with God, in the final resort, one by one, though none of us has ever so come who had not been led *towards* God by Christian friends. To repent is a clear act of the spirit, not any ecstatic swoon or dim craving in the blood. Contrition must be as solitary as sin. Every man who has ever done a real act of penitence, who has looked up into the Face of wounded love and taken from the unseen hand that incredible but never-failing gift of pardon, knows that in the well-remembered hour God and he were alone together, and that the voice he longed to hear would have been drowned and lost in the tumult of common life. The will to face solitude thus is a prerequisite of having our sins forgiven. So narrow is the path to the mercy-seat, and back again, that two cannot walk abreast.

The penitential movement of the soul is also Faith. It is as we cast ourselves on God that the assurance of pardon comes home to us and that very definite inward state, "peace of conscience," gains reality within. To begin with, this involves that the religious value and momentousness of faith resides not in its psychological or reflex effects, but in the Divine object it apprehends; what saves is not faith *simpliciter,* no matter in what, but faith in God our Saviour. Indeed, it is just because faith invariably terminates on God in His character as faithfully and unchangeably Redeemer—to use old-fashioned terms, on the Promiser even more than His promises—that faith is never represented in the Bible as saving men by an inherent meritorious virtue. It is the condition of being taken into fellowship with God, as eating is the condition of being nourished. But the act of eating does not produce food, nor does faith give reality to God's pardoning grace. To speak of merit in such a case, as if we deserved to be forgiven because we believed that God was forgiving us, is preposterous. If I give a man money, he must of course take it if it is to belong to him; but the taking is not a performance I reward by bestowing the gift. To deny this is to turn experience upside down. Faith, for the mind of the New Testament, is the act in which the fundamentally right relation to God is actualised. Personal trust makes the trusting man righteous in God's sight; it is the attitude—in fact, the only attitude—which contents the Father's heart.

This truth that the apprehended object (or God) is that which imparts to the experience of faith its distinctive character, has further consequences. It vetoes, for example, the curious and really sub-Christian idea that we are forgiven by degrees. "Forgiveness," writes R. C. Moberly, "is strictly and absolutely correlative to what may be called the 'forgivableness' of the person forgiven"; and to this he adds that as there is, upon earth, no consummated penitence, so neither is there any consummated forgiveness. "It is not consummated perfectly till the culprit *is* righteous: and love does but pour itself out to welcome and to crown what is already the verdict of righteousness and truth."[3] We are pardoned, then, by instalments, in proportion as we are forgivable. This, we may fairly say, is either a truism or an error. If "forgivable" means simply "capable of being forgiven," no one will of course demur. We have already seen that penitence and faith are the spiritually necessary preconditions of our receiving Divine pardon; an unforgivable man, on these terms, is the man who neither repents nor trusts. But Moberly's allusions on the one hand to forgiveness inchoate and provisional and to forgiveness consummated on the other, clearly show that this is not his meaning. He envisages a forgiveness on God's part which is conditional, subject to revision, in a real sense precarious and asymptotic.

This notion, that when God forgives the sinful what He actually does is not to take them back to His heart, freely and unreservedly, but to take them on trial, is, I think, manifestly out of touch with so central a part of Jesus' teaching as the Parable of the Prodigal. So far from pardon being represented there as a matter of degrees, of the calculated less or more, we are shown once for all how it is the transcendent

[3] *Atonement and Personality,* pp. 56, 60-61.

property of love at the sight of penitence to break through the barrier of wrong, and run to meet the wrong-doer as he stumbles up the path, and bring him in, and robe him, and set him down at the table loaded with the feast of fellowship. That is a picture of forgiveness full and unqualified. No other conception appears ever to have been in the apostolic mind. And indeed, provisional pardon is an idea scarcely fitted to evoke a joy unspeakable and full of glory, or to inspire the tempted with unwavering courage. What the New Testament exhibits is a company of men proclaiming the infinitely glad and daring gospel that we sinners can have full salvation now, in the sense that now, and before we become better men, God will treat us, unreservedly, as His dear children. On the other hand, it is fatal to the exhilaration of Christian living if the reality of God's fatherly communion with us be made dependent on the growth of our acquired goodness. When character is thus taken as the ground of our acceptance by God, what is it but a new legalism? Writing to a friend about the *Life* of Pusey, to whose massive and exalted piety he pays tribute, Dale observes: "The absence of joy in his religious life was only the inevitable effect of his conception of God's method of saving men; in parting with the Lutheran truth concerning justification, he parted with the springs of gladness." God's love in Christ, in its full measure, is offered not to those merely who are believing enough, or penitent enough, or reformed enough in their lives. It is offered to all who will cast themselves on God, though it be with "faith as a grain of mustard seed." The earthly love that shows likest God's is never apt to put its penitent loved ones on probation, but rather accepts them just as they are. And our thoughts of God's mercy must be not less wide.

This may seem a doctrine that ministers to laxity or induces presumption, but, provided the nature and cost of the Divine pardon be realised, the effect ought to be of an opposite kind. Surely there is less presumption in taking my complete forgiveness from God's hand at the outset and always later, as a purely loving gift, than in coming to Him afterwards, at intervals, with the sense that I am now a better man and therefore fitter to be forgiven. Nothing more apt than this to breed self-consciousness could be imagined. The truth is, when securities for a good life are demanded from the sinful before forgiveness full and free is placed in their hand, the result is to turn Christianity into a form of morality rather than a religion.

The paradox that it is not the worthy but the unworthy that a pardoning God receives is a point indicated somewhat technically by Ritschl in his well-known monograph. He insists that God's judgment of forgiveness is not analytic but synthetic.[4] These formidable terms suggest a point of real importance. When we are on our knees in penitence, the inward question cannot but arise: What does God, the Holy One, think of us? Some real answer to this we must have if we are to live at peace with ourselves and the world. And if He receives us, if He will not cast us out but gives us a place in His fellowship, on what is this gracious estimate of us based? On our character, on what by good endeavour we have made of ourselves? Is it not rather on what His pure grace bestows? If we chose the first of these alternatives and held that God accepted us for our (in any degree) excellent character, at once our own badness would also confront us. In short, we should have to listen to the verdict of conscience on ourselves, and *that* would certainly insist that from a God who "marked iniquity" we should deserve no mercy at all. Thus, it turns out, the consequence of claiming that our good shall count with God is that our evil must count too. We cannot have it both ways; we cannot rank as self-made men when our virtues are in the scale, but, when our sins come uppermost, say to God: "Why didst Thou make me thus?" So that from the nature of the case forgiveness is a marvel that baffles all logic: God can recognise only those who feel that they are utterly unworthy of recognition. That the Holy One should receive sinners is to natural logic a contradiction in terms. But in this wonderful life of ours it is not quite unfamiliar. Something of the same paradoxical kind emerges as we have seen for a man who finds that he has won the love of a good woman—it is all of grace, he con-

[4] *Justification and Reconciliation*, p. 79 ff.

fesses, and nothing of desert. He has been gifted with a great new boon on which he had no claim. So it is here: the God who by His holiness shatters our claim to live before Him nevertheless by His love gives us a new life. And by the phrase " a synthetic judgment " this fundamental point is emphasised, that the forgiving grace of God does not presuppose our worth but calls it into being. His pardon is not a tribute to our character; it is not a function; rather it is a creative volition in which the Father affirms the real being of that which was not there apart from Him. In a word, He thereby inaugurates a new relation between Himself and unworthy men which is grounded not in their virtue, but in His pure and perfect grace.

But at this point someone may demur. Must there not after all be something *in men* which differentiates the forgiven from the unforgiven? How can you explain the simple fact that certain people do live with God on the footing of pardoned sonship, and others do not? That distinction cannot be rooted in chance, for Christianity is not a casual religion; it must be relevant to some quality or attitude in individual men. What then is it in a man which makes God forgive *him* but not his neighbour? Plainly, whatever it is, it must be something present in him now, not merely something yet to be. Now, if forgiveness be a miracle of grace, this question cannot be fully answered or disposed of; but we may go a certain distance towards answering it if we consider carefully the nature of penitent faith.

Faith, we have seen, is as it were the receiving surface for Divine pardon. Where it exists, the soul has awakened to reality; there is a new longing for righteousness; there is, deep down, a self-identifying with Jesus and all He stands for. But this means that while as far as personal identity goes the man still is continuous with his old being, in a yet profounder sense what he was has ceased to be. Though he might not dare to say it of himself, an omniscient onlooker might fitly apply to him the apostle's strange but triumphant words: " I live, yet not I, but Christ liveth in me." God's love in Jesus has changed the man transformingly. That is fact not one whit less than his old identification with self and evil was fact. And, in our stumbling fashion, we have no option but to say that God sees this. Indeed, in that which God sees it is the principal and determining fact; and there is a real relation connecting it with the Father's attitude to him now. Faith means admitting Christ to an inward union with your mind and heart and life. By God, who looks on the heart and sees things as they are, the man who has faith is seen as one with Christ, and thus, astoundingly but not immorally, is forgiven.

But the sinner so forgiven is still imperfect, it is urged. Undoubtedly he is; but why, it has been well asked, should we go on perpetually assuming that God can and will accept only what is perfect? Were it so, none could ever hope for pardon. We must remember the infinite significance of even the faintest believing contact with Christ; as one with Him, however imperfectly, we are become new men. Quantitatively, if we may employ so gross a term, the penitent sinner is and will always be unequal to his idea; qualitatively his attitude to God is now the one attitude of soul which the Father seeks in a child—he is willing to receive as a son receives. True, to the end there is mystery here for the man guided merely by moral principle; God does not treat the man as he deserves. But does love anywhere do that?

Already we have implicitly touched upon the next problem: How can we *know* that we are forgiven? Clearly if forgiveness counts for us as inestimably precious, we shall wish to be quite sure of it; it is therefore not surprising that the past debate regarding what is called "Assurance" has been long and spirited.

The best thing ever written about assurance is two sentences in one of Denney's books. "Nothing," he writes, "is more characteristic of Churches than their attitude to assurance, and the place they give it in their preaching and their systems of doctrine. Speaking broadly, we may say that in the Romish Church it is regarded as essentially akin to presumption; in the Protestant Churches it is a privilege or a duty; but in the New Testament religion it is simply a fact."

Allowing for the edge of epigram, this is sound and memorable.

The Roman thinker disposes of assurance in his own fashion; it is given, at all events for the moment of absolution, in the voice of the absolving priest. What seems most out of line with New Testament faith in this conception as a whole is not the interposition of the priest, as God's official representative, nor is it the demanded performance of meritorious satisfactions in penance; it is rather the belief round which the entire theory is built that with every new mortal sin the sinner forfeits his standing in grace; or, to put it otherwise, that with each voluntary transgression he has ceased to be God's true child and must regain his status by the pathway of penance. And this breeds the mood of painful suspense.

Nor could much comfort be drawn by the anxious-predestination. If the metaphysical predestinarianism of Augustine, Calvin, or the Synod of Dort be laid down as the foundation of theology, if, that is to say, the "elect" are a certain number of souls which can neither be increased or diminished, and if, consistently with this, the sovereignty of God be dwelt upon in abstraction from His fatherly love for all men, how natural that men should fall into doubts regarding the good-will of God to them personally! The question, "Am I one of the elect?" when asked by a timorous and self-distrustful heart, is a question that from this point of view is by no means sure of its answer.

Within the past two or three centuries different answers have been offered to the inquiry: How shall I be assured that God forgives me, and forgives me now? People have been advised, for instance, to consider their own increasing love for spiritual things, their undeniably good works, and the like. Yet it is difficult to see how this could help much; if they are persons of genuinely spiritual feeling, they must know that they cannot be really good without God, and the point at issue precisely is whether or not they are in fellowship with God. Ritschl counsels them to exert their faith in Providence, and assurance will return. As we shall see presently, this is valuable in a way, though not exactly for the point we are now considering, which is the ultimate ground of assurance rather than the pathway of experience by which we reach it. One thing, surely, is entirely clear: whatever it be that evokes assurance, it cannot be anything in ourselves, for it is just regarding ourselves that *ex hypothesi* we are in doubt. One man may say: I am sure that I belong to God, for I can remember a day when He vouchsafed me an overwhelming impression of His forgiving love. Another may say: God is mine and I am His; I know it, for I now love Christlike things to which once I was indifferent. But both are building their house upon the sand. Assurance must depend on present reality, not on past events; on what confronts us unchangeably, not on the soul with its ups and downs.

We can have no trustworthy guide here but the New Testament. It does not make two problems where there is only one. Assurance for apostolic men is not something alongside of faith as an added perfection; it is neither prior to faith and preparatory for it, nor subsequent to faith and derived from it; nor is it a privileged reward for what faith has achieved. It is simply the mark showing faith to be of the right kind. When we look believingly at God in Christ, where is the presumption in being quite sure of His compassion to the sinful? Can we be too sure of it, too trustful in claiming it for our own deep need? If then a man should say: I long to be reconciled to God, but a glance at myself unsettles me again and my felt unworthiness makes me unbearably doubtful whether He will receive me, our answer ought to be unhesitating. Get into the company of Jesus and into the atmosphere of compassionate love He bears with Him, and let this tell upon you. Stay in His presence, as St. Mark pictures Him; bring your mind in earnest to bear upon Him, as He lives, as He dies, and your heart will open to complete certainty that God is not casting you out. Forget yourself, and allow Jesus to make Himself so familiar that you know God's very self is touching you through His holy love. Thus we escape from subjectivity, as the New Testament invariably does, to the great fact of Christ and God's trustworthiness in Him.

But all this, it is very possible, may not happen in a flash; in many cases we may be sure it will not; and it is at this point that suggestions like those of Ritschl are helpful. He taught, we have seen, that the right method of obtaining assurance is to exert an active faith in God's providence, such a faith as exhibits itself in the patient bearing of hardship. On the main point this is scarcely adequate; for if assurance of the Father's grace has weakened, the resulting and characteristically Christian faith in providence will have weakened along with it. None the less Ritschl does point to an important truth. That truth bears not on the object or evoking cause of the faith that we are now forgiven—which must always be the redemptive self-manifestation of God— but on its experiential verification. The trust that God has received us cannot be verified by rehearsing an argument, by repeating or listening to words. The problem cannot be talked out, but it can be lived out. It is one thing to enter the relation of pardoned sonship; it is another to live oneself into the felt enjoyment of this wonderful new possession.

All kinds of experience, it is plain, will minister to the verification of a man's conviction that God has given him His fellowship. But two, in especial, may be singled out. In the first place, the reality of our communion with God in prayer will be its own evidence. We discover, as a simple fact, that we have access to the Father and that our petitions are heard. Trusting God for power to destroy sin, we find that sin is destroyed. No convulsion of our nature occurs, no voice peals through us proclaiming absolution; but our communion with God, once begun, continues and deepens. Secondly, we gradually waken up to the fact—than which nothing in life can be more humbling—that God is permitting us to co-operate with Himself in doing good. He is giving us a share in the tasks of His Kingdom. He is using us as instruments for a purpose greater than ourselves, and in the process is training us in freedom from the world and mastery over its temptations and fatalities. These experiences, and others like them, confirm and nourish the assurance that our sins—for we sin daily—are by God's unwearied grace not being permitted to separate us from Him. Not that we base our hopes upon them, otherwise our certainty of a gracious God would wax or wane in accordance with our success and failure. The foundation-stone of faith that can be lived by is, always and unconditionally, the love of God in Jesus Christ our Lord.

CHAPTER XI

THE MORAL INSPIRATION OF FORGIVENESS

The most crushing evil under which men suffer is the guilt of sin. When we speak of redemption, therefore, we are able to say in advance that nothing can possibly be of such cardinal importance as that we should be redeemed from the fatal load of guilt, from that sense of felt distance from God, of dread and concern, of dull, helpless resentment by which the guilty are plagued. In the foregoing pages it has been argued that pardon is the primary thing in the Christian gospel, the gift which leads in all other blessings by the hand. It precedes and by its nature implies the breaking of sin's power. The heart must be thrown open by the welcomed certainty of forgiveness before the long process of what has usually been called sanctification can begin, and the evil promptings of our lower nature be gradually subdued. Here lies the secret of the profoundest moral catharsis and of revulsion from evil. Forgiveness is the experience by which we pass from Christian truth to Christian duty.

We must now seek to understand how new resources for increasing moral victory flow, naturally and intelligibly though none the less spiritually and supernaturally, from a man's reception of pardon through the love of God in Christ. It has been wisely said that almost all really new ideas have a certain aspect of foolishness when they are first produced. And to the moralist it must always have a sound of folly to say, in the sense of the New Testament, that the only good man is in point of fact the man whose heart has been made tender, and his conscience sensitive, by submitting to have his sins forgiven. Yet pardon, in its Christian meaning, has the background of the one ethic which pierces to the heart of moral experience. The sense of it, far from being a barren and inert emotion, running its course idly within the mind, is a fruitful and energetic conviction, charged as no other conviction is with explosive power to change lives and destroy social wrong. There is no intention to deny the mystery of grace, as the saving personal influence of God, when we say that the connexion between pardon and right character can be made psychologically luminous, and that motives called into being by the life-giving knowledge that God is our friend can be exhibited in their transparent clearness. It is demonstrable that from the new consciousness of the Father engendered by a wonderful experience there flows, with a moral inevitability, a new attitude to life and its tasks, inward blessedness, confidence, love, obedience and courage. Faith cannot but translate itself into action—action which is the spontaneous outcome of a will now in principle one with the will of God.[1] It is indeed no enigma that goodness should issue from peace with God. Were it otherwise, our intelligence would be put to confusion by the discovery that we were living in a moral chaos.

[1] When we speak of right living as the *spontaneous* outcome of faith, this is not to say that obedience is either immediate or effortless. In such a chapter as the present, the perspective of growth in Christian character is necessarily foreshortened, and principles are chiefly in view. Faith gives the impulse to obey as well as the power, yet this impulse may have to fight and overcome other impulses. So for Keats poetry must always come " as naturally as the leaves to a tree, or it had better not come at all "—and this, no matter how arduous the thought, how desperate the suffering out of which it was created. There is no nature-process, moving automatically. It is tempting to say that the highest Christian life will be effortless, yet this will depend on circumstances and the particular allurements that have to be resisted. There was struggle in Gethsemane.

Especially in social relationships, faith is confronted by an ever-growing and widening moral task. The conception of duty, as it becomes increasingly clear, becomes also increasingly intricate and exacting. The more we know of the social ideal, the harder it is to be morally adequate; and there is nothing in the Gospel which relieves us from the difficulties of sustained reflection on the part Christian insight is called to play in industry, commerce, civic government, national politics, international affairs.

Thus while " good works " may in part become more and more easy of performance, this itself implies a struggle after an ever-expanding moral ideal, which, as it is progressively attained, relegates the lower reaches of activity to what may be called unconscious habit.

Forgiveness as an experience means at least that a new gladdening and commanding idea of God is planted decisively at the centre of our inward life. Now, we have good ground as psychologists for saying that ideas do move us; let them obtain possession of the mind and corresponding results will follow. If they are permitted or encouraged to hold the field and develop themselves, action ensues. Great ideas, above all, have their effects and influence further living. Quite apart from religion, they can modify and control our appetites and desires; and it has generally been allowed that religious ideas are amongst the most potent and irrepressible forces in human life. Hence we are entitled to start with the presumption that the assurance of Divine pardon, if held steadily, will influence conduct deeply in positive ways. What these ways are, and the reason for them, we have still to ask; but the general character of the human mind and its normal modes of working are enough to indicate that they will neither be negligible nor obscure. The conviction that God forgives sin, and that He is ours, will, like other convictions, be accompanied and sustained by the emotional dispositions that befit its meaning.

Nor ought it to be forgotten that in inquiring precisely how and why to be made pardoned is to be made good, we are engaged not in speculation but in the scrutiny of fact. Unless men are incapable of forming true judgments about their fellows it is certain, first, that innumerable persons have been observed to become noticeably better in character after (by their own account) they had taken pardon from God's hand, and secondly, that they themselves would unhesitatingly have traced this release from the shackles of evil to their apprehension of the Father's love. What we have before us, accordingly, is not a merely curious hypothesis but an actual condition of affairs; we are trying to explain what happens constantly, not raising the question whether conceivably it could happen. Our point of departure is the circumstance that trust in a forgiving God does have ennobling effects, and that of this some intellectual account can be given.

The supreme secret of goodness, which carries all else within itself, is of course the new fellowship with God on which the pardoned man has entered. This of itself makes him a new person and turns the world he inhabits into a new and astonishingly hopeful place. To be in filial contact with the Father has once for all abolished the painful and disabling *solitude* of the moral conflict; it affords the certainty of an inward presence by which moral weakness will be sustained because the deepest springs of joy have been unsealed. I feel that at this point our thoughts about God cannot be too human. Every great friendship is felt by us as a fount of animating and uplifting power, and the first question we ask regarding a person of uncertain or immature character is whether he has good friends, whose stronger nature will fortify and inspirit his efforts to be brave and true. And the most important thing about the forgiven man, from the standpoint of ethics, is just that his eyes have opened to the amazing truth that God is his Friend, who can be trusted never to let him down. Whatever his temptations, whatever the weakness bequeathed by previous failures, God is still there, unchanging in faithful love as well as in exacting stringency of precept, so that never again need he face alone the onset of evil. That friendship, that communion, that overshadowing presence—whatever be the theological terms used for its designation—have changed his moral prospects utterly. For the first time he has learnt from Jesus, most of all from His passion, what God is, and is for him; and the perception has recreated him in moral being.

If we know much about ourselves, the thought of being good does not, apart from God, merely attract us; in part it scares and depresses us. We know that in following the ideal we cannot wholly count upon ourselves; our worse nature betrays us, stabbing us in the back at the moral crisis like a treacherous house-mate. The garrison of the beleaguered hold is torn by civil war. But to have touch with Jesus, as the self-revealed love of God, gives us back our nerve because amongst other things it gives us inward unity. We have grown aware at once that the great Companion of man has offered and made ours a fellowship which He will never withdraw, so that henceforward the nature of things is with us, not against us, in our struggle; and that it has thus become possible for us to gather all the impulses and desires of life round one all-commanding aim, so that we have emerged from the bewildered distraction of the past into an inward harmony of being. It scarcely needs saying that this harmony, born of reconciliation, is far from being fully actualised from the outset, and is given at first only in principle. But then it *is* so given; and we have simply to keep ourselves under the conditions which led to its first bestowal in order to secure that it shall steadily gain predominance over our inward life. Nothing, in short, can give us inward peace, " a heart at leisure from itself," but surrender to One who both humbles us by His holiness and accepts us in His unimaginable love, One in whose presence we feel even more vividly our powerlessness for life, yet are filled with a new courage to live.

All this may be put otherwise. Everything in the growth of character depends on where our centre of interest is placed—in self or in what is not self. The morality which rests on and revolves round self has upon it the sentence of death. But no man can react honestly to the message of Divine forgiveness without *eo ipso* renouncing self and giving Christ, in the familiar phrase, " the right of way through his life." The effects of the Gospel are in tune with its meaning; and its meaning is that it brings men the knowledge of something that God has done, and bids them rejoice in a salvation He has wrought. It thus sets men free from the chains of their past, transfers the centre of their expectations and opportunities from themselves to God, and calls them to a life of unrestricted fellowship with Him. It has frequently been argued that Christian religion is self-centred, interested and prudential; but the truth properly understood is simply that apart from such religion of the loftiest kind—in which the majesty of God's holy love overshadows all—morality cannot attach itself to what stands sublimely at once above the individual and above society, and evokes the reverent and self-abandoning homage of the soul. To owe everything to God, as the pardoned do, is to have taken the first decisive step in escape from self-absorption—even though that may have been the not ignoble self-absorption of seeking out ways in which the inner independence and harmony of the individual soul may be maintained. But when the focus of a man's interest has been definitely occupied by the great friendship and transcendent claims of God who has blotted out all his offences, a new principle of moral health has been implanted. And it is this emergence from egoistic isolation, this opening gateway into the immeasurable world of Goodness, Truth and Beauty, all dependent on a Father who makes His children free of its wealth, which renders a man for the first time capable of wholly unreserved fellowship with others.

One simple and conclusive fact of which we ought not to lose sight is this, that the man who has known the joy of being received to God's mercy despite his sin has thereby awakened to a new ideal for his own life, since he personally is bound to exhibit to others the loving mercy shown to himself; and that this vision of a new and lofty ideal is itself an immensely important moral event. The recognised obligation binding him to the same exhaustless love as God has shown, the call to forgive others as God for Christ's sake has forgiven him, does, if reflected upon, convey a fresh and undreamt-of conception of what moral practice may become. We have now no choice but to review our own conduct and character in the light of what the cross has proved God's nature to be. Only as we endeavour to walk in this light, this love great enough to take the unworthy to its heart, can we have true fellowship with God and with each other. The forgiven man, conscious that God has not dealt with him legally by reckoning up individual offences and balancing against them individual merits but in the way of pure, unbought grace, realises that in his neighbourly relationships he too is summoned by the Father to display, not the calculating temper of moral prudence merely, but a certain spirit—the love that never fails. He is beginning to learn not simply that in morality fellowship is the one thing needful, but also that fellowship, if real, is costly.

This truth, that the consciousness of pardon generates a new moral ideal, is of singular moment; and it is of importance that its meaning should not be misapprehended. It does not mean, for example, that the individual's previous moral experience has now lost its value. On the contrary, we have repeatedly made the point that nothing except a serious and unreserved acknowledgment of moral obligation can prepare men either to seek or to appreciate forgiveness. As the Gospels show, the ethical demands of Jesus, and above all the spectacle of His goodness, stirred those to long for pardon whom the rigid, metallic exhortations of the Pharisees had left cold and impenitent. So too within the Christian life, moral precepts are so far from having lost their point, that we are perpetually being stimulated by the sharp demands of particular commandments to inquire whether we do in fact possess that longing for personal fellowship which alone can enable us to fulfil them as they ought to be fulfilled. And as we have unceasingly to confess that here we are unpardonably at fault, we are spurred on unceasingly to seek more and more of the sheerly indispensable spirit of love. To have grasped a new moral ideal, and to have found contact with One from whom we can gain increasing power to attain, is to have had our moral resources indefinitely multiplied. It is once for all to be shaken out of self-satisfaction. Ethical complacence is impossible for the man who thinks often of Jesus Christ. Were he for a moment to imagine that forgiveness renders moral precepts superfluous, it would prove his failure to reflect at what cost and for what end forgiveness had been imparted. Were he to dream that moral precepts and compliance with them made forgiveness unnecessary, it would show that temporarily he had forgotten how august and exacting goodness is. Or to put it otherwise, the Law *in* the Gospel is more stringent by far than Law apart from Gospel. It may seem easier because Jesus formulated it so briefly: "Thou shalt love the Lord thy God with all thine heart, and thy neighbour as thyself." All the endless multiplicity of legal enactments has dropped away. But examined more closely, the moral task has now become infinitely more exalted. The effect of Christ, always, is to confirm the moral demand, rendering it more inward, more spiritual, more searching. We have seen God in Him, and know as never before what we ought to be. And in this sight, this knowledge, there is a constraint that goes to produce a new morality.

All this is the more true, because the production of morality is not the immediate purpose of forgiveness. Paradox though it may sound, it is strictly the fact that the ethical influence of pardon is all the more fruitful and abiding that its primary aim is not to affect character but to rectify our personal relationship to God. When religion has been presented as valuable chiefly for the ordering of life, it has been misrepresented. This obviously holds true, for instance, of worship. Nothing so tends to destroy the very sense and soul of worship as preoccupation with the ethical benefits to be derived from it. Men cannot adore except as they lift up their eyes and abandon themselves with awe, solemnity and tenderness to Him that loved them with a love passing knowledge. Their first impulse, their controlling impulse at each moment, must be that of response to an unspeakable gift which went far beyond all they could ask or think. "There is nothing so characteristic of the Church's life as doxology." When the bearings of worship are taken from any other standpoint, side-glances being thrown perpetually at the ethical profit of the worshipper or the impression made upon a gazing world, justice is never done to the central motives of adoration; and what is even more relevant now, the ethical profit itself is missed. No act not done for its own sake can react beneficially on character. Worship, like poetry, is not *for* something else; it is its own justification, it embodies an absolute and independent value. There is an epigram to the effect that to get pleasure you must forget it; similarly, worship loses its savour and grows ethically barren when we persist in asking ourselves whether it is yielding moral excellence. Leave the soul to itself in presence of the Eternal, and it will bow down in simple adoration. There is no gain for character to be had on any other terms, no elevation of feeling, no release from self, except as the sense of God fills our thought and our souls kindle under it in reverent and impassioned praise. It is the same with the consciousness of being pardoned. Here too the saying holds good that "conduct is a by-product of religion—an inevitable by-product, but not the main point." Just because men do not seek forgiveness primarily in order to become better men (any more than they fall in love to improve their character), but to regain touch with God and have peace with Him, ethical consequences ensue which would elude them to the end if sought directly. The grateful surrender to God which forms a living element of faith in His pardoning love creates goodness by the way; it is a well-spring yielding the richest and most enduring moral incentives by which a righteous life is rendered not only possible but certain. Not the torturing or hypochondriacal manipulation of the soul calls out the Christian virtues, but the thankful contemplation of One whose love lifts up and comforts the soul that His holiness had cast down.

These are truths which hold good for the continuance of the Christian life no less than for its inception. To be a Christian is to prolong the line which the first movement of faith began to trace. Take, for example, religious discipline. Now the idea of discipline is at bottom an acknowledgment of the fact that there is such a thing as Christian character, and that the followers of Christ are bound to take steps to secure its existence in themselves. It is incumbent on us to make a sustained effort to raise life to the Christian level and to keep it there.[2] But the impulse and dynamic necessary for this object can only be found in the same means as went to initiate Christian experience. It is still the same realisation of God as holy and absolving love which will refine and sanctify. You cannot convert men by thoughts of gospel, then form them by thoughts of law. Steady pressure can be kept upon conscience, life can be raised above moral common-place, only as we live within the influence of God's forgiving mercy. We need not think about it all the time, but we shall always know it is there; and to know this will make a whole world of difference. We do not really make most of the moral conflict or of neighbourly service by contemplating ideals, as if this were the surest method of escaping from self and living nobly. To give ideals by themselves the com-

[2] Cf. Denney, *The Church and the Kingdom*.

manding place in thought is to foster in ourselves the notion that nothing decisively significant has yet been achieved, and that we have to achieve it. There is more inspiration by far in the vision of God, in the remembrance of great things He has done for the sinful. That vision, that remembrance, is our one ground for optimism. It is as we open the mind more fully to His cleansing love that our responsibility for Christian character will come home to us more subduingly, in company with great motives impelling to its attainment.

Thus from every side we are consistently led to the insight that it is fellowship with the God of holy and sin-remitting love which forms the fertile secret of Christian goodness. To have seen in the face of Jesus Christ the revolutionising certainty that despite our evil God is ours and we are His, is to have embarked on an assured career of hope. In such a faith some great convictions are implicitly contained: two especially may be singled out. In the first place, as has already been noted, we are now inwardly united to One whose love is constantly available, with participating sympathy, in our desperate emergencies. Temptation can be borne and can be repelled, if God is with us. A man will stand up and close the dock gates, pushing back the ocean with his two arms, because behind him are all the resources of hydraulic engineering; evil, too, in its darkest shape, he can confront with the certainty of triumph if the resources of God are within his reach. He now knows that his prospects are dear to the Father who gave Christ that men might have forgiveness. In the second place, the Power upon whom we can reckon is omnipotent over the world. Alike in the individual life and in society ethical progress, in the last resort, depends upon trust in a power which will not suffer the fruits of sacrifice and effort to be swept away by the annihilating forces of change; a trust that will inspire men equally to break with evil habit and to defy the tyranny of social custom and assail the established order of things. Thus the supreme power of God is the background of unshaken moral confidence, for self and for others. As we survey those who are troubled in their minds, not concerning God's love—of that Jesus is the full guarantee—but concerning themselves, their waywardness and infirmity of purpose, we cannot but ask, What is going to banish those fears which are crippling their endeavours after self-mastery and robbing them of joy? What is going to countervail the doubts springing from their sense of weakness? Nothing will do it, as experience proves, but the conviction that for the inward struggle we have an omnipotent Ally, who will take our victory as His concern. But *sinful* men can gain this unshakable conviction only from the assured knowledge that this omnipotent God, who also is the Holy One, has *forgiven* them. There is an almighty Power, to whom belong the moral issues of life and death; in Jesus we have met this Power, and found Him forgiving all our iniquities.

So far then is pardon from being a moral sedative, that it is the most powerful stimulus to self-forgetful goodness of which we have any knowledge. It is when we know our sin forgiven that we have the heart to fight and forsake it. We search in vain for any inducement to right living which is comparable to the liberating and inspiring sense that the Father in mercy has taken us into His personal communion and let us see in Christ that we have unrestricted access to Himself. Once for all the sinner has thereby been lifted out of the region of law—which never touches the heart, and therefore cannot unseal the richest springs of moral energy—into the sphere of the felt love of God. An atmosphere is now about him in which aspiration can unfold. In St. Paul's great words: "What the law could not do, God did, sending His own Son."

We are perpetually being assured that this way lies ethical laxness, and that the one effective method of preventing a thoughtless or a deliberate antinomianism is the method of moral exhortation or even menace. Men obey most eagerly, it is held, when they hear constantly the bracing threats of the commandments. But it is not so. A suggestive analogy may be found in the institution of slavery on its economic side. On the assumption that the object of industry is the maximum of production, the problem for solution was, by which method can this object be attained most fully, by slave labour or free? In Greece, in Rome, even in the modern world a hundred years since, the question was answered unhesitatingly by many in favour of slave labour. Yet emancipation had only to be accomplished to prove that, economically no less than socially, freedom was incalculably the more advantageous of the two. And thus it is in religion. Let men believe that they must purchase union with God by hard, grim toil, as bond-slaves of heaven, and their hands will sink in despair and weakness. But tell them that in Christ they are the forgiven children of God our Father, and grateful wondering love will call out a wealth of devotion of which, on any other terms, it would have been useless to dream.

It is a grateful love; and to the psychologist, interested in motivation, gratitude must always appear a profoundly important element in the situation we are now contemplating. The impelling reason why people who are conscious of owing everything to God do one thing and leave another undone, will in countless instances be found in a deep though perhaps quite unobtrusive thankfulness. They have been ushered into a new world of hope and gladness; the Spirit itself now bears witness with their spirit that they are the children of God; the cruel hard weight of felt guilt has been lifted off: and they wish to make some return. Let it not be forgotten that this sense of thankful indebtedness is itself ennobling. Psychologically, we cannot keep up gratitude except to one who we feel has really benefited us. Often, it may appear as if we gave our heartfelt thanks without discrimination; but if, in ministering to our pleasure, a seeming benefactor has really done us harm, and we know it, the flow of gratitude is checked and inevitably changes into bitterness. But gratitude to a mother, a wife, a hospital nurse, a loyal friend is of itself morally elevating; it raises us, so long as it is felt, to a higher plane of being. Of this, clearly, gratitude to God in Christ is the limiting case. He has redeemed us at so great a price, He has drawn us so close to Him, that we are our own no longer. Nothing so good morally can happen to a man as the habitual consciousness that he belongs to one higher than himself. It is a feeling, of course, which is possible only towards God, or One in whom God is personally present; for as Lincoln put it, "no man is good enough to possess another man."

The obverse side of such gratitude as animates the genuinely Christian life is fear. By many thinkers the notion is assiduously fostered that fear, as such, is unworthy of a place in the believing mind, and that actions or forbearances motived by fear are therewith stamped as unfitting. But this is a simple misapprehension. Fear, so far from being always ignoble, is a temper well befitting many occasions. If I fear by a certain course of action to forfeit the respect of those I venerate, my emotion is ethically worthy. And if I fear sin, lest by indulgence I should lose fellowship with God, hurt the Church He has redeemed, and weaken my own power to serve men, my feeling is the natural consequence of a right attitude to these definitely evil things. In practice, we are much more deeply influenced by good people than by goodness as an abstraction; we shrink from losing their respect much more than we abhor this or that vice in and by itself. For here "persons influence us, voices melt us, looks subdue us, deeds inflame us." And in religion similar effects flow from a vividly realised personal relationship to God, such as is naturally associated with the experience of being pardoned. Loving gratitude to Christ will constrain to service which other motives could not have engendered; fear to lose contact with Him will expel temptations that might have carried the day. The part which feelings play in the conscientious regulation of life is of high importance. A recent writer on ethics speaks of "the tortures of remorse and the bitter cry of the man who feels himself smirched with sin."[3] Who can feel shame and self-abasement, yielding powerful restraints for the next temptation, like the man who has just realised his betrayal of the Lord that bought him?

This study of the emotional forces released by forgiveness is a long business, and we cannot think to exhaust it. To have looked into God's face and recognised Him as mercifully and changelessly Redeemer brings with it, for example, a new and creative moral exhilaration and an abolition of

[3] Laird, *A Study in Moral Theory*, p. 134.

that sense of inherent frailty, that depression and unexpectancy, which are the sure precursors of moral defeat. We now know that God the Forgiver, who hates sin, will never place us where we cannot obey Him. Jesus redeems our weak wills because He grants us, in the prophet's words, "a future and a hope." So long as we look ahead, questioning doubtfully what is to become of us, surveying life with its disproportion between our task and our powers, and death with its impenetrable shadows, we are weakened and discouraged. The great absolution of the Father changes all that. The man who knows, as the pardoned do, that he will assuredly grow into his Lord's mind, partake of His victorious Spirit, and eventually enjoy His actual presence—this man possesses a new heart of courage.

Nor is the victory we thus envisage a merely individual thing, capable of being actualised or enjoyed in solitude or complacent self-absorption. Though space fails, and we cannot here develop the principle in all its bearings, it cannot be too emphatically said that the content of the new morality inspired by forgiveness is social in its constitutive essence. We cannot have God apart from our neighbour. To put it in its simplest form, the pardoned man has made the discovery that fellowship is the all-inclusive secret of human life; and that this fellowship, through which alone self can be realised, embraces all who are the objects of God's love. It is not that love to others springs from an impulse parallel, as it were, to grateful love to God, altruistic morality thus forming an external supplement to a religion that at most tolerates it beside itself. The truth is, moral life is itself a living element of communion with God. To be blessed in pardoned fellowship with the Father is to be conscious of the impulse, which will not be denied, to share our lives with all for whom God cares. Thus a vital connexion exists between forgiveness and the Church, or rather all mankind. The pardoned life, when equal to its idea, is a life in which each is debtor to all the rest.

CHAPTER XII

FORGIVENESS AND THE CHURCH

If they were frank, a good many Christian people would confess that the idea of the Church with which at the moment they are most familiar is one of which they find it curiously difficult to make religious use. It has somehow fallen from its former high estate. It is not on a par with the idea current and influential in the great epochs of Christian history; still less is it equal to the conception set forth in the New Testament, and always implied there. They hear men censure the Church as a society, membership of which is inconsistent with intellectual or even with spiritual freedom, and affords no guarantee of energetic interest in social reform; and they hardly know what reply to make.[1] In a word, the idea of the Church does not inspire or subdue them as anyone can see it subdued and inspired St. Paul. Nothing in their experience, as they are accustomed to interpret it, would spontaneously lead them to give the Church a place in the Creed, alongside of other supernatural elements of the Gospel. And when they repeat the Creed, it is with a certain feeling of mystification, not to say unreality, that they pronounce the words: "I believe in the Holy Catholic Church."

The argument for corporate Christianity cannot be set out here in its full compass. A living and continuous society is obviously needed to interpret God in Christ to the generations, and to act as a nucleus and rallying-point for men of good-will who are striving to promote the felt unity and brotherhood of mankind. Christianity is, in a unique sense, the historical religion; but history does not consist in a mere succession of external events or changing ideas. We begin to find the conception of history intelligible and impressive only when we realise a truth or principle which underlies all human life, viz. that the moral being of the individual

[1] Cf. Denney, *The Church and the Kingdom.*

231

has its roots in a larger personal fellowship, which is heir and trustee of the achievement of the past. Moral life springs not merely from the powers and impulses of the single soul but from that interwoven context, that vital and vitalising community, of single lives in which the hard-won possessions of the race are funded. It is this which makes history conceivable. The possibility of history is given in the fact that, supremely in an ethical point of view, the fellowship is the essential presupposition, because the soil and substance, of the individual career. Apart from history, a man would not be himself on a reduced scale; he would not be himself at all. These ethical truths have their last and highest exemplification in the Church of Christ. It is what the generations hand on to each other, of devout and living conviction, that alone makes possible a personal and contagious faith.

In this chapter attention will be called to a single crucial aspect of this great theme. Religion in essence is fellowship with God; and this fellowship, as we have seen, presupposes and includes as a vital element the forgiveness of sins. In Jesus' preaching of the Kingdom forgiveness took rank as a chief blessing offered to faith, and where Christianity has remained true to type, it has kept this perspective tenaciously. The point I now desire to make is that apart from the Church, the communion of believing men, forgiveness is devoid of meaning. Were the Church to disappear, the reality of Divine pardon would disappear along with it. The two are indissociably one.

We must not, however, confuse this position with one for which Ritschl has made himself sponsor.[2] As is well known, he insisted strongly that the proper and, so to say, original object of Divine justification or forgiveness is not really the individual, but the Christian society as a whole. The boon of pardon is conveyed by primary intention to the Church; the individual serves himself heir to the blessing by joining the society in faith. It is as if God were conceived to say : " I forgive, I admit to fellowship with Me, despite their unworthiness, all who hereafter shall adhere believingly to the

[2] Cf. *Justification and Reconciliation* (E. T.), p. 108 ff.

Church of My Son." Two kinds of argument were led in defence of this. In the first place, it is in line with Old Testament religion. The great sacrifices were primarily meant for "the congregation of Israel," and it was only as a member of the community that the individual Israelite profited by them. Secondly, confirmation is found in New Testament passages—like "the Church of God which He purchased with His own blood"—where a plural or collective noun or pronoun is used to denote the object of Divine redemptive action.

If we understand Ritschl to be arguing that in the New Testament God is represented as forgiving the Christian society first of all, the individual only in the second place and inferentially, refutation is not difficult. No passage in which the Church is mentioned bears directly on forgiveness; on the other hand, there are verses in which God is explicitly said to pardon the individual. He is "the justifier of him that has faith in Jesus."[3] It was also Ritschl's intense conviction that in this point of doctrine he had reverted to the forgotten but sound and authentic views of the great Reformers; Luther in particular, he held, had taken this line strongly, and it was a miserable fatality that Melanchthon should have gone wrong, and misled other people as well. In point of fact, Luther seems to have expressed himself as in thoroughgoing agreement with his friend.

At the same time, something of real importance can be learnt from Ritschl's line of approach. If we put aside his tendency to set the Church and the individual over against one another as opposites, and to speak as if forgiveness were imparted to the Church quite irrespectively of the persons who might come to compose it, like a government concession granted to a trading company (which is very inaptly to transfer to the Divine mind the conditional quality of human knowledge of the future), we may realise freshly under the impact of his words how vital a part the Church actually does fill in mediating forgiveness. The life of the Church, it may be asserted without hesitation, is for each of us the

[3] Rom. 3.26.

medium of Divine pardon, and a medium which, so far from being accidental or arbitrary, is ethically indispensable. This follows from one or two familiar considerations.

In the first place, the Church forms the channel by which forgiveness reaches men, because it is solely through the Church's witness that they become aware of the Gospel of Jesus. Some people will persist in speaking as if the pardoning love of God were obvious, and had only to be stated to commend itself to all normal minds. In more unguarded moments they even fall into expressions which suggest that it is a truth of " Natural Reason," whatever that may mean. In sober fact, it is either ignored or denied by much more than half the human race. Old Testament believers themselves possessed a partially uncertain or conditional apprehension of the great truth; and the world had to wait for Jesus Christ before a society grew up, in His company and under His influence, the members of which were quite sure that " there is joy in the presence of the angels of God over a single sinner who repents."[4] Now the Church is this society as it exists to-day; it is the fellowship which perpetuates the revealing influence of Christ, and through which, in the power of the Spirit, the assurance of God's forgiving love is conveyed to the world.

Such a position has of course been scouted as pedantic and artificial. This, however, is the result of a too narrow identification of the Church's influence with that of preachers; and in the light of this assumption it is not unnaturally asked whether we mean to contend that no one attains to the lifegiving certainty that his sins are remitted except under the powerful impression of a sermon. Not indeed that this idea is so absurd as may be thought; for it is unquestionably through the preacher that numberless souls in every age have obtained the assurance of pardon. When a devout and selfforgetful man stands up to bear witness to Christ, pleading with men to come home to God and to come at once, in the conviction that there and then, with their sins upon their head, they may have all God's love for their own, it is the most natural thing in the world, if also the most super-

4 Luke 15.10.

natural, that they should believe him, and that a new joyous sense of acceptance by the Father should fill their heart.

It is however not through preaching alone that men are made aware of the gospel for a world of sin. Phillips Brooks, in his Yale Lectures, gave the memorable definition: " Preaching is the communication of truth by man to men. It has in it two essential elements, truth and personality." If we look closely, we can I think see that this covers a good deal more than preaching. If we take friendship, one of the friends being supposed a Christian who persuades the other to cast himself on God; or if, better still, we take the life of a Christian home, where the young people grow up in the trust, built into the very substance of their being, that there is forgiveness with God just as there is with their mother—in both of these cases we obviously have the same fact, " the communication of truth by man to men "; and also the same two essential elements, " truth and personality." Wherever, accordingly, the smallest group of friends is to be found, one of them a Christian, or wherever a Christian home exists, there a sub-section of the Church is present, and the witnessing influence of the Church is being disseminated. Apart from this witness of the fellowship, faith in God's redeeming love cannot begin. Let the Church cease to be, and the faith also will cease to be. All this seems only a special case of the more general truth that personal fellowship is invariably the *prius* and the gathering-ground of individual moral life. The initiative lies with the pre-existing higher form of common spiritual consciousness; it is the condition of the emergence of better things in the attitude and character of the individual.

If then we are to leave abstractions aside, and get back to reality, this tie between forgiveness and the Church must be allowed for. Apart from the society of believers, forgiveness is a mere word without the impulse of personal witness behind it, a word that will never be heard unless there are forgiven men to speak it. And at the moment the only people anywhere who utterly believe that the pardoning love of God is *there* as an objective datum, as something offered to us all which carries with it or within it every other blessing, are those who gather round Jesus. If we ask how we ourselves made the great discovery, our reply must be that it was through those who, after winning our trust and reverence, gave us by voice or bearing to know that we need not continue to bear our guilt hopelessly and alone, but that God's pardon and friendship might be ours as it was theirs. They stood surety to us for the truth of the remission of sins. Through their instrumentality we found our way, by degrees or suddenly, into the presence of the Father.

In such dependence upon social testimony and personal contagion, belief in Divine pardon is not of course by any means singular. Of all beliefs that touch the inner life the same holds good. No man really values truth but he who has lived close to those for whom truth is sacred. None loves purity but the man who has mingled with the pure. In like manner, no one will rank the forgiveness of God as possible or worthy of belief except as he has shared the life of those who themselves are forgiven. The isolated man—isolated, I mean, from the Christian brotherhood—might well long for pardon; he might feel profoundly that pardon was the one thing needful, if by him goodness was ever to be won and held; but over and above all that he must meet it as a possessed and experimental reality in other lives contiguous with his own, if he is to dare the personal apprehension of it. Faith is a venture, always; and courage for the venture is never the product of spontaneous generation within the single life, but of the contagion of richer souls.[5]

In experience this means that all who long for pardon need, before the longing can be satisfied, to encounter those who have seen and believed the love of God in Jesus Christ. Or, to put it otherwise, they must encounter the Church. In an essay on the greatest things in the *Confessions* of St. Augustine, Harnack has called attention to the truth and

---

[5] In *The Sadhu*, by Canon Streeter and Mr. Appasamy, a striking case is recorded of a man being converted simply by reading some torn pages of St. John's Gospel that had been flung out of the window of a railway carriage. This instance of "solitary conversion" may be taken as the exception which proves the rule I have tried to state above. And even here the indirect mediation of the Church in circulating the New Testament is evident.

insight of the opening paragraphs. St. Augustine first speaks of man's inborn disposition or instinct for religion, but he does not stop there; instead he passes on to the historical factor, the definite message or testimony, which must enter in, if true religion is to appear, to fructify this inward matrix of piety. The disposition alone by itself is good for nothing. Hindrances of every sort crush and stifle it. But let a message supervene, a gospel inspired by history and carried by human lives, and from the conjunction of the two —disposition and good tidings—a new life will spring up in which man not merely seeks God, but finds and praises Him. Similarly, the conviction that there is forgiveness with God can never arise where men are flung back simply on their own desires and hopes. They can only be helped by witness to a gospel, witness borne with affectionate good-will by people whom they trust. And this means that apart from the forgiven life of the Church, the company of the faithful, pardon for the guilty could be nothing more than a bleached and empty phrase.

The Church, however, makes Divine forgiveness credible not only by this heartfelt testimony to its reality and blessedness, but by the ethical attitude of Christians to each other. The forgiveness of God is only believable in a certain psychological atmosphere. For that atmosphere two ingredients are essential: first, the living witness of pardoned men to the truth in which they themselves have found life and power, and secondly, the Christian habit of *practising* forgiveness. In other words, the Church is not merely a society called to proclaim that loving Divine pardon which confronts the penitent alike in the Gospel and the Sacraments; it is a society in which men are accustomed to forgive each other. This second requisite is as vital as the first. Without it the good news of pardon can make no impression. It is only when we have met those who themselves forgive injuries that we find it possible to rise up to the stupendous and at first sight all but incredible truth that God forgives. Here, then, we find one cardinal reason why the Church of Christ is in the world; it is there in order that by the spectacle or experience of mutual placability and long-suffering, men may be persuaded that the Father, against whom all sin is done, Himself pardons freely.

It is therefore natural that throughout the New Testament we should find a striking juxtaposition of Divine forgiveness and human. This vital connexion between the two has been tolerably widely acknowledged in doctrine, but much less in practice. A placable or forgiving spirit is perhaps the least warmly admired of all the Christian graces, even in religious circles. It is apt to be dismissed with lifted eyebrows or half-stifled yawn, as though it implied some not altogether wholesome strain of character—quixotic, viewy, feeble. The sight of unfeigned readiness to pardon offences is apt to excite a curious impatience in otherwise Christian minds.

Yet it is clear our Lord spoke of this matter repeatedly and with exceptional directness. He proclaimed a Divine love as free as sunshine, He sealed the proclamation with His blood. None the less, one absolutely binding pre-condition was invariably made plain. To be pardoned of God we must pardon others. The rule is stated both ways—positively and negatively. "When ye stand praying, forgive, that your Father also may forgive your trespasses"; "if ye do not forgive, neither will your Father forgive you."[6]

We do not need to say that Christianity is the only religion which has inculcated the forgiveness of injuries. But it does stand by itself in its representation of loving pardon as an act in which the human spirit as it were shares the life of God—does what God does, not merely because He does it, but through Him and with Him. Pardon is no longer a Divine injunction simply; it is a grace in which the Father enables us to co-operate with His own attitude to the sinful. "Love your enemies," Jesus said, "and ye shall be the children of the Highest."[7] "'Forgiving one another,'" St. Paul wrote, "even as God in Christ has forgiven you."[8]

No one who has reflected deeply on human life and character will feel surprise at the prominence given by Jesus to this subject. To pardon a bitter injury—to self, still more to loved ones—is indubitably the hardest of all moral tasks. It is so very hard, not merely because the injury has evoked

[6] Mark 11.25; Matt. 6.15.   [7] Luke 6.35.   [8] Eph. 4.32.

passionate resentment but because it at first sight looks as if forgiveness were a confession of our fault in being indignant; whereas in our deeper mind we realise that such indignation was right and worthy, and that its absence would stamp us as not better men but worse. And yet, despite the fact that it is the hardest duty of all, Jesus with unequalled moral daring ventures to make it the condition of our being forgiven by the Father. That is a singular though frequently overlooked indication of His confidence in the new regenerating motives He can bring to bear.

These two great realities, then—man's pardon of a neighbour and God's pardon of the man himself—confront us; and according to Jesus, they are inseparable from each other. But if the relation is so vital as this, it may be contemplated from still another point of view; and this we must now attempt. If the presence of a forgiving spirit is an indispensable prerequisite of our receiving pardon—if the Father's love can only be perceived when man's love is felt—then it is only as non-Christians are forgiven by Christian neighbours that they can believe in the forgiveness of God to them personally. And thus, from a new angle, we come upon the indissociable bond between a gospel of pardon and the Church.

It is a frequent question, why the Christian message has not made a deeper mark on the world. Many reasons, doubtless, can be adduced; but surely part of the answer is that this human co-efficient of forgiving love, required to add momentum to the good news, has in great measure been absent. We all of us know what happens in religious circles where an implacable spirit has gained the upper hand. Whether owing to theological controversy or to purely personal antipathies, the new conditions inevitably produce an immediate fall in spiritual temperature, accompanied by a greatly diminished credibility of the Gospel. In such circumstances and amid such companions, it becomes all but unthinkable that God should forgive. Nay, the very idea of forgiveness loses colour, charm, persuasiveness. No preacher who stands up with a sense of grievance is in a position to bear witness to Christ eagerly and affectionately; his rankling heart puts an edge on what he has to say that wounds the hearer and makes him indisposed to be reconciled to God. And if the grievance is not in the pulpit but in the pew, if men listen with hearts hot with the recollection of unappeasable resentment on the part of others, then appeal and argument have to get through a barrage of hostile emotion which checks the impact of the most delicate and winning testimony. It is only when the air is warm with brotherhood that the Gospel sounds true.

It is interesting to conjecture what thoughts would arise in a man presented with the message of God's love in Christ, if we suppose him never once to have encountered genuine and loving friendship. Would words like "mercy" and "reconciliation" possess a meaning for his mind? Would the idea of being at peace with God have any reality that he could apprehend? Would he see what salvation is for? It may well be doubted. And from this point of view we begin to understand afresh the significance of the fact that, broadly speaking, the Church is made up of Christian homes. For it is in the home that the profound and beautiful and creative meaning of the word "forgiveness" is first learnt; not only so, it is learnt in circumstances which at every point make human forgiveness a fit parable of Divine. When children are told of God's pardon of their sins, it is all interpreted for them by the familiar attitude of a loving mother in taking a naughty child who is sorry back to her heart and her confidence. They know that such a mother does not stand over them as a taskmaster or a judge; they know that she opens her arms as soon as they long to return to her bosom; they know that to be at peace with her makes everything different. When penitent, they are not kept waiting or put on probation, but accepted just as they are. But I do not see how anyone can traverse such experiences as these without certain conclusions regarding the nature of the world in which he lives having registered themselves, more or less definitely and explicitly, in his mind. It is obviously a world, for one thing, in which forgiveness is not only possible but actual, and in which broken relationships between persons can be reconstituted. No mechanical necessities have any relevance to what he has experienced. Free, immediate, unqualified reconciliation has taken place between the heart he has wronged and his ashamed self. Love, he now perceives, is such that even this amazing thing is not beyond its power; it can refuse to cast off the wrong-doer; it can throw a bridge over the estranging gulf; it knows how to deal with evil so as to rob it of its alienating power and renew the severed bonds. But all this supplies to the child's estimate of life, its possibilities and resources, an element which is obtainable nowhere else. If he is ever to know, altogether irrespectively of religion, what forgiveness means, and what the import is of those profoundly impressive moral experiences into which the reception of forgiveness can usher him, he must learn it in the home; or, if his home be unhappy, in some circle of true and persistent good-will that fills its place. Furthermore, if in youth he has opened his nature to the faithful and patient kindness of those who love him, he will also have learnt that forgiveness is not to be conceived as something morally impotent or self-contained. On the contrary, the truth that forgiveness is the most regenerating thing in the world can be verified through our common relationships day by day. To be restored to fellowship with those whose fellowship we crave and to whom we look up, is to begin to live in their light.

These things indeed are not merely the antecedents or occasions of personal religion; in a true sense they are the inception of it. As Herrmann somewhere puts it: "To reverence persons, to bow inwardly at the presence of moral power and goodness, is the root of all true piety." Experience of what personal communion and redeeming influence mean inside a worthy home is the stepping-stone to a right apprehension of God in His personal bearing on our lives. The Psalmist puts all in a word: "Like as a father pitieth his children, so the Lord pitieth them that fear Him."[9] But such fathers and such mothers, who in pardoning yet reveal a sense that they themselves need a pardon still higher, are found only within the Church. If they have helped us to an understanding of what is signified by personal reconciliation, we are in their debt for ever. They have done for us an

[9] Ps. 103.13.
C.E.F.   O

inestimable thing: they have made it possible for us to be religious in a fashion morally transparent.

St. Augustine begins the eighth decisive book of the *Confessions* with these words: "Thou hast broken the chains that bound me; let me offer to Thee the sacrifice of praise. How Thou hast broken them, I will now relate." And what follows? The narrative of his contact with a stream of personal religion in others which gathered him also into its reviving and cleansing tide. Lingering memories of childhood counted for much; Ambrose too for something; most of all, perhaps, the story he had heard of the conversion of Victorinus and his comrades. The certainty of forgiveness, which gave him back to himself as a moral being because it restored him to God, came to him not as a personal inspiration, but through the common religious life he was asked to share. The past history of believers reproduced itself in St. Augustine's heart by the vital contagion of life and word. Thus does the power of God's mercy go down from one generation to another, reaching triumphantly over space and time. Among the forces that operate recreatingly on our will is the unremitting pervasive influence and vital tradition of others' faith, imparting the courage to believe that the new joy they found in a forgiving Father may also be ours.

It is in this region, perhaps, that we may fitly look for the deeper meaning of certain New Testament words, which some readers may be tempted to put aside as of merely antiquarian interest. "Is any sick among you?" writes St. James; "let him call for the elders of the church, and let them pray over him; and the prayer of faith shall save the sick: and if he have committed sins, they shall be forgiven him."[10] Again, the Fourth Gospel reports the saying of Jesus to His disciples: "Whosoever sins ye remit, they are remitted unto them, and whosoever sins ye retain, they are retained."[11] Conceivably this is a late allusion to what came to be known as "the power of the keys," a notion which afterwards blossomed or faded into the belief that the Church as an hierarchical institution has authority to admit to or exclude

[10] James 5.14-15.
[11] John 20.23.

from the benefits of salvation, in this life and the next. And to that as it stands grave objections, presumably, could be raised. But is there no truth behind, to which experience bears witness? If a Christian has fallen into scandalous sin, does it not in fact, to an extent we dare not limit or define, depend on the attitude held towards him by his fellow-believers, that is by the Church, whether the realised peace of reconciliation with God will ever again be his? If in judgment they are merciless, if they draw away their skirts from the pollution of his touch, how can he again open his heart spontaneously to the compassion of the Father? If he finds none here who can give and receive freely the blessed experience of reconciliation, with its incalculable power to neutralise and transcend the past, will he soon believe that the Lord of heaven and earth can pardon and restore the soul? Or is it not only too likely that the pitilessness of man will hide the pity of God? Even if under these harsh conditions he should attain to something like faith in Divine absolution, it is all but certain that contact with men who can only be softened and appeased by a variety of penances and satisfactions (though they may not be called so) will also infect his thought of God, and of the terms on which He too will grant peace. On the other hand, it is difficult to assign limits to the renewing tenderness and power with which the Father's absolving love may flood his heart, if his fellows have frankly forgiven him and taken him into confidence again. Thus, from a new angle, we may see how the Church has much—all but everything—to do with what the forgiveness of sins may mean for the guilty.

Or again, it is agreed by all that a vital condition of receiving Divine pardon is the lowly heart. We are sure that God resists the proud and gives grace to the humble. But lowliness is not relative to God merely. It is an attitude bearing on those with whom our life is shared. Now, the experience of receiving God's pardon involves the consciousness that we form part of a pardoned company; it means that we are content to share and share alike with them, for in the Kingdom of God none can be saved in isolation. " God," it has been said, " has no blessing for me apart from the rest of the family." This is the true humility, which God takes to His heart; and it consists not in telling dejected lies about ourselves but in quelling the passionate impulse, natural in all, to make special claims or insist on privileged exceptions or look askance at the company God has given us. This willingness to be lost in the great multitude who owe everything to Him, this eagerness to join in the doxology of the reconciled and in thankful adoration take their confession and praise as ours, acknowledging that like them we have nothing which we have not received, forms a real element in the experience of being forgiven. Pardon is invisible to the man whose eyes are dark with pride. Thus on every ground alike of thought and life we must recognise the vital bonds between these two great realities—Forgiveness and the Church.

It is just because the Church is a forgiven community, rejoicing in fellowship with the Father of men and suffused with the spirit of forbearing love, that to-day she is called as never before to play, alike in international difficulties and industrial disputes, the part of a Society of Reconciliation for the world. In all generations she has believed that in her Divine Faith she possessed the secret of human life and welfare; after these last years of passion and sorrow she is more sure of it than ever. To avoid war, Lord Grey has said, "the most effective change would be that nations should dislike each other a little less, and like each other a little more."[12] It may seem a modest hope; yet in point of fact it is the one method by which to secure an associated, instead of a competing and hostile, humanity. It is, in short, the one hope for a spiritually recreated race. And of this we may be certain, that such a hope can never fulfil itself by the operation of any natural law. Not merely between Church and Church, or class and class, but above all between nation and nation the wires must be laid over which the messages of love and brotherhood may move. None can lay these wires so well as living members of the pardoned Church of Jesus Christ. The forgiveness of God must be our incentive. Our

[12] *Twenty-five Years,* vol. ii, p. 276.

common reception of His love in Christ must be our bond of unity. Only through the gospel of the reconciling Father and the reconciled family of His children can the old yet ever-new ideal of international trust and amity be carried to realisation in the teeth of those vested interests of capitalistic commerce and military ambition from which no people is free. Short of a world so purged by mutual faith, posterity may yet learn that the Great War was fought not merely in vain, but at a ruinous loss to the moral resources of civilised mankind.

CONCLUSION

Throughout the foregoing chapters we have studied a single topic, endeavouring to catch its outlines and estimate its purport and significance from a variety of points of view. The subject is one which persists in claiming a central place. Jesus Christ has done many things for the world; the chief thing He has done is to mediate the forgiveness of sins and to impart the assurance of its reality.

It may possibly help the elucidation of the theme, as now presented, if I once more retrace the argument.

Forgiveness is central in Christianity; it is a truth, an ingredient, without which the faith created by Jesus Christ would lose its identity. It may be objected that pardon is unnecessary, or impossible, or immoral, or that insistence upon it must affect unfavourably the interests of moral education; but these objections can be answered. Had not the Gospel held this blessing at its heart, we should not have been able to recount the triumph of Christianity over other, less sufficient, worships. This, indeed, may be called self-evident, once we have understood what God's forgiveness is. When God forgives a man He does not merely cancel exterior penalty or surrender the right to reprisals; much less does He simply agree to overlook faults. Even between men pardon signifies far more. To forgive, on God's part, is in pure love to draw the sinner, despite his sin, into communion with Himself and to take the first step in doing this amazing thing. There is nothing in the assured results of modern psychology which has rendered all this less credible than before. Plainly, the grace that rises to meet sin must be wonderful; for sin, as we are here concerned with it, is the refusal to trust the Lover of our souls. We cannot describe it adequately as misfortune, we cannot extenuate its gravity by tracing all to ignorance. Sin comes out of the self and renders us accountable to God.

These reflections are met and corroborated when we turn

to Jesus Christ as the New Testament depicts Him. By being what He was He enabled friendless sinners, as they stood before Him, to believe that the Father was pardoning their wrong. There is virtue in this historical fact to which nothing comparable can be found either in common life or in the conjectures of philosophy. And the significance of Jesus for Divine pardon is clearest in His death.

In his own manner St. Paul proclaimed the same truth when with impassioned earnestness he taught the doctrine most intimately associated with his name, viz. justification by faith. We can pierce beneath the thought-forms of the apostle to a meaning which perpetuates the message of Jesus. For long, in official theology, this insight was obscured by legal accretions of belief and custom; but when, at the Reformation, Luther drew men back to the historic Christ, the old announcement of free and unreservedly gracious pardon once more fell upon human ears. Luther's problems, in their stark urgency, are still ours, and in our efforts to solve them we must still work in the light of his religious intuitions.

Pardon, it next becomes clear, is intelligible only as we relate it to the character of God. Forgiveness takes its quality from the Forgiver. He is holy; therefore sin is something He must condemn and even punish, though the worst punishment of all is to lose communion with Him. But also He is a personal Father, a Father who can interpose directly and supernaturally to put us right with Himself. And when in Christ He does so interpose, it is at an inestimable cost; when we speak of atonement we mean the cost of forgiveness to God. What essentially it costs God to forgive sin we behold in Jesus, and supremely in His death. The Cross of Christ is at once a manifestation—which nothing can equal or outgo—of the Father's love to the sinful and a decisive exhibition of His hostility to sin. We find ourselves pardoned and received into His fellowship when by faith we unite ourselves to Christ and are thus in spirit identified with His perfect sacrifice.

Faith is, on its other side, penitence; to turn towards the great Absolver is to turn from sin. There is assurance even for the most self-distrusting in the aspect of Jesus. And the consciousness of pardon is the source of all true and victorious morality. In such an experience a new ethical ideal is apprehended; a new Divine companionship is enjoyed; new motives spring alike from gratitude for undeserved love and from an able fear to be unworthy: all these conspire to evoke personal goodness and to equip men with the unselfishness requisite for the best service of mankind.

The gospel of forgiveness, however, has reality and persuasiveness only within the Church, only as the Church proclaims it both by word and life. To an extent we dare not limit, it depends for credibility on the forgiving spirit of those who follow Christ. The coefficient of kindness and love must give power to words about Divine pardon if they are to win and change men.

At various points in the argument we are led to illustrate and interpret the forgiveness of God by the forgiveness imparted by man to man. Yet how rare in human life, how all but unknown, is the noble pardon of great injuries! So rare, in fact, that we are left with an inescapable conviction that nothing less than the Cross could have persuaded men that God *does* blot out their sin. Except for Jesus, living and dying, such love had not entered into man's heart to conceive.

Yet the wonder of forgiveness is the measure of its necessity. And the deep, personal certitude that there is forgiveness with God is the true spring and cause of all evangelism. In every age the guilty must be told of the remission of sins— it must be brought close to them by self-abnegating friendship—if their life is to be commensurate with the Divine thought of reconciliation. "With the Lord there is mercy, and with Him is plenteous redemption"—this is the note of authentic Christianity. And it is a note which men love to hear in a preacher's voice.

INDEX

I. INDEX OF SUBJECTS

II. INDEX OF AUTHORS

III. INDEX OF REFERENCES

Other Fontana Religious Books

MERE CHRISTIANITY

C. S. Lewis. Here at a popular price is a revised and amplified edition of C. S. Lewis's three famous books, *Broadcast Talks*, *Christian Behaviour*, and *Beyond Personality*, brilliantly presenting the author's modern revaluations of Christian apologetics, ethics and theology.

THE SCREWTAPE LETTERS

C. S. Lewis. This witty and profound analysis of Christian strength and weaknesses outlined in the letters of the elderly devil Screwtape to his young nephew, is a classic of religious exposition.

SURPRISED BY JOY

C. S. Lewis. How could Professor Lewis, author of so many works radiant with the sense of God, ever have been without the sense of God himself ? And how in the end did he attain it? In this autobiography these questions are answered straightforwardly and comprehensively.

THE PROBLEM OF PAIN

C. S. Lewis. The author gives his views as a layman on the Christian doctrine relating to all aspects of the problem of pain and explains the existence of pain in a Christian world.

LETTERS TO YOUNG CHURCHES

J. B. Phillips. The author's most famous book, this is more than a mere translation of the Epistles. It has already become a contemporary classic of Biblical interpretation, a valuable guide for all those who in their groping towards a maturer Christian faith, encounter and are perplexed by the vital but difficult Pauline doctrines which constitute the foundation of Christian Theology.

MAKING MEN WHOLE

J. B. Phillips. Undoubtably one of the author's finest books— a vigorous and searching appraisal of the place of both Christian and non-Christian in the modern world and of their part in God's purpose.

THE GOSPELS IN MODERN ENGLISH

J. B. Phillips. " It is all to the good that we should be given a translation in straightforward English, and Mr. Phillips has a flair for doing this that none of his predecessors in the task seem to have had."
Times Literary Supplement

THE YOUNG CHURCH IN ACTION

J. B. Phillips. " A simple, clear and unsophisticated account of what happened to the world when a group of people surrendered themselves to the direction of the Holy Ghost."
Spectator

Other Fontana Religious Books

SCIENCE AND CHRISTIAN BELIEF

C. A. Coulson. The author sets out to show that, far from out-dating and nullifying tradi-tional Christian beliefs, science is essentially a religious activity, playing its part in the unfold-ing of the nature and purpose of God.

THE MEANING OF PAUL FOR TO-DAY

C. H. Dodd. Professor Dodd suggests the place of Paul in the history of religion, and seeks to bring out the perma-nent significance of the apostle's thought, in modern terms, and in relation to the general inter-ests and problems which occupy the mind of the present generation.

THE PERENNIAL PHILOSOPHY

Aldous Huxley. The author illustrates and develops pass-ages from the writings of those Saints and Prophets from all monotheistic religions who have approached a direct spiritual knowledge of the Divine.

"A mine of curious and erudite learning."

New Statesman

CHRISTIANITY AND HISTORY

H. Butterfield. With force and profundity the author states his belief that history testifies to Christianity and Christianity interprets history.

THE JOURNALS OF KIERKEGAARD

Ed. Alexander Dru. A unique combination of notebook and diary in which Kierkegaard's spiritual and intellectual devel-opment are intimately re-corded.

CHRISTIAN DOCTRINE

J. S. Whale. The author des-cribes and meets the difficulties which the great Christian doc-trines raise for us to-day, and shows how the Christian faith understands human history and death.

A SHORT BIBLE

Arranged by Austin Farrer. "I am more than pleased, I am excited, by Austin Farrer's book. I don't know that I ever learned so much (from anything of the same sort and on the same scale) as I have done from his introduction. This is a brilliant popularisa-tion as we are ever likely to see." *C. S. Lewis*